M000188475

GERMANS
in the
Southwest
1850—1920

GERMANS
in the
Southwest
1850—1920

Tomas Jaehn

University of New Mexico Press
Albuquerque

© 2005 by the University of New Mexico Press.
All Rights Reserved. Published 2005

09 08 07 06 05   1 2 3 4 5

Jaehn, Tomas.
  Germans in the Southwest, 1850–1920 / Tomas Jaehn.
      p. cm.
  Includes bibliographical references and index.
  ISBN 0-8263-3498-9 (cloth : alk. paper)
  1. German Americans—New Mexico—History. 2. German
Americans—New Mexico—Ethnic identity. 3. German Americans—
New Mexico—Social conditions. 4. German American literature—New
Mexico—History and criticism. 5. New Mexico—History—1848–
6. New Mexico—Ethnic relations. 7. New Mexico—Intellectual life.
I. Title.
  F805.G3J34 2005
  978.9'00431—dc22

                    2004028622

Book design and composition by Damien Shay
Body type is Minion 10.5/14.
Display is Disturbance and Birch.

für meine eltern
&
for pilar and leah

Table of Contents

—ɯ—

Figures

—◆—

Tables

—◆—

Acknowledgments

The list of those whose support, guidance, and knowledge were instrumental in the completion of this manuscript is lengthy and spans both sides of the Atlantic. The list includes friends, colleagues, teachers, and family. Without their involvement, this work would have been difficult to complete.

Across the Atlantic I thank my parents who encouraged me as only parents can and who so patiently functioned as "go-between," corresponding with descendants of those who immigrated. Without hesitation, they copied materials at German universities as I chased yet another potential lead. Their transcriptions of letters written in an old German script were invaluable to me as it was faster and easier to verify their writing, than to spend hours upon hours deciphering a style with which I have only a passing familiarity.

On this side of the Atlantic, Richard Etulain of the University of New Mexico guided the initial project for years and patiently read many earlier drafts, as did Ferenc Szasz, Garry Scharnhorst, Henry Tobias, and the late Gerald Nash. Frederick Luebke and Gus Seligman, too, were kind enough to read a draft and make suggestions. I thank them all.

I must thank countless archivists and librarians at the Angélico Chávez History Library (before I started to work there) and the New Mexico State

Records Center and Archives in Santa Fe, the University of New Mexico General Library's Center for Southwest Research in Albuquerque, and the Bancroft Library and Stanford University Libraries in California. They patiently pulled seldom-used manuscript collections from among their holdings and found books for me through interlibrary loan from obscure places. Bonny Hardwick of the Bancroft Library, who did not really know me until I started work across the Bay, assisted me with her extensive knowledge of the collections holdings at the Bancroft Library, and Kathy Ferris and Rose Diaz at the University of New Mexico helped me when other commitments kept me from going there myself. Albert Cota, friend and former colleague at the Stanford University Libraries, assisted me with his expertise in computer technology, and my current colleague, Blair Clark, assisted me with photographic reproductions.

I am especially grateful to Bill Tydeman, now Associate Dean at the Texas Tech University Libraries in Lubbock. From my first meeting with Bill at the University of New Mexico through our time together at the Idaho State Historical Society, to the time we parted ways professionally, he readily and willingly, and on more than a few occasions, read the "last draft" of this manuscript. His candid discussions, countless coffee talks, and occasional pool games have been invaluable and have made me, I believe, a better historian, archivist, and librarian.

Finally, I would like to thank my wife and friend, Audrey Moore, for her patience when I needed to be alone or needed a sounding board, for her ideas, and for her countless reviews and suggestions to improve my sentence structure and to detect my "Germanism."

Introduction

Hundreds of thousands of German immigrants left the Old World during the nineteenth century, in pursuit of a better life in the United States. Aside from major urban centers such as New York, Philadelphia, or San Francisco, Germans sought their future in the West, which had "already long been a metaphor for opportunity."[1] Driven, in part at least, by the myth of cheap and unoccupied land, they arrived individually, with family, or as a communal venture and settled in western towns and farming communities. While their immigration experiences may have differed from each other, and a "typical immigrant experience," as has been argued, may not exist, it remains a fact that most Germans in the nineteenth and early twentieth centuries encountered the dominance of Anglo-American culture.[2] In time, usually after periods of isolation and segregation, they acculturated and adapted.

It has often been assumed when considering acculturation processes that the American culture is distinctly Anglo-American (which in itself is a problematic assumption considering that the "United States is composed almost entirely of people whose origins can be traced to other lands"[3]). While it is true that regional characteristics and distinctions in, for instance, the mid-Atlantic region or the Midwest shaped German immigrants' acculturation process differently, the process was nevertheless tied to an Anglo-American society. More to the point for this study, an exception to this process was found in the Hispanic Southwest. Germans who moved to the Southwest experienced a distinctly different society and "place characteristic."[4] In 1846, Adolph Wislizenus was disappointed in Santa Fe with its "irregular cluster of low, flat roofed, mud built, dirty houses." Nearly two decades later Balduin Möllhausen reiterated that Santa Fe had "little appeal"; and in the 1880s, traveler Robert Schlagintweit was still amazed at Santa Fe's cultural differences and doubted that it could be considered "still in the Union."[5]

This study analyzes German acculturation processes under these ethnically diverse circumstances. Different from the Midwest, where German Americans "invented the institutionalized ethnic community,"[6] it is my contention that Germans who arrived prior to the coming of the railroad in New Mexico in the early 1880s were more interested in acculturation than cultural preservation. Their individual and group behavior demonstrated very little that could be labeled ethnic and consequently moved toward a relative multicultural equanimity. But the impact of railroad and the subsequent rearrangement of socio-economic activities marked significant changes. As Anglo-Americans entered the territory and supplanted Hispanics as the dominant cultural force, ethnic Germans became more concerned about their cultural identities and undertook more activities designed to preserve cultural traditions.

This study of Germans will not emphasize religious differences among Germans. This means particularly that Jews from Germany are treated first as Germans and then as persons of a religious persuasion.[7] On the whole, my research confirms the conclusions of other historians, such as Henry Tobias and Moses Rischin, that anti-Semitism was insignificant in the West. As recently as 1992, journalist Rafael Seligmann pointed out that "Jews were Germans and wanted to be seen as such."[8]

Germans in the Southwest examines several aspects of German life in the Southwest and German perceptions of the Hispanic Southwest. It evaluates German-language literature about the region; sketches a demographic portrait of German ethnicity in New Mexico showing trends in this multicultural region; and discusses political, economic, and cultural aspects of German life in New Mexico. In political and economic experiences, especially, Germans were part of a new system of capitalism emerging when a United States takeover drastically altered New Mexico. The book also provides a brief discourse of World War I in New Mexico, one of ethnic Germans' most difficult experiences in the United States, which, in turn, closed an era of German immigration to the Hispanic Southwest that had begun in the 1840s. The entry of the United States into the war against Germany and shifting immigration laws in the early 1920s essentially ended German immigration to the United States.

German experiences in New Mexico both reflected and diverged from those of Germans in other parts of the United States. Historian Frederick Luebke found that in 1854 Nebraska's Germans quickly gravitated toward building distinct communities and organizations. He concluded that this behavior was a reaction to the strange environment and to the pressure to conform to the Anglo-American host society.[9] The more than two hundred Germans who had settled in New Mexico by 1850 did not resort to public ethnic behavior, suggesting that they did not perceive New Mexico's geography and the Hispanic host society as unfriendly. In their experiences with Native Americans and Hispanics, Germans in New Mexico remained restrained in displaying ethnic behavior.

Only after the arrival of the railroad in New Mexico and migration of considerable numbers of Anglo-Americans to that territory starting in the 1870s, did Germans and German Americans begin to exhibit ethnicity. Ethnic organizations formed in New Mexico for the same reasons Luebke documented in Nebraska or Kathleen Conzen in Milwaukee, Wisconsin: Ethnic behavior "lessened pressure to abandon quickly old cultural habits."[10] German immigrants showed signs of "behavioral assimilation" into both the Hispanic and Anglo-American societies during the first two decades of the territorial period, but the increase in Anglo-American presence in New Mexico in the latter part of the nineteenth century retarded that process.[11] Germans in New Mexico, then, followed the broader experiences of Germans in other parts of the United States.

In the end, Germans in New Mexico added to the ethnic experiences in the United States, even though in the larger context of the Hispanic Southwest they were considered "Anglos." But the Hispanic cultural environment allowed them to adapt to their new environment more freely than in predominantly Anglo-American surroundings.

Regarding terminology, even though *Hispanics, Native Americans,* and *Germans* should be understood through their usual ethnic meaning, *Anglo-Americans* will be treated generically rather than ethnically, as a composite term for all others of European descent. I have chosen the term

Hispanic over the more contemporary *Hispano* because it is gender-neutral indicating Spanish-speaking people of the Southwest. In addition, I use the term *German Americans* to mean those who have at least one parent or grandparent born within the borders of Germany by the eve of World War I (which is essentially the current Federal Republic of Germany and coastal sections of Poland and Lithuania).[12] For consistency's sake, I have united Navajos, Apaches, and Pueblos under one term, *Native Americans* or *Indians.* I use all these terms not to oversimplify or neglect the many differences among these groups, but to streamline the organization of this book.

To gather all this information on Germans in New Mexico, I have consulted many archives and libraries, often looking for what seemed the proverbial needle in a haystack. Aside from examining U.S. population and agricultural census reports for ethnic Germans, I have found most of my information in the collections of the Center for Southwest Research at the University of New Mexico, which holds a wealth of rare books, manuscript material, and oral history collections. The New Mexico State Record Center and Archives and the Angélico Chávez History Library at the Palace of the Governors in Santa Fe also possess considerable material about Germans in New Mexico. Additional information was obtained from the Rio Grande Historical Collection at New Mexico State University in Las Cruces and from smaller historical libraries and institutions in Taos, Roswell, and Las Vegas. Outside the state, I have drawn on the resources of the National Archives in Washington, D.C., the Bancroft Library at the University of California, Berkeley, historical libraries in Texas and Arizona, the Bayerische Staatsbibliothek, München, and the library at the Ludwigs-Universität, Göttingen. In addition, I have conducted interviews with immigrants and descendants of immigrants in New Mexico, California, and Texas. I have also exchanged numerous letters across the United States and Germany to gain additional information.

During the course of my research, two books were of special help for their research findings and methodological insights. Henry Tobias's *History of the Jews in New Mexico* was an invaluable tool in identifying Germans since so many Jews were German or of German descent. In addition, Kathleen Neils Conzen's works, particularly her *Immigrant Milwaukee, 1836–1860: Accommodation and Community in a Frontier City*, provided many of the critical questions and conceptual ideas for this study.

Although this study focuses on New Mexico or the Hispanic homeland, it has broader implications. The patterns found here could apply
as well to the rest of the Southwest. The Hispanic settlements along the
Rio Grande from Taos to Socorro are, after all, the heart of Hispanic expansion.[13] In the end, Germans in New Mexico added to the ethnic experiences in the United States, even though in the larger context of the Hispanic
Southwest they were considered "Anglos." But the Hispanic cultural environment allowed them to adapt to their new environment more freely
than in predominantly Anglo-American surroundings.

CHAPTER ONE

The Hispanic Southwest in German Literature

In the nineteenth and early twentieth centuries, when Germans wanted to inform themselves about the Southwestern region of the United States, they looked for printed material but were often hard pressed to find appropriate literature. German authors, claiming to write about the larger West, inflated their titles and nearly always ignored the Hispanic Southwest.[1] Still, the Germans' interest was considerable. Stories about Western adventurers were logical successors to the romantic sagas of German heroes like Siegfried or Thor, "who battled evil to win out for truth."[2] The German book market offered abundant fictional and travel literature about the larger American West. Moreover, toward the end of the nineteenth century anthropological and ethnic interests resulting from Germany's colonial quests added to the preoccupation with the American West and the Hispanic Southwest.

It is difficult to determine how German emigrants perceived literature of the Southwest. Was it reality or fiction?[3] Karl May's novels, for instance, were often regarded as authentic. His use of real geographic locations and his public insistence that he had met his two fictional heroes,

Old Shatterhand and Winnetou, contributed to this illusion. May's works became one of the most popular sources of information for early twentieth-century Germans who wished to learn about the American Southwest.

Travel accounts, scientific reports, literary works, and even the much maligned popular literature by Germans, and by American writers whose works had been translated, represented important sources for the potential immigrants. As one scholar notes, "thousands of Europeans knew America only...from the travel literature and emigrant guides that appeared in all the leading European languages."[4] The authors, most of whom had traveled extensively in the American West, not only provided readers with a sense of the region through colorful tales, but also included general statistical data and historical detail. As one German scholar argues,

> Germans longed eagerly for books.... [They] enjoyed the adventures and pictures of the New World, pretended to be on the prairies, in the land of the Indians, got sucked in by the Dollar millionaire, the "rich uncle in America" presented on German stages or in German novels, ate up reports about Germans who made their luck overseas.[5]

These "western image-makers" helped shape German understanding of the Southwest.[6]

Influenced by the works of early "western image-maker" James Fenimore Cooper, German adventure and travel writers gradually seduced readers into a Germanized Southwest.[7] Writers like Balduin Möllhausen interspersed immigration information with Cooperesque stories of heroic women and men who struggled with the environment, hunters and traders who battled Native Americans or outlaws, and farmers who labored on the soil. These conflicts generated both excitement and hope for potential German emigrants and at the same time appeased the commercial interests of the publishers and met the expectations of the general German reading public.[8]

Democracy, individualism, and frontier struggle were central themes of many German publications. From the beginning, Germans were fascinated by America's "Noble Savages,"[9] echoing Cooper's treatment of Native Americans. In fact, as one scholar has noted in a study of Western travel literature, "this romantic tendency toward noble savagery is evidenced in virtually all German-language fiction about Indians, regardless of the author's background." More recent scholars have coined the term "Indianthusiasm" signifying the Germans' fascination, then and now, with American Indians and everything Indian.[10] These writers, with Eurocentric overtones, introduced German readers to a noble savage doomed to vanish. Few German publications dealt with Hispanic traditions in the Southwest. Instead, New Mexico was often described in terms of uninhabited plains and high mountains, reminders for travelers of the hardships they had to endure and the hostile Native Americans in the West.[11] To nondiscriminating German readers, novels, travel accounts, and scientific reports about the region were sufficient to quench their thirst for information. It did not matter whether it was Cooper's West in New York, Gerstäcker's West in Arkansas, or Karl May's West everywhere between Missouri and Kurdistan in Persia. Clearly, for Germans, the Southwest was only a region of the larger West. The cultural and historical uniqueness of the Southwest was rarely emphasized or explained.

General descriptions of the West did not supply the serious German reader with sufficient information to understand regional characteristics of the Southwest. The first detailed account of New Mexico to surface in Germany was a translation of Josiah Gregg's *Commerce of the Prairies*.[12] German publishers considered his famous work, issued originally in 1844, sufficiently important that a translation was marketed in 1847.

Since 1831, Gregg participated in several other overland journeys between St. Louis and Santa Fe. His memoirs, detailing flora and fauna, geography and topography, manners and customs of Hispanics and Indians, and the history of the region, were popular. Archibald Hanna in his introduction to a later edition of *Commerce of the Prairies*, attributes this success to Gregg's ability to communicate what he saw to his readers: "The blood of even the most confirmed city-dweller still responds to the tale of high adventure in the unknown territory beyond the edge of civilization."[13]

Focusing on economics and emphasizing southwestern aridity and the limited potential for mining and agricultural ventures, Gregg's observations interested many Germans. New Mexico, he claimed, enjoyed little civilization and possessed only a few agricultural advantages such as the fields around Santa Fe that had "no doubt been in constant cultivation over two hundred years."[14] The mixture of information, eyewitness account, and "tale[s] of high adventure" included in *Commerce of the Prairies* enlivened the works of later authors such as Frederick A. Wislizenus and Balduin Möllhausen and made them equally popular among German readers.

Germans writing about New Mexico, however, faced a dilemma: New Mexico was not typical of the American West because Hispanic culture pre-dated Anglo-American domination. As mentioned earlier, observations like Schlagintweit's, a German scientist who visited Santa Fe in the early 1880s, were typical: "It is unbelievable that one is still in the United States."[15]

German writers took different approaches to manipulate the Hispanic Southwest's deviation from Anglo-American understanding of the West. Frederick A. Wislizenus, for example, who presented the earliest, if brief, account about New Mexico, attempted to remain purely scientific. Settling near St. Louis, he undertook two trips to the Southwest, the Rocky Mountains, and Mexico for "recreational purposes." Wislizenus's discussions were void of commentaries, primarily scientific, and concentrated on the Mexican territory south of the Rio Grande. As one early scholar has noted, Wislizenus "was no part of the fur trade. He was no part of the missionary movement to save souls, and he was not looking for a homestead."[16] Wislizenus's books, which were published in German and English and also in installments for the German newspaper *Anzeiger des Westens* in St. Louis, reflected this attitude.[17]

In his second work, *A Tour of Northern Mexico, 1846–1847*, Wislizenus describes in far greater detail the land and scenery of New Mexico, and, as such, this book presents a more important value to German immigrants. Trying to remain on objective grounds with scientific data and observations, he repeated the limitations of New Mexico due to its climate. Yet, he predicted success for agricultural endeavors in the valleys through methods of dry farming. He also elaborated on the neglected industries of livestock and mining. In Wislizenus's view, both endeavors, if attended to carefully and intensively, had great potential.[18]

In all his detailed scientific research and observations in New Mexico, Wislizenus barely mentioned the region's Hispanic and Native American populations. In 1846, appraising his second trip through New Mexico, Wislizenus briefly recognized the "deep rancor of the Indian race against the white [that] has continued to the present time" and characterized the Pueblo population as industrious, frugal, sober, yet poor.[19]

In applying a scientific approach to New Mexico, Wislizenus circumvented promoting the virtues of German and Euro-American civilization. He also avoided mythical issues like civilization versus wilderness and the West as a place of true democracy and individualism. Since New Mexico already had a well-established, though small population center with a long history, it was a difficult task for Wislizenus to picture the territory in the same way as Cooper had previously described his frontier. Nonetheless, Wislizenus predicts that when "the waves of civilization will draw nearer and nearer from the East and the West," the virtues (and the vices) of civilization will come to New Mexico.[20] Until then, Wislizenus implies, German immigrants would fare better elsewhere.

Aside from his eagerly awaited letters from the Southwest in the *Anzeiger des Westens*, Wislizenus's influence on immigrants is difficult to determine. No sources speak of the reception of his second book, which went on the market in Germany following political unrest. But Germans, hoping for less restrictive political conditions and for better economic situations, were likely attracted to Wislizenus's observations about the Southwest and New Mexico.

Another German author reporting on New Mexico was Balduin Möllhausen. As a topographer and travel writer, Möllhausen's wanderlust led him frequently into the Southwest and, in his publications, he displayed first-hand knowledge of the region and its people. After his return to Germany, he became a skillful fiction writer. As Robert Taft points out, "Möllhausen's Western experience formed the basis of his career as a writer."[21] In assessing New Mexico's economic future, Möllhausen described the area as "waterless sand deserts and impassable high plateau canyons."[22] In addition, he portrayed the territory as a cultural wasteland with little hope of improvement. Nevertheless, his visual geographic descriptions made it easier for the German reader to understand the region. For instance, he compared the Navajo region to the Sächsische Schweiz, a sandstone region along the Elbe River, but concluded that the tribal land was not as inviting or as friendly as the German region.[23]

Möllhausen did include philosophical and political themes in his works. He realized that a well-established Native American and Hispanic population precluded promoting the frontier virtues of democracy, individualism, and civilization. Instead, Möllhausen, influenced by the Humboldtsche Weltbild of the time, portrayed the Native American population as part of a larger macrocosm.[24] Within this intellectual context, Möllhausen treated Native Americans as part of the universe and accepted their cultures, their habits, and their traditions. Following the tradition of Cooper, Möllhausen saw the Pueblos as perfect manifestations of noble savages: "Happy people with your semi-civilization; may the real civilization never reach your peaceful home."[25]

His travel experiences made him painfully aware that contact between Europeans and Native American cultures almost always worked against the latter.[26] In rating the consequences of Western civilization on the Native way of life, he lamented Native Americans' conditions: "They are slaves in their own country, sinking deeper and deeper under the influence of this civilization and coming to know that having dark skin annihilates the right to justice."[27] Still, Möllhausen believed in the adaptability of Native Americans to new situations and blamed the insensitivity and intolerance of the U.S. military and of land speculators for the Native Americans' dismal situation. Instead, Möllhausen favored the "honorable class" of fur trappers and traders as a transitional group between civilization and wilderness. Not surprisingly, roaming the endless prairies with a shotgun on his back, he considered himself part of that group.[28]

Möllhausen left a deep impression on German readers. Inexpensively produced in small paperback format and appearing in journals like *Die Gartenlaube, Das Ausland,* and *Der Hausfreund,* his fantastic and colorful descriptions of the American West enlightened generations of Germans.[29] His prolific creativity, demonstrated in numerous novels, short stories, and semiscientific essays, illustrates his success in Germany. In addition, he also claimed the rare honor of having one of his works contain a pleasant preface by Alexander von Humboldt.[30]

Another German author, Armand, overlooked the demographic and cultural differences altogether. Armand was the pseudonym of Friedrich Armand Strubberg, the former director of the Mainzer Adelverein, a German organization that settled in Texas. His obscure autobiographical work, *Amerikanische Jagd- und Reiseabenteur,* discussed a tour along the Pecos River into the Sangre de Cristo Mountains and north to Taos.

In romantic prose Armand wrote of a hunting trip from Texas to northern New Mexico possibly during the late 1840s or early 1850s. On his journey, he frequently successfully hunted big game and met members of tribes not native to New Mexico (the Delaware, Shawnee, Osage, Creek, and Choctaw). Although he intended to go to Santa Fe and from there to Taos, he neglected to confirm whether he actually arrived, although his ambiguous geographic descriptions suggest that he was in their vicinity.[31] While extensively detailing his and his friends' adventures in New Mexico, and describing the mountainous landscapes of the territory, he failed to mention meeting any Hispanics or New Mexico Indians. Still, Armand's book was guaranteed success since it was published by the famous Stuttgart publishing house J. G. Cotta, which had a history of publishing North American travel accounts. Armand's misconceptions spread widely and fostered the stereotype of New Mexico as an empty wilderness.[32]

The same misinterpretation of New Mexico as a region where trappers and hunters encountered "savages" appears in the writings of Karl May, one of Germany's most famous novelists. Although celebrated for his stories about the American West at the end of the nineteenth and early twentieth centuries, May never visited the West or New Mexico; he drew his information from published sources.[33] Much more skilled than Armand nearly half a century earlier, May used literary devices to mold New Mexico's collection of cultures into a mythic, adventurous place where German individualism could flourish.

May shaped millions of German readers' views of New Mexico and produced best-selling novels about the American West until his death in 1912. Indeed, his work and fame continued to appeal to Germans well after his death. Karl May's popular appeal, German news magazines have maintained, was greater than that of any other author between Johann Wolfgang von Goethe and Thomas Mann, outshining famous German writers like Karl Marx, Friedrich Nietzsche, or Berthold Brecht. They compare the cult behavior surrounding "the Pop Star of Saxony" and his "Villa Shatterhand" to that of Elvis Presley and "Graceland."[34] May's message of German nationalism, his emphases on chivalry, manliness, and adventure, appealed to German audiences.[35] May's portrayal of Native Americans in New Mexico, similar to that of Balduin Möllhausen, yet with greater Germanophile overtones, acknowledged that Native Americans were a distinct ethnic group with a distinct cultural heritage. In the preface to *Winnetou*, May claimed that "the Red Man possesses no lesser right for existence than the White Man and should have the opportunity to develop societal and state skill in his own manners." Through his characters, May makes clear that Native Americans did not lack the capacity to create a viable state of their own, but that "the evil influence of the white men [particularly Anglo-Americans, and never Germans] ... led the noble redskin astray."[36]

Although one journalist noted the obvious when she wrote that "May's basic message ha[d] little to do with the American West and everything to do with spreading the message of Christian brotherhood,"[37] May was familiar with the American West and with New Mexico's history and culture.

Having read the works of Cooper, George Catlin, Robert von Schlagintweit, and perhaps even Möllhausen, he imparted to his audience a reasonably accurate picture of segments of New Mexico.[38] May repeatedly details the area along the Pecos River, home of his fictitious Apache tribal chief Winnetou; elaborates on one of New Mexico's unique cultural groups, the Pueblos; and for adventurous plots utilizes extensively the Llano Estacado in eastern New Mexico.[39]

Within these geographical and cultural contexts of New Mexico, May developed his plots. Ever present are the dichotomy of civilization versus wilderness and the themes of democracy and freedom so often displayed by Cooper and others. They appear not only through the German protagonist Old Shatterhand and his Apache friend Winnetou, but also through the supporting casts of warring tribes, bandits, scientists, and the increasing number of German immigrants.

Karl May often deviated from New Mexico's realities. He makes little mention of the Indian wars in the Southwest at the time that forced Navajos and Apaches more and more into reservations. Since he wrote during a time of surging German nationalism when German newspapers were filled with theories about the superiority of the Teutonic race, May felt pressed to advance Germanic morals and idealism and occasionally compromised accuracy for ideological purposes. In order to depict Native Americans as noble savages and to suit his German audience, May placed the Apache tribe in cliff dwellings or in a pueblo;[40] the Apache tribal chief appears well educated according to European standards; and Winnetou's sister, like many fictionalized Native Americans before the twentieth century, was equally Europeanized, styled after the Greek ideal of beauty.[41] In addition, Teutonic traits appeared in all of May's adventure stories. In *Winnetou*, Old Shatterhand teaches immigrant Germans, Anglo-Americans, and Native Americans Teutonic wisdom and manners; in *Krüger Bei*, Winnetou visits Karl May in Dresden, Germany, and even the chief of the Navajos is fluent in German (he happens to be married to a German woman!).[42] As one authority points out,

> so thoroughly has May transplanted German customs to
> America that the United States often resembles a German
> colony. May's western heroes drink German beer, hear
> German music, sing German songs and read (authentic)
> German newspapers.[43]

In short, Teutonic ideals replaced authenticity in Karl May's Southwest. In promoting these ideals, May took part in what Ray Allen Billington calls "Europeaniz[ing]" Native Americans, endowing them with the traits and ideals drawn from Western civilization, while they still possess the natural nobility that made them valuable allies.[44] Tailored to German ambiance, this pro-German tendency contributed to the continued success of May's novels.

May was clearly the most influential German writer to comment on New Mexico and the Southwest. By choosing to write in the first person, he subsumes Native American culture and values under his own *Weltbild* and thus makes himself the spokesperson for Native Americans. This style of narration inevitably implied German superiority.[45] Although his approach sold millions of copies, May's information was too inaccurate for those seeking information about the Southwest.[46]

The most qualified person to attempt an assessment of New Mexico for German immigrants was Robert von Schlagintweit. Unlike Josiah Gregg, who "set out to tell the partisan story of the Anglo-American residents of Santa Fe,"[47] Adolph Wislizenus, who had limited exposure to foreign cultures, or even Karl May, who had not even visited the western United States, Schlagintweit was accustomed to foreign cultures. A well-known scientist and researcher, he participated in many expeditions to remote regions in Asia and South America; and he was familiar with the customs and conventions of the United States, having undertaken several trips across the country in 1868–69 and in 1880. In addition, he delivered numerous lectures before German-American organizations during his stays in the United States,[48] so he was acquainted with the needs and interests of Germans.

Schlagintweit saw New Mexico on his way to California from a railroad car traveling from Raton in the northeast to Deming in the southwest. Except for brief visits in Santa Fe and Albuquerque, he spent little time in one place. Equipped with a personal letter of introduction from Interior Secretary Carl Schurz, he visited tribal lands for anthropological studies. Schlagintweit may have interrupted his trip long enough to visit Tesuque Pueblo near Santa Fe and Isleta Pueblo near Albuquerque.[49] Drawing on these side trip expeditions, Schlagintweit offered his audiences a broad array of detailed descriptions and observations about New Mexico, ranging from seasonal temperatures to annual rainfall and from population statistics to postal routes. Schlagintweit elaborated on the territory's

historical developments, its distinct architecture, and the work habits of its multicultural populations.

In his section on New Mexico in *Santa Fe—und Südpacificbahn*, Schlagintweit relied heavily on material by other Germans like Möllhausen, Adolph Bandelier, a German Swiss, and ornithologist Julius Fröbel.[50] Thus, his information and broader understanding of the Southwest resembles that of the German writers who almost half a century earlier portrayed the ethnocentric sense of economic and cultural superiority of Euro-Americans.[51] In addition, Schlagintweit emphasized the economic potential in New Mexico. In 1884 he reported on successful mining activities in the territory, but cautioned that Native American hostilities and water shortages limited the industry's capabilities. New Mexico's plateaus, Schlagintweit concurred with earlier German observers, were excellent for cattle ranges, but they were not rich in water.[52]

Schlagintweit's comments extended beyond geography and economics. A scholar, but also German to the core, he could not omit "superior"

Figure 1:
"Eine Strasse in Alt-Albuquerque"
by German artist Rudolph Cronau
pictures a street scene in the
early 1880s. Courtesy Museum
of New Mexico, neg. #148393

judgments. This ethnocentric attitude was apparent enough to an editor of the *California Mail Bag* in San Francisco that he ridiculed "Professor Von Schlagintweit [who] is rather obviously of German extraction" for his Teutonic and academic values.[53]

Schlagintweit's contacts with New Mexico and New Mexicans were limited, and his views reflected contemporary events. He visited the Southwest on the Atchison, Topeka and Santa Fe Railroad in the late 1880s, an experience that was dramatically different from that of previous travelers. As historian Anne F. Hyde noted, "safety, comfort and speed made the trip more pleasant and faster, but also changed the perceptions of travelers."[54] The deficiencies he observed—lack of steam engines, inadequate transportation, and the absence of gaslights—were all signs of inferiority and barriers to immigration to New Mexico.[55]

Unlike most of the other German authors, Schlagintweit visited the territory at the height of the Indian wars in Arizona and southern New Mexico, and so concentrated on nomadic tribes. Touching on the situation of the

Pueblos only briefly, he criticized the nomadic tribes at great length for their murdering, looting, and other acts of violence.[56] Accordingly, he viewed favorably the reservation policy of the United States. After having visited tribal lands, his judgment was that they were adequate and did not resemble "Pferche" (pens) as critics had claimed. Eurocentric in outlook, he negated the value of Indian culture and emphasized European virtues of law-abiding citizens whose positive influence on social conditions and on morality would have a permanent impact.[57]

Despite occasional excursions into cultural and political spheres, all German publications, to varying degrees, emphasized the economic possibilities of New Mexico and the plights of its Native American inhabitants. It was easy for Germans to overstate New Mexico's economic potential, to downplay its economic disadvantages, to paint a dramatic portrait of the territory's wilderness, or to picture the Native Americans as noble savages. Yet, they struggled to integrate the Hispanics and Hispanic culture of the Southwest into their accounts. German myths about the American West held no place for an already established Hispanic culture and certainly not for the monarchical and Catholic influences of the Spanish culture.

Understandably, New Mexico's long Hispanic tradition of politics, its civic duties, and its cultural development under Spanish and Mexican dominion made it difficult for German writers to promote frontier democracy, religious freedom, and other Anglo-American ideologies. Where the Native Americans were treated in a manner benignly appropriate for the time, the Hispanic population of New Mexico was harshly criticized. The benevolent tolerance often shown toward Native Americans was not apparent in comments about the Hispanic population and their communities.

Literary works that appeared in Germany revealed a discouraging perspective of Hispanics in New Mexico. Josiah Gregg exhibited virulent prejudice toward Hispanics and had "very little good to say about the Hispanic people of New Mexico and of the compatriots in the interior."[58] Profit-oriented, like all merchants of the Santa Fe trade, Gregg was especially keen to reproach Hispanics for their trade restrictions (New Mexico was then still under Mexican authority), and his mercantile outlook often confused his understanding of the Hispanic culture.[59] He showed contempt for the Hispanic work ethic and for Mexican officials. In Western capitalistic terms, Gregg identified freedom as free trade, a system he thought New Mexican Hispanics hindered.

German writers either overlooked Hispanics or blamed them for what they thought was wrong with New Mexico. Adolph Wislizenus, for instance, in his scant treatment of cultural New Mexico, barely touched on Hispanics and displayed a stereotypical disrespect for them. He characterized them as indolent, deceitful, treacherous, and cruel.[60] Möllhausen, too, on rare occasions reported on Hispanics, observing, for instance, that New Mexican children were neglected and unkempt.[61]

Schlagintweit's opinions were no different from those of his fellow writers, but his Germanophile attitude was more pronounced. To Schlagintweit, Santa Fe, the cultural center of the Southwest, seemed to have existed only because of the economic and social activities of Germans. His observations about the local "greasers" was limited to their dirty shoes and their lack of white shirts.[62]

Interestingly, but not surprisingly, most German assessments of Hispanics differentiated between the genders. Möllhausen, for instance, stereotypically identified señoritas as flirtatious and señores as vain. Wislizenus described Hispanas as handsome but Hispanos as ill featured.[63] Here, German writers were participating in a stereotype that many other male visitors of the Hispanic Southwest believed. As one historian of the Hispanic Southwest noted,

> [male visitors] were frequently impressed by the beauty,
> kindness, and flirtatiousness of Mexican women. In forming
> this positive stereotype, American males allowed their hor-
> mones to overcome their ethnocentrism.[64]

To reassure Germans that the West was a wide open and largely uninhabited region removed from aristocratic restraints and saintly, Karl May avoided writing about Hispanics. He reaffirmed German expectations of the West as a place where democracy could develop, and thus, acknowledged the existence of Santa Fe only as a faraway place where one could restock one's supply of cigars and provisions, and he had Old Shatterhand briefly visit Albuquerque once.[65] But instead of becoming embroiled in Hispanic and Anglo-American conflicts, his characters interacted largely outside New Mexico, from California to Wyoming to Missouri. Occasionally, Hispanics appeared in May's novels in minor roles, but, measured against the German values Old Shatterhand exhibited, they generally emerged as vain, arrogant,

Figure 2:
Karl May often emulated Old Shatterhand, his fictional Teutonic hero,
which in turn led many of his readers to believe this character was real.
Courtesy Southwest Collection/Special Collections, Texas Tech University

and elitist characters whose Iberian indifference was often the root of the Native Americans' deplorable situation.[66] May's simple plots of good versus evil, or civilization versus the wilderness, existed outside of Hispanic culture. In omitting Hispanics, he, like other German writers, deprived German readers of a more accurate picture of New Mexico's culture.

These objectionable portrayals had several causes. Americans and (non-Catholic) Germans held deeply rooted prejudices against Catholicism and royalty. Indeed, for many Germans religious and political restraints in the German principalities were often reasons for leaving the old continent. Anti-Catholic views found a receptive audience in Germany and in ethnic centers across the United States. Demographic changes resulting from the Mexican-American war also kept uneasy feelings alive in the Southwest. Wislizenus, for example, remarked that Spanish priests favored a mixture of Catholicism and paganism as a method of control over Native Americans.[67] Karl May's Old Shatterhand was a strong German with true Protestant religious values. There was neither room nor need for a Catholic antagonist.

Balduin Möllhausen was the only German author who elaborated on what he considered the regressive and dubious influence of Catholic priests on the New Mexican population. During his visit to the Zuni pueblo, Möllhausen described the local Mexican priests as lazy and dirty alcoholics and accused them of preaching and baptizing children only against payments. For Möllhausen, priesthood symbolized the decadence of the Catholic Church and the evil influences of civilization, and priests were among the "contemptuous creatures."[68]

In addition to their criticisms of Catholicism, German writers harpooned the political and cultural remnant of the royal Spanish system. New Mexico, with its monarchial bureaucratic hierarchy and the remnants of an *encomienda* (tributary labor) system, did not appeal to the German travel writers. They conveniently forgot that landholding aristocrats in Germany, too, operated a feudal or semifeudal system of compulsory labor. German reasoning followed the suggestion that Phillip Wayne Powell offers in *Tree of Hate*: "We [Anglo-Americans] transferred some of our ingrained antipathy toward Catholic Spain to her American heirs."[69]

Although anti-Hispanic descriptions and enlightened tolerance toward Native Americans continued into the first two decades of the twentieth century, the 1880s marked a change in attitude with the appearance of a new generation of writers such as Charles Lummis. Not until Lummis's appearance in the Southwest "would there be any Anglo traveler of prominence who voiced an appreciation for the 'Spanish' element."[70] As editor of the weekly journal *Out West*, he provided a forum for ideas contrary to those depicting Native Americans as "a hazy cross between a cigar-store wooden eikon [sic] and a dime-novel scalp-taker."[71] To Lummis and like-minded women and men, New Mexico was no longer a backward and undeveloped place, as German travel writers so often described it. Rather, he described the "unexpected hospitality, warmth, and friendliness of the Hispanic and Indian citizens of New Mexico."[72]

Lummis represented a period of growing awareness of Spanish contributions to American civilization and was important "for the touristic marketing of New Mexico."[73] His works, unfortunately, were never translated into German. That absence made the Swiss German Adolph Bandelier the most important advocate of the southwestern region for German-speaking people. Bandelier, who arrived in New Mexico in 1882, spent nearly a decade in the Southwest. Interested in the Native American and Hispanic cultures and their representation in the world, Bandelier "viewed archeology as a lengthening arm of history-gathering hobby."[74] *The Delight Makers*, his best-known work which appeared first as a German novel and public lecture in Germany on delight makers, provided significant commentary on the Southwest.[75] Yet, as editors of Bandelier's *Southwestern Journals* caution, the ethnographer was inconsistent in utilizing Humboldt's theories of the grandeur of Native Americans, and his loyalty to the Catholic Church may have forestalled "any real empathy for the Indians."[76]

Like others, Bandelier had to overcome his ethnocentric bias. Architecture, language, native conduct—everything indicated that he was visiting a new people with different customs.[77] His initial portrait of New Mexico was not positive. Bandelier's descriptions and photographs, the German-language weekly newspaper *Highland Union* noted, "do not entice us to exchange our present home for the bleak and sandy high plateau of Santa Fe." In addition to Bandelier's comments, the newspaper warned people of encouraging news in other newspapers that advertised the fertility of New Mexico's soil. Rather, the editors suggested, mining speculations were responsible for most of the population increase in New Mexico.[78]

After the initial culture shock had worn off, however, Bandelier began, in subsequent trips to the Southwest, to appreciate the cultural diversity.

Figure 3:
Adolph Bandelier visited the Mission of Santo Domingo Pueblo in 1880.
Courtesy Museum of New Mexico, neg. #4299. Photo by George C. Bennett

His reports to the Highland newspaper reflected a larger recognition of these cultural differences. To be sure, he and his wife missed the wheat fields and fruit orchards of Illinois, but their descriptions of Santa Fe, for instance, were cheerful. Bandelier was restrained in his comments about the Native American population. He defended the policy of reserving fertile land for the Native Americans against intolerant Euro-Americans.[79] No friend of communal ownership, however, he contended that the villagers were communists "who could teach certain modern Socialists a few things."[80] Like Möllhausen before him and May after him, Bandelier believed that this communal form of living could be altered with the help of a supportive and tolerant white American population.[81]

Unfortunately, Bandelier's influence in Germany was limited. Although an authority on New Mexico and the Southwest, Bandelier did not publish nearly as much as did Möllhausen and May. Conversely, he had a larger audience in the United States, specifically in the Midwest. His reports were published not only in the *Highland Union* in Illinois and the *Belletristisches Journal* in New York, but also in the *Anzeiger des Westens* in St. Louis.[82] This may have helped influence interstate migration among German Americans who started to arrive in significant numbers in New Mexico in the 1880s. Bandelier promoted the Hispanic culture of New Mexico at the end of the nineteenth century until his death in 1914. This promotion was too little too late. Not only was Karl May's popularity still rising, but translated works by Zane Grey began to appear on the German market to continue the romantic tradition of the West.[83]

Germans interested in New Mexico and the Hispanic Southwest had limited material with limited perspectives from which to extract pertinent information. Romantic adventures too often dominated the German literature of the Southwest. From Wislizenus's first visit to the Spanish borderlands in 1839 to Karl May's fictitious visits to the Pecos in the early twentieth century, New Mexico was portrayed as a territory with few attractions for home seekers. The multicultural experience in New Mexico presented cultural challenges German writers could not or would not meet. Thus, New Mexico stood in stark contrast to the fertile, inviting places in the Midwest and elsewhere.[84]

Obviously, the Southwest was more than the land of heroic trappers and Indian fighters described in the works of Möllhausen, Armand, May, and others. Into the region's tapestry were also blended Mexicans, Native

Americans, Chinese, American Hispanics, and women.[85] In the writings of Germans during the nineteenth and early twentieth centuries, New Mexico appeared only as an exotic place to visit for adventure and perhaps for quick profits; but it was neither an alternative to the old continent nor a land of opportunity. New Mexico could not compete with more popular destinations for Germans in the American West.

CHAPTER TWO

A Profile of the German
Ethnicity in New Mexico

Most accounts of Germans in New Mexico single out individuals; but these interpretations illustrate only the literate, affluent, and prominent German immigrants in New Mexico. The persistent emphasis in New Mexico history on the few German merchants like the Hunings, Spiegelbergs, Ilfelds, Jaffas, and Beckers creates a distorted picture of German activities. Focusing on these few well-known men, lesser known Germans and German Americans are distorted or neglected.

In fact, German women and men of other professions far outnumbered merchants. But the reasons for the emphases on the German merchants are obvious: They were well educated, financially successful, and often left behind personal and business records for historians. Few of the other Germans and German Americans left any records. The lack of personal accounts dealing with the "silent masses" requires reconstructing Germans' and German Americans' lives through United States census data and other historical records.[1]

This profile of German men and women in New Mexico from the 1840s to the 1910s is largely based on the census records. These records are, as Margo

Anderson has noted, a "full-fledged instrument to monitor the overall state of American society."[2] The findings serve partly as background information about all Germans and German Americans in New Mexico and place into perspective ethnic German activities. Primarily, though, it will be a demographic history of the ethnic German population in New Mexico and the changes this group experienced from 1850 to 1920.[3]

U.S. census returns have limitations. Not only was the census taken in decennial intervals, but also federal agents occasionally collected false information or omitted entries.[4] Despite these limitations, the U.S. census returns reveal a wealth of information: birth place, age structure, occupational standards, and ethnic concentrations. This study is a simple percentage analysis of the ethnic German group to reveal trends and tendencies in its numeric strength, influences, and experiences in New Mexico.[5]

A primary problem in any study of Germans as an ethnic group is identification. Prior to German unification under Bismarck, the census showed numerous German kingdoms, principalities, and duchies as birthplaces; but after 1880 the census determined those born within the political boundaries of the newly created nation as simply German. Although this solution was probably the only sound one, it creates numerous obstacles for one using census data. In his study on Germans in Nebraska, for example, Frederick Luebke had to deal with the enigma of German nationality.[6] As he points out, an Alsatian after 1871 was German by nationality but French by culture and upbringing. Further problems arose with states like Austria, Switzerland, and Luxembourg, which also contained segments of a culturally German population but were not, by definition, German. A similar question occurs with Germans from Russia, Hungary, and other Balkan states.

The census following German unification in 1870 requires much guesswork concerning the ethnic origin of a native of Switzerland with its diverse German, French, Italian, and Roman ethnic groups. The same is true for immigrants from the multiethnic states of Austria-Hungary and Russia. As Luebke correctly points out, "the basic challenge ... [is] to decide which Swiss, Austrians, Alsatians, Russians, and Schleswig-Holsteiners were actually Germans."[7] For accuracy and consistency of the statistical data, the German ethnic group in this work will include only persons born in and to parents of Bismarck's Germany as it existed in 1871.

Though they played a small role numerically in the settlement of the territory, ethnic Germans are an important part of New Mexico's history. They constituted the second largest European ethnic group in the period from 1850 to 1920. The territorial census of 1850 lists 292 Irish and 224 Germans, with the German population thus representing a mere 0.3 percent of the total 61,547 New Mexico population (Native Americans are not included). Germans comprised 10 percent of all foreign-born men and women in New Mexico. If one takes into consideration that more than half (1,365) of the foreigners claimed Mexico as their place of birth, the German share of other foreign-born rises to almost 28 percent. Like Germans, other foreigners in New Mexico came predominantly from northern and central European countries.[8]

Over the decades, German migration to New Mexico remained relatively constant. In 1860 Germans represented 8 percent (545) of the foreign population and 0.6 percent of the total population, with Irish immigrants leading the European countries.[9] Even though the population of the New Mexico territory in 1864 declined because of the creation of the territory of Arizona and new border alignments with Colorado in the north, German numbers in the 1870 Census only dropped to 7.5 percent (422) of the European contingency and to 0.4 percent of the total population. This small decrease suggests the scant attraction Arizona held for Europeans.[10] In 1880, the German element took a narrow lead over the Irish in New Mexico. The census shows 684 (0.5 percent) Germans in the total New Mexico population and a nearly one-percent increase to 8.4 percent of the foreign populace.[11]

The arrival of the Atchison, Topeka and Santa Fe Railroad in the territory brought a decline of the German share in the total population. The railroad promoted interstate migration of many American laborers and foreign settlers, with increasing numbers of such ethnic groups as Bohemian miners and Chinese railroad workers and miners. Despite this, Germans remained a significant ethnic factor in New Mexico.

By 1900 the picture had not changed. German immigrants took the lead, this time over English immigrants. Listed in the census are 1,257 persons born in Bismarck's Germany, representing 9.1 percent of the foreign population and 0.6 percent of all New Mexicans, illustrating a small increase from the previous (1880) census. While Germany and the Northern European states dominated European immigration, Italian immigrants, primarily miners from the region around Raton, were steadily increasing. Still, residents of Mexican descent accounted for about half of the foreign population in New Mexico.

The 1910 Census statistics indicate a decline in immigration to New Mexico. Germans now represented 7 percent (1,629) of the foreign numbers, second to the Italians and ahead of the Austrians. Both Italians and Austrians were concentrated in the New Mexico mining areas near Raton, Gallup, and Silver City. The decline in German immigration to the territory reflected the general decline of German immigration to the United States and is partially explained by a nationalistic resurgence in Germany.[12] The deteriorating situation in the first decade of twentieth-century Europe that led to World War I and changes in U.S. immigration laws after the war resulted in further decline in German immigration. The 1920 Census reports that only 3.9 percent of the foreign population in New Mexico were of German birth, just 0.3 percent of New Mexico's population.[13] The low German percentage in New Mexico, always far below the 12-percent national average, suggests little attraction of New Mexico for German immigrants.

The addition of second-generation Germans does not significantly affect a change in the German immigrant picture. No adult German American appears in the 1850 and 1860 immigration statistics, and in the 1870 census only one second-generation German is listed. During the decade between 1870 and 1880, however, significant numbers of German Americans began to gravitate to the Southwest and New Mexico. Among the top attractions were the railroad industry, which provided jobs and easier access to the territory, and the opening of new lands under the Homestead Act during the first decade of the century. Yet, even after one factors in these second-generation German adults, the German presence in New Mexico never exceeded 1.1 percent (in 1900) of the total population between 1850 and 1920.

In New Mexico towns, Germans never achieved the ethnic dominance as did, for example, the Irish in Butte, Montana, or the Italians in some of the San Francisco districts. The Irish, for instance, "could build an Irish community to their own specifications" since no other ethnic group hindered their activities. San Francisco, on the other hand, had such a large population that newcomers felt compelled to settle initially in ethnic ghettos to ease the difficult sociocultural adjustments.[14]

New Mexico's cultural geography presented different challenges for immigrants. Centuries of cultural, social, and political influences from Spain and from Mexico left a strong imprint on New Mexico. As cultural geographers have noted, one culture often dominates a particular region. In the case of New Mexico, the influx of Anglo-American immigrants, and their politically and economically powerful presence, did not noticeably change the cultural tendencies of the Southwest, particularly those of northern New Mexico.

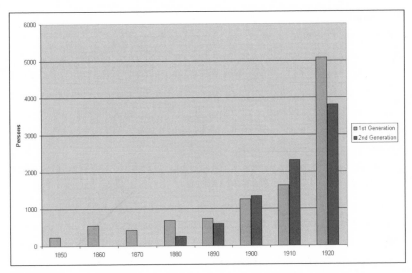

Table 1:
German Population of New Mexico.

Cultural influences from neighboring Old Mexico continued to be present and kept cultural pluralism alive in New Mexico. As one cultural geographer pointed out, "the Hispanic Southwest remains a battleground of cultures, [and] the major example of cultural pluralism in the United States."[15] With the arrival of the railroad and the limited mining boom in the 1880s, New Mexico underwent a slow transition to an Anglo-American industrial economy, but communities in the territory were never large enough to develop an ethnic neighborhood. In 1870 in Santa Fe, for instance, European Americans were evenly split in their choice of residence: One-third lived with Mexican neighbors, another third resided in a mixed neighborhood, and the last third stayed in an American cluster. Until the arrival of the railroad impacted the towns along its tracks, residential segregation was insignificant not only in Santa Fe but throughout New Mexico.[16] Some historians and sociologists have argued that this lack of ethnic clustering eased assimilation since buffers between German newcomers and the larger Hispanic society were missing.[17]

True, New Mexico had few major communities, and its urban proportion was the lowest in the West until 1920,[18] but the census clearly shows that these few communities were the locations where many Germans settled. Throughout the second half of the nineteenth century and the first two decades of the twentieth century, Santa Fe and Las Vegas, New Mexico, maintained a steady population of Germans. Yet, beginning in the 1870s Germans and German Americans gravitated toward Albuquerque. The city evolved as the economic center after the arrival of the railroad and matured into the spearhead to the southern and western parts of the territory. Other towns along the Santa Fe Trail and the railroad tracks, too, grew into small economic centers. Locations of interest to German immigrants were Grant County, during the mining rush in the 1890s, and Colfax County, where mining ventures also developed.

Most Germans who arrived in the territory were well educated in either the German Gymnasium system or the vocational tradition. Nearly all appear to have been literate in their native language. In fact, in no decade was the percentage of illiteracy among Germans larger than 3 percent. Unfortunately, the U.S. Census Bureau was not interested in an immigrant's ability to communicate in Spanish. To be sure, communicating in English was an essential tool in the United States. In the Hispanic Southwest, however, under Spanish and Mexican influence since the late 1590s, the Spanish language was still of enormous importance. It was the language of the street and of business. Enumerators, unfortunately, were provided with only one column to record immigrants' ability to speak English or their native tongue. Throughout the territorial and early statehood periods, Germans satisfied the census taker's requirement for English. Never more than 3 percent were unfamiliar with English, and the number of men and women unfamiliar with English declined further in the twentieth century. Some individuals were raised speaking Spanish because of their proximity to Spanish-speaking population clusters in the northern part of New Mexico.

In general, the German language simply was not a factor in territorial or state affairs as it was in the large, German-speaking states of the Midwest or large urban centers across the United States. There, German language was considered a birthright that should not be sold out for a "Yankee pottage."[19] The Germans and German Americans scattered across New Mexico did not feel the need for such culture-preserving German institutions as the church, school, or press. The dominant cultural force in New Mexico was the Catholic Church, influencing not only religious matters but schooling as well; the nearest German newspaper was published in St. Louis, Missouri.[20]

German ties were further weakened through intermarriage with non-Germans. During the early years of the territory, no unmarried German woman came to New Mexico, so affluent German merchants went east or

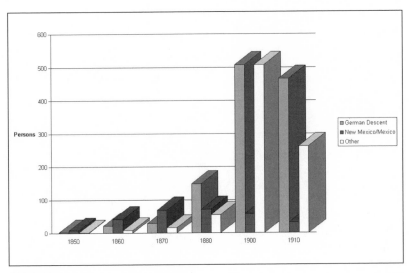

Table 2:
Marriage Trends – 1st Generation

to Germany to find a German bride. Many less prosperous and less prominent men, however, married locally. These cross-cultural marriages were not
unusual in the Southwest. Indeed, as one historian has written, "continuous and intimate contact between Hispanic and Anglo spouses helped to
bridge cultural differences."[21] However, in a few cases, rather than easing acculturation into the Anglo-American society, intermarriage resulted only in
acculturation to the Hispanic way of life. Children born into some German-
Hispanic families were able to speak only Spanish.

The experiences of cross-cultural marriages suggest that German immi-
grants, particularly outside the urban centers in New Mexico, internalized
the Hispanic culture rather than becoming acculturated to the Anglo-
American culture. Until 1880, when the marriages between Germans and
Hispanics dropped off dramatically, almost two out of three (ca. 70 percent)
German men married Hispanic women. Marriages between Germans and
Hispanics decreased after 1880 when more and more immigrants and migrants
came to New Mexico. Then married couples came to the Southwest but more
single women arrived in the territory as well. By 1910, only 7 percent of all
Germans married a Hispanic spouse.

Marriage patterns, of course, are also reflected in the age stratification
of Germans coming to New Mexico. The first German men to the Southwest

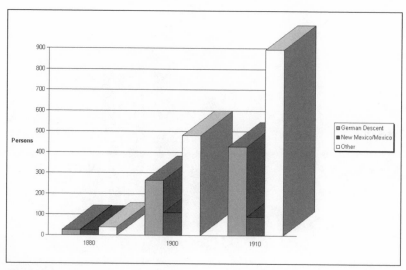

Table 3:
Marriage Trends – 2nd Generation

were young. Through 1870 more than 50 percent of the immigrants were between twenty and forty years of age, but the majority was under thirty. Because travel to the Southwest was difficult and the establishment of a homestead in the Southwest required strength and stamina, few people over fifty immigrated to New Mexico before 1880. The pattern changed noticeably in the late 1870s. A safer, faster, and less strenuous means of transportation was available when the Atchison, Topeka and Santa Fe Railroad crossed the Raton Pass into New Mexico in 1878 to reach Las Vegas and Lamy, and eventually Albuquerque. As a result, more older German and German American women and men arrived in New Mexico. Farmers, particularly those who came at the beginning of the new century and who "normally took up land and cultivated it as families," changed the demographic picture.[22] Women and men between forty and seventy and a surprising number of people between the ages of seventy and eighty appeared in the censuses, indicating not only that older persons were immigrating to the area but also that early German settlers to New Mexico were coming of age.

At first, New Mexico seemed to have little need for "Eastern ways and occupations." But the arrival of the railroad benefited the Anglo-American immigrants more than it did Hispanics and Native Americans. As one historian noted, "with the railroad came commercial opportunities, which New

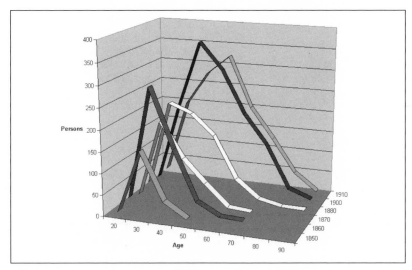

Table 4:
Age Distribution – 1st Generation

Mexico's business-minded minority immediately recognized."[23] Clearly, the railroad not only offered Hispanics some employment opportunities, but also dramatically improved the job prospects for Euro-American immigrants.

Through the occupational information of the decennial census data, one can form not only a picture of an individual ethnic group's economic situation, but also monitor its social mobility.[24] German professionals such as engineers, physicians, pharmacists, educators, and clergy were consistently the smallest group to find its way into New Mexico. In a group that never represented more than 4 percent (1880 and 1910) of the German work force, only a few German engineers made a living in the state. Even mining and railroad developments that required university-trained skills did not attract a significant number of German engineers to New Mexico. An occasional pharmacist or doctor opened his office, and a few German lawyers practiced law in New Mexico.

German educators, too, showed little interest in New Mexico. The public school system in New Mexico was in the early stages of development, with few public schools in the nineteenth century. Instead, immigrant women often taught their children at home to ease the financial burden. In this regard, however, Elliott West in his study on children in the West concludes that "on balance, frontier home education was better than adequate."[25] Likewise,

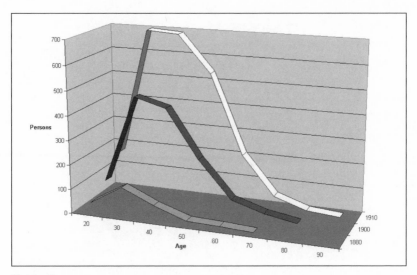

Table 5:
Age Distribution—2nd Generation

German priests and nuns never constituted a significant professional group in New Mexico. Occasionally they served in New Mexico, but their numbers were never as influential as, for example, the German Jesuits in Arizona or the Italian Jesuits in New Mexico.[26]

Other occupational groups came to New Mexico in relatively small numbers. Unskilled laborers did not come in large numbers until the 1880s, when mining and railroad activities called for unskilled labor in that field and when growing retail businesses of urban centers needed increasing numbers of salespersons. For example, although only one salesperson was listed in the census up through 1880, economic and demographic developments expanded those numbers in later decades: The 1900 census lists thirty salespersons and the 1910 enumeration is forty.

Overall, the number of unskilled German laborers slowly expanded from 12 percent in 1850, but never rose above 16 percent of the German work force. Instead, Hispanics continued to fill unskilled jobs.[27] The unskilled work force remained constant. Few large-scale employers, who often provided newly arriving immigrants with their first jobs, resided in the Southwest. Other regions were more attractive, and New Mexico's rural, agricultural traditions precluded structured factory work. As one English labor historian pointed out, men and women who were "accustomed to work for subsistence, not for maximization of income," rarely moved easily into industrialized life.[28] This resistance was even more difficult for Hispanic New Mexico where agriculture predominated. Industry was centered around domestic workshops and family farms, and New Mexico withstood the industrial development of workplace longer than did other states. The availability of new agricultural land in the 1890s held the territory in its preindustrial stage, providing additional opportunities for unskilled laborers to secure jobs. Generally, unskilled labor remained a small portion of the German labor force, but competition for low-paying jobs was as intense as in New York or Milwaukee.

Semiskilled professions, which required a "modern" economic infrastructure and capital-intensive manufacturing, were even less represented. Semiskilled workers, primarily employed in transportation businesses as teamsters and drivers until the 1880s, grew in number with the discovery of precious metals in New Mexico. Still, New Mexico's territorial mines were, in comparison to other lodes, modest and remote. Poor road maintenance in the mining regions and Indian hostilities in the southern parts of the territory hampered vigorous exploitation. Even when these obstacles lessened in the 1880s, progress in the mining operations was limited for German miners and prospectors.[29]

German miners and prospectors in the West realized that, when working independently and without capital investment, profits were difficult. In a Marxist-influenced study of miners, Norbert Finsch suggests that the ideology of free labor was hard to maintain. Independent prospectors usually wound up in the employment of a mining company or had to move to other occupations.[30] If German prospectors stayed in mining, they joined other miners in the coal fields near Raton, which grew in importance after the arrival of the Atchison, Topeka and Santa Fe Railroad in New Mexico in the late 1870s.[31] In contrast to Italian, Bohemian, and Austrian laborers, who concentrated in ethnic clusters near mines in the northeastern part of the state and near Gallup, German miners did not establish ethnic communities but dispersed throughout the territory.

The appearance of the railroad also opened numerous semiskilled jobs, like brakemen and switchmen, within the railroad system. Mining and railroad enterprises drew individual wage earners to the Southwest and attracted "a different civilization that injected new social and economic practices throughout the Hispanic Southwest."[32] But industrial growth in New Mexico was slow, creating only limited opportunities for Germans, with the percentage of semiskilled laborers among the German workforce in New Mexico remaining constant until 1900. Thereafter, fewer German semiskilled workers entered the territory, partly as a result of the general decline of German immigration to New Mexico and the United States.

Clerical jobs in New Mexico remained limited as well. After a peak of 14 percent of the German workforce in 1870, these occupations consistently declined to a low of 4 percent in 1910. In part, the slowly developing territory, entrenched in what William Parish called "petty capitalism,"[33] frequently required that businesspeople be both employer and employee. This rudimentary economic framework in New Mexico during the territorial period did not require many clerical workers.

Thus, it was difficult for clerical, unskilled, and semiskilled workers to make a living in the Southwest. Unlike the East and Midwest, the Southwest lacked a manufacturing and industrial foundation. While land was the main inducement to come west, laborers often, as one historian has written, "could not escape westward regardless of the availability of free land,"[34] lacking sufficient start-up capital for such a passage.

Available land notwithstanding, New Mexico did not advertise itself well to Anglo-Americans as an agricultural region. In fact, prior to the arrival of Anglo-American farmers, the rural life of the Hispanic people was "unhurried if frugal," dependent on unspecialized labor in the sheep industry.[35] The agricultural environment, so different from Germany's geography and culture, attracted only the most adventurous farmers. As has been demonstrated in a comparative study of German farmers in Russia, the American Midwest, and the Brazilian pampas, new and strange environments required a good deal of adaptation.[36] Even New Mexico's territorial promoters acknowledged the limited farming potential: "Agriculture is confined to the valleys, where irrigation can be made available; and lands thus available are of sufficient breadth to supply home demand."[37] What promoters generally neglected to mention was the uncertainty of titles to Spanish and Mexican land grants. As one historian of the territory noted, "in New Mexico it was the spurious claims, instituted largely after American occupation that proved the greatest deterrent to settlement."[38]

Only in later years, after the railroad was established, did New Mexico attract significant numbers of German and German American farmers. Unlike California, which "exhibited many of its distinctly twentieth-century characteristics" early on, New Mexico was neither highly mechanized nor dependent on a large force of migrant workers in the late nineteenth century.[39] In 1880 German farmers and a few stockraisers represented 11 percent of the German workforce. But after large segments of New Mexico's eastern territory were opened for homesteading, the number of farmers doubled between 1900 and 1910. Similar to settlements elsewhere in the United States, German farmers in New Mexico settled in the wide, eastern plains of the area, "rejecting proprietary plans for settlement in rural villages, scattering instead on isolated homesteads."[40] The jump from 11 percent in 1900 to 23 percent in 1910 made farmers the second-largest group among the German workforce in New Mexico.

Most visible among Germans in New Mexico were the proprietors and managers. Since few managerial positions were available in mining and manufacturing, this group was by and large service oriented. They catered to local markets, Santa Fe Trail migrants, military posts, and railroad or mining interests. Often, in cooperation with local Hispanic entrepreneurs, German merchants could be found in the forefront of economic development.[41] They were active even prior to the American takeover of the Southwest.[42] The early appearance of Germans in New Mexico is not surprising when one recalls the economic importance of the Santa Fe Trail, a caravan route from St. Louis to Santa Fe, the brainchild of merchants trying to fill the needs of Mexico's neglected province.

Within this entrepreneurial group, merchants made up by far the largest numbers. Men and women working in retail, food, and hardware represented more than half of this group, followed by persons in hotels, saloons, and restaurants. In 1850 every individual in the entrepreneurial group was a merchant. Although the numbers of merchants dropped during the following decades, as late as 1910 German merchants comprised more than half of the entrepreneurial group.

The German entrepreneurial group remained a constant force in New Mexico, representing up to 26 percent (in 1880) of the German labor force. Even after the territory's border realignment, creating Arizona in 1864, the entrepreneurial group experienced an increase. Many German entrepreneurs not only supplied New Mexico with much-needed goods and merchandise, they also provided the predominantly barter society with a primitive banking system. "The merchant credit system"[43] which all residents of New Mexico alike utilized, fulfilled banking needs into the 1870s, when the first banks in Santa Fe and Albuquerque opened.[44]

Even larger in number than the entrepreneurs was the skilled segment. In fact, skilled workers represented the largest portion of the German workforce throughout the period between 1850 and 1920. A number of occupational opportunities attracted German skilled labor to the Southwest. The dominant professions in this group were woodworking occupations (primarily carpenters), bakers, and smiths. The lack of restrictive guilds typical in German states, along with the opportunity to work as an independent craftsperson with a chance to own a business, may have influenced the decision of craft workers to come to the territory. Since, as one historian notes, "[their] pride in craft became an important community value," many of these laborers located in the urban areas of New Mexico such as Albuquerque, Santa Fe, Las Vegas, Las Cruces, and even Roswell.[45] By the beginning of the twentieth century with industrial growth reaching New Mexico, urban centers offered jobs in the building trades and in mining and railroad construction.

The economic well-being of Germans on the southwestern frontier can only be inferred during the decades from 1850 to 1870. Whereas the census form provided for a column of real and personal estate, the numbers reflect only general information about economic and financial welfare of people in New Mexico, especially since definition of real estate (land and home) and personal (financial) holdings were unclear.[46]

The most profitable occupations were undoubtedly those of the entrepreneurs, whose financial strength dominated. In 1850 nearly two dozen entrepreneurs, all of them merchants, accounted for nearly 86 percent of German real estate in New Mexico. The picture never changed. In 1860 the entrepreneurial group held 64 percent ($132,067) of German assets. The total rose over the next ten years despite only a three-percent increase in German entrepreneurs. In 1870, businesspeople enlarged their holdings to 75 percent ($222,300) of all German real estate holdings in New Mexico.

Not just the capitalists benefited in New Mexico; other Germans, although their incomes were much smaller than those of the entrepreneurs, improved their economic status as well. Skilled workers, the other dominant group among Germans in New Mexico, slowly but consistently expanded their holdings. Although the first skilled laborers who came to New Mexico in the 1840s had accumulated, as a group, only $1,635 in real estate, these holdings swelled by 1860 to almost $27,000. Parallel to expanding population, property accumulation in the 1860s likewise increased; the 1870 census reveals a total of $39,855 in property.

The financial holdings of other groups are more difficult to evaluate. Although their ownership of real estate and personal estate often seems considerable, a closer look shows that one person in the respective group often held most of the wealth. For example, the semiskilled group's real estate holding for 1860 was $10,000, but it was all in the hands of one individual, the owner of a mine in Doña Ana County.[47] Farmers are another group that can be assessed with limited certainty. In 1850 ten farmers' real estate holdings amounted to $1,855, but in 1860 these holdings increased to $25,150 for eighteen farmers and ranchers. In 1870, the total plummeted to $15,920 for twenty farmers and ranchers, perhaps because of difficulties over land grant titles and the separation of Arizona territory in 1864.

The picture is similar in personal property holdings. Entrepreneurs in 1860 held $647,520, or 74 percent of all German personal holdings; in 1870, the share increased to 83 percent or $527,470. New Mexico's colonial conditions suited entrepreneurial Germans well. Likewise, skilled laborers slowly but consistently increased their savings. Their share in German holdings was $44,500 in 1860 and $65,475 in 1870. That same year, 1870, the individual from Doña Ana County who had significant real estate holdings had personal property of $106,000, which accounted for nearly all of the assets of the semiskilled group.

In the other occupational groups, one or two individuals also dominated. The professionals' personal estate for 1860, for instance, amounted to $39,340, but $12,000 of this total belonged to mining engineer Fred Brunekowone and $25,000 to civil engineer Herman Ehrenberg. The listings for agriculturalists' holdings are suspect because the census was taken prior to the harvest. In 1860, when personal estate for farmers was relatively high at $25,700, more than half of the total was in the hands of two farmers, Moses Schwabacher of Socorro County, $10,000, and Frank Weber of Mora County, $6,000.

Overall, in the three censuses from 1850 through 1870, when personal and real estate was listed, New Mexico clearly was a profitable region for entrepreneurs. Although it was profitable for individual skilled workers, agriculturalists, and professionals, it was less so for them as a group, and the unskilled and clerical groups experienced only limited financial gains.

The economic status of Germans after the 1870s can be measured only through their ownership of property and through their employment status. Of the 1,241 first-generation Germans in 1900 New Mexico, 36 percent

(454) are listed as owning their house or farm, while 23 percent (287) rented their dwellings. Only thirteen of the renters leased a farm, and 500 Germans did not report their property status. The 1910 census shows a slight drop in home ownership, suggesting that Germans with less income and those who considered the territory only an interim place were moving into New Mexico. Of the 1,629 Germans, 29 percent (468) owned their home (free or mortgaged), only 12 percent (203) were renting, and the rest did not list any home status.

Other than through home ownership, it is difficult to assess Germans' economic well-being since the U.S. Census Bureau ceased to ask economic questions after 1870. Only in 1910 did the census taker again require information about the occupational status of the residents. The answers are limited indicators of German immigrants' economic situation, since the term "self-employed," for example, does not necessarily indicate financial independence. The terms "self-employed" and "employer" do give clues, however, to what extent immigrants in the early twentieth century participated in the "American dream" of individual ownership. In that, nearly half (387) of the respondents to the question of employment status claimed to own their businesses and to employ others, while 401 declared wage labor.

Not until the railroad advanced into New Mexico and new homestead land was opened in the territory did significant numbers of second-generation Germans appear in the New Mexico censuses. The census of 1870 lists only one second-generation German, Peter Subert, nineteen-year-old son of farmer John Subert and his Hispanic wife, Emma, who resided in Bernalillo County. Of the 227 second-generation Germans in 1880, 27 percent were unskilled laborers, 21 percent skilled laborers, and 17 percent entrepreneurs. Semiskilled, clerical, and agricultural workers followed. The smallest numbers were professionals.

New Mexico experienced a considerable increase in second-generation Germans in the last two decades of the nineteenth century. In fact, in 1900 children of German immigrant parents outnumbered the German-born for the first time in New Mexico. The distribution of the second-generation Germans among the various occupational groups changed notably. Of the 807 gainfully employed second-generation Germans in 1900, only skilled laborers and professionals increased their share while the other groups lost shares. The increase in skilled laborers, farmers, and professionals and the decrease in the other groups indicated a turning point in New Mexico: Its rural, self-sufficient towns and regions were turning slowly into more metropolitan centers that developed an increased need for skilled professions and educated people. By the same token, the need for German unskilled labor and entrepreneurs like prospectors slowly decreased as did the mercantile market for the merchants.

These occupational trends continued in the first decade of the twentieth century, with professionals and agriculturalists increasing their shares among the occupational groups. Among the 1,889 gainfully employed second-generation Germans, 25 percent, or one-fourth of the workforce, labored in the agricultural field while 8 percent were professionals. All other groups lost shares or remained stagnant. The skilled laborers, still the second largest group with 413 workers, and the semiskilled workers lost considerably with 8 percent and 7 percent respectively.

When one compares first-generation and second-generation Germans, the percentage of the unskilled labor force of the second-generation Germans was consistently larger than the percentage of this occupational group among first-generation Germans. Second-generation Germans were more prone to accept less stable, "on-the-move" jobs that characterized the unskilled job market in New Mexico. Particularly from the 1880s to 1900, many unskilled second-generation German laborers found employment in rising urban centers such as Albuquerque, Las Vegas, and Las Cruces. Railroad expansion also provided jobs for unskilled labor, whereas mining, another industry of employment for unskilled and semiskilled laborers, was never an attractive industry for Germans of either generation.

Of the other occupational groups, skilled laborers of both generations were strongly represented in the workforce, indicating that Germans with a trade were always sought after in the territory. Of the remaining groups, first- and second-generation German farmers streamed into the territory in equal numbers when new homestead lands opened after 1900 and made up the largest share of workers in 1910. Numbers of clerical and professional workers continued to remain small. They may have found New Mexico unattractive or lacking in employment opportunities.

Second-generation entrepreneurs and skilled workers remained constant ingredients in the German workforce, but second-generation German entrepreneurs were never as numerous or influential as first-generation entrepreneurs, revealing that over the decades the Santa Fe Trail lessened in importance and the impact of the railroad reduced the trade hinterland for general mercantile businesses. Otherwise, retail and specialized stores were on the rise, and competition with other Euro-American and Hispanic merchants increased.

Unfortunately, the census data, aggregated for Germans as an ethnic group, reveals little about women. Although a strong masculine preponderance among Germans in frontier regions like New Mexico was to be expected, German and German American women presented an integral part of New Mexico's development. Many studies of the 1980s and 1990s have shown that women's experiences in the West went beyond taming the social conditions with "quiet force."[48]

Generally, few women, and even fewer gainfully employed women, arrived in the early period of territorial New Mexico, but their numbers increased steadily in the following decades. In fact, just one German woman, Catharina Deus, entered New Mexico via the Santa Fe Trail prior to 1850. She was reunited with her husband, a brewer, in Santa Fe. Only fourteen more German women came to New Mexico in the 1850s. This represented slightly less than 3 percent of the Germans in the territory. During the decade of the 1860s, the number of German women in New Mexico rose by only two women. Sixteen women (4 percent) resided in the territory. Overall, these small numbers of German women confirm that until 1880 Euro-American women were scarce in New Mexico.[49]

Conversely, by 1880 the number of German women in New Mexico dramatically increased. Ninety-two German women (and fifty-five women of German parentage) came alone or with family to New Mexico, a 10-percent increase since 1870, and for the first time second-generation German women resided in the territory. Two decades later, 398 first-generation and 558 second-generation German women lived in New Mexico. These numbers increased to 433 and 1,040, respectively, by 1910.

Throughout these decades, employment opportunities for women were limited. Women either did not seek employment or census takers did not list their occupations. Despite these omissions in the census, women and children from middle- or low-income families had to contribute to family income by taking in boarders, washing clothes, participating in farm work, or serving as helpmates or partners to their families. As Sarah Deutsch discovered in her cross-cultural study of women in northern New Mexico and southern Colorado, "villagers' economy depended on the labor of each family member."[50]

Although ethnic background was a factor among women seeking and accepting wage-earning jobs, the market for women was so confined that ethnic factors should not be overemphasized.[51] In the limited job market, female workers, regardless of ethnicity, had few jobs and were poorly paid. In 1860 only one of the fourteen German women in New Mexico was gainfully employed; the census listed her as a merchant. The number of German women who worked for a living did not increase significantly over the next ten years. The 1870 census lists three women gainfully employed: one hotelkeeper, one seamstress, and one servant.

Although the number of German women increased in the 1870s to ninety-two, the percentage of employed women remained low, with only ten women gainfully employed. In 1880 most German women were employed in skilled and unskilled jobs: three servants, one laundress, two cooks, and one midwife. Moreover, teaching assignments, one of the few jobs readily open to women, were not attractive for German women, probably because these jobs, which often lasted only for a three-month period, had little security and were prone to moral scrutiny.[52] In 1880, at a time when the Catholic Church still controlled much of the territory's educational system, only one German woman was teaching. Equally rare were clerical and entrepreneurial jobs for German women. Nascent industries in New Mexico did not yet demand the clerical staff many eastern companies required. Only one clerk and one wool merchant were listed in the 1880 census as earning a living.

The picture for second-generation German women in the workforce was not much brighter. Of the sixty women listed of German descent, eight were gainfully employed: five unskilled servants and laundresses, a nun, and two entrepreneurs (dance hall owner, saloon owner). The limited number of women in the workforce suggests that the "domestic ideology" "was central to the world view of Anglo women in the West."[53]

Nineteenth-century New Mexico may have had limited opportunities for women seeking employment. The new century, however, with its economic and technical changes expanded, if marginally, the work possibilities for women. In 1900, forty-seven of 398 German women recorded were wage earners, a one-percent increase from the previous census. Similar to general occupational groupings of previous decades, these women were employed in entrepreneurial (11), skilled (12), and unskilled (13) fields. The opening of the farming frontier in New Mexico, too, allowed women to work the land. Yet women in agricultural enterprises (5), similar to women in clerical (1) and professional (5) jobs, remained limited. The small number of German teachers may indicate language difficulties but also suggests that opportunities for advancement in this profession were not quite as promising as some historians have suggested.[54] An increase in women teachers came in the early twentieth century when more emphasis was placed on public education.

Small percentages of second-generation German women were also employed. The 1900 census indicates that only 69 women out of 558 were gainfully employed. These employed women were predominantly in unskilled (33), skilled (13), professional (9), and entrepreneurial (8) fields. German women seemed to show little interest in or were not being hired for jobs that required semiskilled, farming, and clerical experience.

By the beginning of second decade in the twentieth century, the picture had changed a little, with just over 25 percent of 433 German women holding jobs in New Mexico. This was in spite of the fact that the new century brought new demands to the job market. Only three women worked in clerical positions. Of the thirty-four unskilled workers who earned an income, fifteen were employed in domestic services. In the entrepreneurial group most of the thirty-three women listed a generic "own income" as their means of livelihood, suggesting they had family savings or investment incomes. The third-largest group, skilled workers, was comprised of twenty-five women, most of whom were in nursing (18). The remaining two groups, farmers (8) and professionals (11), remained small.

The occupational situation for second-generation German women was similar. In 1910, 1,040 ethnic German women were living in New Mexico, with 29 percent of them (302) gainfully employed. Unskilled jobs (99), particularly in sales and domestic services, and those in skilled professions (60) again topped the list, with nurses and textile workers leading the groups. Entrepreneurial jobs, including those listed under the generic term "own income," included forty women. But other occupations, which previously provided little opportunity for women in New Mexico, increased dramatically in the 1910s, not only for German Americans and other Euro-Americans but also for Hispanics.[55] For instance, the advancement of industry and population in New Mexico required more educators, with German American teachers making up forty-six of the fifty German professionals. Clerical jobs, too, were more accessible in the first decade of the twentieth century. Of the twenty-nine German clerical workers, eleven were stenographers. Likewise, women working in agricultural jobs increased in accordance with the general pattern: twenty-four women worked in the fields.

One aspect of women's occupational careers, buried under census statistics, must be taken into account. Many women with unlisted professions were part of a family unit and as such were enumerated as kin to the "head of the family" without any occupation or as "keeping house." Only after the death of a husband did the responsibilities and holdings fall into the hands of his widow. Quite often, despite an occupational listing of "house keeping," women like Catherine Fritz of Lincoln, Yetta Kohn of La Cuinta, or Johanna Blatt of Santa Fe were full-time workers and partners in the family enterprises.[56] Other women who had generally been raised to be dependent, as was, for instance, Agnes Morley Cleaveland of Mora, adapted to the new situation without a husband and managed the family business.[57] In short, only after the deaths of their husbands did many women gain an identity of their own in the censuses for managing farms, stores, or ranches.

Not all women married; some chose to remain single. The 1880 census does not reveal, unfortunately, the economic status of the thirteen first-generation German women and the fourteen second-generation single women. The enumeration of 1900, on the other hand, indicates that almost half of the thirty-one first-generation single German women were gainfully employed. Working primarily in unskilled waitressing jobs or as teachers with equally low pay, these women rarely held any property. One woman owned her farm, and two others rented their houses. Other women lived with their extended families or rented apartments or rooms.

Over time, the occupational situation of second-generation single women did not improve significantly. Of the eighty-five single women in 1900, thirty-eight were gainfully employed. Although most of them earned their livelihood in unskilled jobs as servants and waitresses (21), women also worked in professional (7) and skilled (6) vocations. Only three women found employment in the clerical field. Property holding for these women was as limited as it was for their first-generation counterparts: One woman owned her house, whereas four rented theirs.

The new century, especially in the advancing industrial system, brought moderate opportunities for single women. In 1910, among the fifty-seven first-generation German women, forty-three earned incomes. Typical unskilled service jobs were available and skilled jobs in the clothing, food, and health industries as well. The 1910 census listed fifteen unskilled and sixteen skilled jobs for German women. Professional, clerical, entrepreneurial, and agricultural jobs were still unlikely jobs for women. Only one woman employed other women, and another was listed as self-employed. Although women's job opportunities improved some, their status as possible property holders did not. Only two women were listed as owning property, whereas two others rented their houses.

The workforce of second-generation single women also increased in numbers in the twentieth century. In 1910 more than half of the 212 women were earning compensation. Again, although employed primarily in unskilled jobs (45), women also worked in professional (22) and skilled (21) fields, and industrial and technological advancements provided additional jobs for clerical workers. For instance, twenty-four women were telephone operators and stenographers. In other areas, five women tried their luck in the entrepreneurial field, and the end of the agricultural depression that plagued the West in the late nineteenth century encouraged some women to consider agriculture as a means for earning an income. Not only did seven women join men as field workers, the changing economic situation allowed them to own some of the land they worked. Although all seven of these farmers owned their farms, only five women working in other professions owned their houses whereas three rented.

Generally, then, job opportunities for ethnic German women in nineteenth- and early-twentieth-century New Mexico were not abundant. But it would have been unusual if they worked outside their homes, for until the end of the nineteenth century the ideology of "domesticity," a middle-class virtue, was stoutly maintained. Toward the end of the nineteenth and in the first two decades of the twentieth century, when more and more working-class immigrants settled in New Mexico, less affluent German women did join the workforce. Not having the "benefits of society's moral sanctions regarding domesticity, they were too busy trying to survive on a day-to-day basis."[58]

Overall, the U.S. census records between 1850 and 1920 show that although they were numerically a small group in New Mexico, Germans represented either the largest or second-largest ethnic group among the European-born and their children. As a group, ethnic Germans showed few signs of the economic depression, characterized by unemployment, illiteracy, bad housing, and poor diets.[59] A substantial segment of them owned property and dwellings, and unemployment among them was rare and often only seasonal. Literacy rates and knowledge of English also were high, and even knowledge of the Spanish language was not unusual.

Obviously, as an ethnic group Germans succeeded economically. A few individuals did exceptionally well. They owned property and were financially secure. Much of this economic success derived from the persistently high numbers of able entrepreneurs and laborers. In turn, ethnic Germans benefited from the presence of socioeconomically lower-ranked individuals in the labor market such as Hispanics, who were often less skilled and less educated in Euro-American traditions.[60]

The arrival of the Atchison, Topeka and Santa Fe Railroad was in many respects a crossroads in New Mexico history. The census records clearly show that the railroad escalated immigration and altered the demography of settlement and marriage. Prior to the railroad, young German-born men settled predominantly in northern New Mexico communities such as Las Vegas and Santa Fe. Most of them married into Hispanic families and adopted Hispanic culture. Some of these families' children spoke Spanish only. A few wealthy men returned east or even to Germany to find a bride.

But in the 1880s, along with second-generation German men and women, other Anglo-Americans and Euro-Americans migrated to New Mexico. Railroad enterprises and land openings in the southern parts of the territory allowed newcomers to move away from northern New Mexico. Gradually the Santa Fe Trail's importance decreased. By the 1880s it had all but disappeared; communities like Mora, Taos, and Las Vegas, and to a lesser extent Santa Fe, lost many German newcomers to rising towns such as Belen, Roswell, Carlsbad, and, particularly, to New Albuquerque. The influx of Anglo-Americans also drastically reduced Hispanic-German marriages. Instead, Germans and German Americans found their spouses among the many other Anglo-Americans who settled in new towns or in new sections of old towns.

CHAPTER THREE

Apathy and Partisanship:
Germans' Influence in Politics

Historians have long tried to determine the influence of ethnic groups on American national and state politics. Studies of this sort, however, are difficult for New Mexico because political interactions and conflicts were seen in racial rather than in ethnic perspectives. Considering all Europeans in New Mexico as Anglo-Americans results in a misleading political picture of the state. It exaggerates the cohesiveness of European groups and the American Hispanics and implies a nonexistent political unity within each group. Clearly, for Germans, geography and religion rather than a shared ethnicity played a greater role in determining political alliances.

It is not surprising that no study of the politics of ethnic Germans exists, as they were almost always considered Anglo-Americans in New Mexico. In addition, unlike Midwestern states or territories or in precincts in major cities like Chicago or Milwaukee, Germans in New Mexico did not congregate in specific counties or precincts. When they did gravitate toward urban centers like Santa Fe, Albuquerque, or Las Vegas, they tended not to concentrate in neighborhoods.

Research of ethnic political behavior in the West reveals that political preferences cannot be easily generalized, although ordinarily Germans tended to support the Republican Party and Westward Expansion policies.[1] A case study in multiethnic San Antonio, Texas, however, found that German- and Mexican-born voters tended to vote Democratic to express their alienation from the Republican Party's nationalistic determination "which mandated their rapid acculturation into the mainstream of American life."[2] Early studies of more densely populated and thus politically more consequential Midwestern states provide a picture of shifting voting patterns and party operations during the second half of the nineteenth century. As historian Paul Kleppner pointed out, "their composite picture is one of an intensely partisan and highly mobilized electorate." The same scholar shows that party voters neither split their tickets nor defected to the major opposition.[3] Studies also demonstrate that political issues, region of birth, religion, geography, and occupation all weighed more than ethnic background.[4] Studies of heavily populated German counties in Nebraska during the Populist era reveal that economic issues, religion, and the liquor question were more important than ethnicity as indicators of party alliances.[5]

New Mexico does not offer a heavily populated German county or town to determine Germans' and German Americans' political behavior and party alliances. In New Mexico between 1850 and 1920, Germans were widely dispersed and lumped together with other "Anglos" as they were rather indistinguishable. Jewish Germans considered themselves, at least until World War I, part of the larger German contingent who settled and developed New Mexico.[6] During the height of German immigration to the United States, Jewish German immigrants were not singled out as a separate ethnic group.[7]

In short, there are few clues as to the political convictions of ordinary German miners, farmers, laundry persons, and craftspersons. Rather, the more vocal, successful, or infamous Germans garner notice. They voiced political preferences, and occasionally attempted to gain political offices. Among them are German merchants, a few ranchers, and an occasional lawyer or craftsperson.

On a national level, it is remarkable that only a handful of Germans attained recognition through federal or state office. As group, then, "the profile of Germans in politics has been almost too low to evoke stereotypes."[8] Unlike the Irish, most Germans were not attracted to American politics. In this regard Germans such as Carl Schurz, Peter Altgeld, and Moses Alexander were the exceptions.[9] Gentile and Jewish Germans alike refrained from seeking political offices. Many historians have suggested that Jewish Germans were reluctant to make political capital out of their ethnic identity partly because of fear of anti-Semitic repercussion. Yet that observation does not explain the reluctance of gentile Germans to involve themselves in American politics.[10] After all, participation in the political life of her or his adopted land often is one aspect of the immigrant's assimilation process.[11]

Following national trends, few Germans in New Mexico tried to attain political offices, and exercised little direct influence in the politics of New Mexico. To understand Germans' limited roles in New Mexico politics, one must reflect on the cultural and political history of the German states. German history is not characterized by political participation of its citizens. Indeed, most Germans were excluded from the political process, and only the upper classes and nobility were in positions of influence. One of Germany's literary greats, Thomas Mann, noted that participation in politics did not benefit the German people; the tradition was one of intellect, epitomized in culture, soul, freedom, and art, and not of politics, exemplified by civilization, society, suffrage, and literature.[12] Minor modifications of German political constitutions between the Napoleonic wars at the beginning of the nineteenth century and the unification of the German states in 1871 did allow for a modest increase in bourgeois participation in state parliaments. However, not until the rise of socialism in Germany at the turn of the twentieth century was the working class able to wield influence in German politics.

This German political climate was not surprising but developed during centuries of divine law and royal rulership; nor was it unique, as other European countries had experienced similar developments. It is remarkable, though, that Germany produced a wealth of influential political thinkers and philosophers. For instance, Immanuel Kant (1724–1804), Johann Wolfgang von Goethe (1749–1832), Georg Wilhelm Friedrich Hegel (1770–1831), and Karl Marx (1818–1883) were influential in the development of world political theory. Yet mainstream Germans did not participate in the political process.

The roots of German political indifference, and even disgust for politics, can be traced to nineteenth-century Germany. As Fritz Stern pointed out in "The Political Consequences of the Unpolitical German," Germans used their greatest achievement, their *Kultur*, to excuse their greatest failure, their *Politik*.[13] Despite a good educational system, Germany did not understand in its entirety the ideas of Kant, Hegel, or Goethe. Sociologist Jürgen Habermas saw a "hidden curriculum" behind the teachings of the philosophers in German *Gymnasiums* that was to promote "elitist self-understanding of academics, a fetishizing of Geist, [and] idolatry for the mother tongue." The goal of higher education was personal, social, and economic advancement, not necessarily a politically aware citizen.[14] Thomas Mann reflected on this attitude already prevalent during World War I when he detected that "intellect and power seem to miss each other consistently in Germany, [and] blossoming of the state and blossoming of culture seem to exclude each other."[15] This trend surfaced in the 1848 uprising when many liberals demanded reforms without a revolution that would have endangered education and property.[16] Rather than use politics to achieve the goal of political freedom, Stern maintained, Germany's upper class "has often disdained the grubbiness of politics."[17] Instead, they thought about legal freedom, freedom from authoritarian powers, and liberation from economic and societal restrictions. Consequently, in pursuing cultural and individual freedom, the German middle class lost sight of the importance of political expression and participation in politics. As a consequence, political indifference was common.

The freedoms Germans sought did not require participation in the politics of the West or New Mexico, even though many had sufficient social and economic stature to do so. Most educated Germans who immigrated to New Mexico cared little for the German thinkers and philosophers. Although immigrants like John Becker of Belen, the Ilfelds of Las Vegas, and the Spiegelbergs of Santa Fe, all well educated, must have been aware of the German philosophers, they immersed themselves in their businesses rather than investing time in the political developments in their new home.

Franz Huning of Albuquerque, a typical German *Freidenker* (free-thinker), illustrates Fritz Stern's apolitical German. Well educated in German public and private schools, he rebelled against his parents' religious beliefs, their sense of law and order, and their wish for him to become a farmer. Rather than paying attention in school, Huning claims in his memoirs, he was more interested in reading his own choice of books.[18] He aborted a mercantile apprenticeship in Bremen and refused to serve in the army in Hanover, his home state. In letters to Franz in Bremen, the elder Huning urged Franz to control his *Freigeist* (free spirit) and to return to God.[19] More than once his father demanded that Franz must quit reading "trashy" novels and stay away from other freethinkers.[20] His parents wrote in vain. Franz maintained friendships with artists, theater people, and other "rebellious" women and men. He remained an atheist.[21] In fact, his final will maintains his disrespect for religious beliefs:

> I direct that my remains be cremated, the ashes put into an
> urn and deposited alongside my children, Lina and Elly. And
> I strictly forbid any and all religious nonsense. If any Old
> Timer should be handy, he may make a speech, but not mix
> up any cant with it.[22]

A list of the books Huning owned in Albuquerque indicates that he never abandoned the books about which his parents warned him. Among others, Huning read Goethe, Schiller, Adalbert Stifter, and Charles Darwin. He also read works by Gotthold Lessing, who questioned the authority of dogmatism and advocated reason. As such, Huning, like many other Germans, lived in pursuit of a life of cultural freedom with a vague but important *Lebensgefühl* (lifestyle). Clearly, Huning's book list underscores Stern's point: Kultur was often a substitute for Politik.[23] Thomas Mann noted of the German character, men and women raised in the German tradition sought to expand their intellect rather than to realize ideas politically.[24] In Albuquerque, though Huning attended weekly theater performances of Goethe, Krug, and Kleist and concerts of Wagner, Beethoven, and Verdi,[25] he remained essentially apolitical and invested his spare time in educational and social activities.

Franz Huning's apolitical style is characteristic of many other Germans and German Americans who settled in New Mexico. Consider, for example, Jacob Korber, educated in German public schools and briefly in a Lutheran seminary, who abandoned organized religion, evaded the Prussian military, and chose immigration to the American West, drifting from Colorado to New Mexico.[26] Making Albuquerque his new home, Korber set up a blacksmith shop that developed into a major venture. Yet despite his

Figure 4:
A few Germans are found among the Albuquerque city officials in this
1901 group photo. Standing: City Clerk C. W. Medler (2nd from left),
Alderman Edwin Harsch (9th from left), Fire Chief Bernhard Ruppe (in
uniform); seated: Police Officer Charles Mainz (far left). Cobb Memorial
Photography Collection. Courtesy Center for Southwest Research,
University of New Mexico, neg. #000-119-0387

success, Korber limited his spare time activities to ward politics, immigrant
activities, and the local Lutheran church.[27]

Other Germans appear to have taken similar paths. Often well educated in German or eastern schools, they achieved social and economic success in New Mexico, but political involvement was limited to local and civic
issues. If they were of Jewish German descent, Reform Judaism encouraged
this trend as it emphasized science in the broadest sense and the German
ideal of *Bildung*, a "constant spiritual self education with a strong emphasis on universal principles such as freedom, equality, and openness." Many
like Albert Grunsfeld and Lehman Spiegelberg accepted appointments to
school boards, whereas a few, such as Lehman Spiegelberg and Abraham
Staab, were elected to county offices.[28]

German women in New Mexico seldom became involved in politics.
On one rare occasion during the *Fasching* period of 1892, German women

of Albuquerque had the opportunity to air political grievances. During this time of fun and satire, Terese Michelbach, probably a second-generation German, took charge and complained on behalf of the women in a rhyme:

> Dies Jahr is ein schaltjahr
> darauf wett ich tausen thaler baar.
> Da deurfen auch die damen wählen
> wen sie auch sonst als nieten zählen.[29]

Generally, though, women, who did not need to work to supplement the family income gravitated toward educational and social activities instead. Flora Spiegelberg, for instance, spent time establishing schools and other educational programs in New Mexico communities. Born in the United States, but educated in German schools, Spiegelberg reflected the bourgeois education of Berlin and Vienna and brought a touch of sophistication to nineteenth-century Santa Fe.[30] Only in later years, at the dawn of World War I, did she become an outspoken pacifist and accused war production companies of making excessive profits. Senator Gerald P. Nye, who headed during Franklin Roosevelt's tenure the powerful and isolationist Nye Committee, is reputed to have told Spiegelberg in 1935, "that he could never quite forgive her for 'stealing his thunder' as far back as 1919."[31]

With only a small number of Germans scattered across New Mexico, political influence was difficult. Germans founded no town in New Mexico.[32] In addition, New Mexico's Germans lacked leaders like Texas had in Prince Carl von Solms-Braunfels and Baron von Meusebach.[33] In these instances, settlements were new, and, as David Emmons has noted, social, economic, and political institutions developed with the respective ethnic group: Butte, Montana, belonged to the Irish in almost the same way New Braunfels belonged to the Germans.[34]

New Mexico, on the other hand, consisted of some of the oldest population centers in North America.[35] Communal and political functions had been in place for centuries. Unlike those in most frontier areas, the institutions of New Mexico at the American takeover in the 1840s were feudal in character, with wealthy men running the towns. The political situation in New Mexico was not unlike that in small German towns headed by secular or religious nobility. Despite studies that try to attribute the patron system to American occupation and capitalistic activities, the system was already in place. Germans and other ambitious immigrants, rather than fighting the system, used or even improved the Spanish system.[36]

The early German immigrants immediately realized that Hispanics shared political power. If they were to succeed in their newly adopted home, Germans had to adjust their behavior to Anglo-American and Hispanic patterns.[37] They did not establish ethnic organizations, such as immigrant societies, to safeguard political and economic success.[38] In fact, the small number of German newcomers discouraged ethnic isolation and favored good relations with the local populations and with the other immigrants in New Mexico.

When Germans did participate in New Mexico politics, they usually did so on a small scale, and even then they rarely concerned themselves with ethnic German issues. Several reasons account for this absence of ethnic concern. First, unlike in Midwestern states, where political issues were highly partisan, in western states ticket splitting was common. For the most part this ticket splitting exemplified a more pronounced tendency toward short-term forces and issues.[39] Second, although voting and political behavior elsewhere in the West was often tied to religious issues, Catholics were so dominant in New Mexico that it was often wiser to avoid religious issues in elections. Clearly, anybody who ran for any office needed Hispanic votes to succeed. Therefore, political clashes over religion were less significant compared to land grant issues, questions about statehood, or Spanish-English language controversies. Third, with very few exceptions, elections and political matters in New Mexico included few ethnic debates that would have mobilized Germans.[40]

Since political-religious tensions were lacking and ethnically relevant issues were absent, Germans usually voted their economic desires and personal convictions. Even in locations of German concentration, as in Albuquerque and Santa Fe, numerical strength was too small to achieve any political control through ethnic power. Instead, they supported Hispanic or other American political agendas and candidates.

Still, the political situation in New Mexico was far from orderly. The factional and constitutional chaos during the first two decades following the United States takeover was a roadblock for any ethnic group to succeed politically. To Germans and other ethnic newcomers, the political environment in New Mexico must have appeared confusing: New Mexico's well-established Hispanic political structure was challenged by the American political system, making it difficult for persons unfamiliar with either system to participate in the process.[41] As historian Howard Lamar has noted, the territory "fitted none of the assumptions of the Ordinance of 1787." A large white population was already present, little public land was available, and no land was suitable for an American farming population.[42] Hispanic political traditions and Anglo-American political modernism created a vacuum that wanted to be filled. Often with the help of the large Hispanic population, farmers and city-dwellers, Republicans and Democrats, Hispanics and Anglo-Americans with different political, social, and economic outlooks wanted to fill this gap. Political intentions ranged from one extreme to the other complicated by numerous "nuances of cultural change and conflict"[43]: from Hispanics who endeavored to preserve their culture and influence on one side to American Anglos on the other who wanted the territory Americanized as quickly as possible. In short, the situation was one of discord, partisanship, and confusion. In fact, political leaders, slogans, and institutions that Germans may have learned about on their way to the United States did not mean much once they arrived in New Mexico. As Lamar points out,

> American party names were used, and each faction had its defenders in Congress, but Republican and Democrat, pro-slave and abolitionist, conservative and liberal, were phrases, which had no real meaning here [in the Southwest].[44]

Even though political confusion in New Mexico was sufficient reason for many Germans to remain politically uninvolved and to attend instead to their occupations and economic aspirations, it allowed for opportunity. Weak party regimentation provided easier access for newcomers, though few Germans accepted the challenge.[45]

Regardless of political agendas, Hispanics held nearly all elective offices. Their ethnic bonds were particularly strong on the county and precinct level and offered only a minute chance for politically ambitious newcomers to get involved. Few Anglo-Americans appeared on the territorial legislative roster, with the first elected German, Bernhard Seligman of Santa Fe County, listed in 1880. More than thirty years elapsed before the first German was elected to the legislature.

On the territorial level, however, politically ambitious Anglo-Americans like Thomas Catron and Stephen Elkins found opportunities for political leadership with positions coming via federal government appointment. Among the few Germans who accepted territorial appointments in the early years of the territory were Charles Blumner, Charles Clever, and William Osterton. But their positions were minor, more civic oriented: treasurer, sheriff, and auditor. The only two Germans prior to 1880 to appear on the territorial assembly roster in nonelective positions were Louis Felsenthal and Clever. Both were listed as clerks of the House (1859) and the Council (1847), respectively.

Even though these early political appointments of Germans are of little significance, they do reveal political alliances and backers. Only when one considers Germans' political associates and acquaintances can one establish their political position, for here was a time when parties were not yet well established and could easily be changed.[46] When the United States Army took over the territory, only one German, Charles Blumner, was prominent in Santa Fe.

Charles Blumner arrived in 1836 in Santa Fe, just in time to witness the 1837 revolt.[47] In fact, Blumner may have been the first German to reside in the New Mexican territory. Unlike many other early arrivals, Blumner did not consider the mercantile business his only opportunity. He gravitated toward politically influential men. During the Mexican period, he worked for Manuel Alvarez collecting debts. Beyond that, "Blumner essentially handled all of Alvarez's business affairs."[48] His association with Manuel Alvarez, the United States Consul in Santa Fe, indicated his desire to have the United States annex and quickly "Americanize" the Hispanic territory. Blumner also accepted Colonel Kearny's appointment as treasurer of the territory and was reappointed in 1851, when Alvarez and Ceran St. Vrain posted a security bond of twenty thousand dollars.[49] In 1858 Levi Spiegelberg and John Mecure secured Blumner's bond as treasurer. The support of German and other well-to-do citizens in Santa Fe suggests that other Germans like Levi Spiegelberg's brothers and Louis Felsenthal may have shared his views of quick Americanization of New Mexico. Blumner's association with these men illustrates a general pattern that American business was often the driving force behind political maneuvering in New Mexico.

Another atypical German immigrant who chose a political career was Charles Clever. Clever joined a wagon train in St. Louis, which also brought Franz Huning to Santa Fe and arrived in New Mexico in 1847.[50] His studies in law, pursued in Santa Fe, benefited his political ambitions. In 1857 he appeared as the clerk of the territorial council, and from 1862 on he was appointed and reappointed as attorney general.

In many respects, Clever was a true politician and an exception to Germans' apolitical behavior. He was interested in the political system and aimed at using it. Through newspaper editorials and in speeches he clearly expressed his political views. Clever, one of the few identifiable ethnic German Democrats (Zodac Staab and Jacob Korber were others), strongly favored Americanization and exploitation of New Mexico as quickly as possible.[51] For instance, Clever supported the 1867 proclamation prohibiting peonage, an announcement that touched a sore spot with some Hispanics as it reflected their ways of life. Views clashed and eventually accelerated to a dispute between J. Francisco Chaves and Clever that is well documented in the Santa Fe newspapers.[52]

Clever's drive for quick "Americanization" was particularly evident in his speech before the national Congress. He painted a clear picture of New Mexico's "American" future. He argued that big business like the railroad had to come to New Mexico to benefit American and Hispanic business elites. In his speech Clever outlined a bright, rich future for New Mexico. To give his speech an authoritative touch, he frequently quoted from the *Santa Fe Gazette*, which he controlled. Clever's apocalyptic vision of "waiting for the day when the rich man with his money will come to be a partner with the poor man with his mine" was undoubtedly an ethnocentric and economically limited perspective. His viewpoint was based on an abundance of available Hispanic and Pueblo labor and the perception that "by mingling our own labor [among the native work force] under proper direction, a healthy industry will be developed, and native artisans [will be] instructed, Christianized and prepared for useful citizenship."[53] Clearly, Clever's exploitative vision was based on a wage system that depended on a racial stratification of labor.[54]

By 1869 Clever had enough political backing to believe that he could become New Mexico's delegate to Congress. Although he won the election, the powerful American Hispanic faction and its Republican candidate contested the election, claiming vote fraud. The claim was successful and J. Francisco Chaves replaced Clever in Washington, D.C. Unfortunately, contesting elections during the 1860s represented a growing distrust between Anglo-Americans and Hispanics.[55] Thus, longstanding disregard for Hispanic values led to Chaves's charges accusing Clever and his supporters of developing the territory for American economic interests. While contemporaries often attributed election improprieties in New Mexico to the Hispanic character and considered it a sign of Hispanics' political ignorance, buying votes was hardly limited to New Mexico or Hispanics.[56]

Though Blumner and Clever chose political careers with mercantile interests as a sidelight, most other Germans who got involved in politics opted for indirect political participation. For instance, many Germans met their civic duty financially. In 1852 Solomon Jacob Spiegelberg advanced the chronically underfunded legislature $4,000 to pay its members.[57] Other financially secure Germans often provided bond monies for Anglos, Germans, or Hispanics who aspired to political offices. Informal politicking was also common. Possibly a casual poker game with Thomas Catron and Jesus Luna or a generous donation to Archbishop Jean Lamy's church fund promoted political and economic interests.[58]

On the whole, however, most Germans stayed away from active territorial politics. They may have voted but did not get involved in party organizations. Business interests guided political matters. Southeastern New Mexico initially tended to be more Democratic because of immigration from Texas and proximity to that state. Ranchers in northern New Mexico may have voted like German immigrant Frederick Gerhardt who "was a staunch Republican, as were most of the early day ranchers, who realized the necessity of a firm tariff on wool, pelts, and hides."[59] Well into the 1920s Hispanic counties were also Republican, but developed Democratic affiliation and mining regions and railroad hubs grew ties to trade unions.[60]

In the 1880s the political picture changed slightly. Early settlers had established their businesses and, because of railroad activities in the territory, towns grew more rapidly. Increasingly immigrants from other parts of the country arrived in New Mexico. By this time, settled Germans were better acquainted with the American political system. Still, most of the Germans' political activities continued to be limited to the local and county level, and often driven by business considerations. When pushing for incorporation of Santa Fe in 1891, the *New Mexican* asked, "will the businessmen of Santa Fe take hold and push the matter to a conclusion?" Many of those businessmen who favored incorporation of the town were German or of German descent.[61] A few Germans, however, were elected or appointed to positions of territorial significance. For instance, John A. Miller, a German merchant living in Fort Bayard, representing Doña Ana, Grant, and Lincoln Counties, was elected to the Territorial Council in 1882, joining Bernhard Seligman as the second German in the New Mexico legislature. Among the influential committees in which Miller participated were Territorial Affairs, Indian Affairs, Finance, and Mines and Public Lands.[62]

Bernhard Seligman, the first German elected to the territorial legislature, was financially established and considered a superb public speaker, who steadily gained political power. Beginning in 1880 he served successfully in both state houses, chaired the Santa Fe County Commission, and was appointed as territorial treasurer.[63] In his first year in the legislative assembly, Seligman was a member of the judiciary and education committees.[64] Not all of his elections were as easy as his first one, however. In 1888, Thomas Catron contested Seligman's election to the Council Assembly, alleging that illegal votes were cast for Seligman, and that the polls in one of the Santa Fe precincts were illegally closed for an hour. The accusations were not substantiated, and Catron's attempt to block Seligman's return to the Council was unsuccessful.[65]

One institution during the territorial period that appealed to Germans was the Bureau of Immigration. Established in 1880 by territorial act, the bureau's mission was twofold: "to prepare and disseminate accurate information" and to present opportunities for "desirable immigration and for the investment of capital." It became, however, more of a propaganda instrument to speed up Americanization in New Mexico.[66] Although a few Hispanics joined the bureau, its membership list reads like an "Anglo Who's-Who" in New Mexico. Many of the members, such as Governor L. Bradford Prince, rancher J. C. Lea, *Las Vegas Optic* publisher J. H. Koogler, and New Mexico Cattle Association counsel Albert J. Fountain, had vested interests in business coming to New Mexico. The organization's German members consisted exclusively of merchants. Lehman and Louis Spiegelberg, William Kroenig, Samuel Eldodt, and Alex Gusdorf, who joined the board a couple of years later, promoted the bureau's agenda and tried to attract more Germans to New Mexico.[67] Obviously, the bureau fulfilled its mission to promote New Mexico's resources. The promotional literature the bureau published emphasized, and not always accurately, fertile soil, salubrious climate, abundant water, and valuable mineral resources. In its quest to "disseminate accurate information," however, the bureau did little to reduce cultural misconceptions about New Mexico. In none of its many promotional publications did bureau members try to rectify any fallacies about Hispanics and

Indians.[68] The failure to discuss Hispanic and Native American populations suggests a hidden political agenda of the Bureau. Attracting Anglo immigrants to New Mexico meant the Bureau could offset the predominantly Hispanic image of New Mexico that many saw as an obstacle to progressive territorial politics and, more importantly, to statehood.

On the local level, Germans in towns like Albuquerque, Santa Fe, and Roswell continued to take active roles in their towns' growth. Although their positions may have been ostensibly political, their real intent was economic. For example, Sydney and Will Prager of Roswell, who had opened a mercantile store with Nathan Jaffa in the early 1880s, became involved in city politics to help protect their real estate and other economic interests.[69] In subsequent decades the Pragers and Jaffa invested money and held municipal offices to further their interests and the town's future.[70]

Germans appeared to shy away from controversial, yet powerful, political organizations and issues. For instance, few Germans were involved in New Mexico's violent Lincoln County war of 1877–78.[71] In fact, none of the influential Germans in New Mexico seemed to have been directly implicated in the dispute, even though Frank W. Angel, a special investigator sent by the U.S. Justice Department to investigate disturbances in New Mexico, made biased assessments (he favored the Murphy faction). His investigation hinted at some indirect involvement of Germans in the political events in the two counties.

Angel indicated that Jerrie Hockraddle, a second-generation German, Charles Probst, born in Prussia, and most likely the German trader Emil Fritz were involved locally in the Lincoln County dispute. Another participant, Robert A. Widenmann, born to German parents, was a close friend of John Tunstall and therefore closer to the events.[72] But in a war of "manipulation" to achieve essentially corrupt ends, these Germans were only minor figures.[73] On a larger scale Angel also warned the new governor, Lew Wallace, that the Spiegelbergs and Staabs were unreliable. The German mercantile dealers of Santa Fe had economic interests in the outcome of the dispute. Angel's warnings also demonstrated, not surprisingly, that politics and economics were often hard to separate. In this case, Angel concluded that the mercantile businesses of the Staab Brothers and Spiegelberg Brothers were bidding for Mescalero contracts.[74] Incidentally, Widenmann, in a letter to fellow German and Secretary of the Interior Carl Schurz, also implicated the two merchants "of defrauding both the Government and the Indians."[75]

Later, in the 1880s and 1890s, Germans remained absent from major political disputes occurring in New Mexico. No Germans were directly involved in the Santa Fe Ring. This is somewhat surprising, as the ring "reflected the corporate, monopolistic, and multiple enterprise tendencies" of the business community—a group in which many wealthy Germans were intensively involved.[76] Two men, Charles Spiess and Abraham Staab, are occasionally referred to in discussions of the ring. The former was a well-established American with possible Germanic ties, and the latter, a German, was best known for an occasional poker game with ring members.[77]

The absence of German ring members is less surprising if one recalls Fritz Stern's assessment that Germans lacked political ambitions. Undoubtedly, wealthier Germans of Santa Fe were informed of what was going on in the ring; but their primary concerns were personal and cultural freedom and the economic success that many lacked in the East or in Germany. In New Mexico they achieved these goals without political commitment.

This lack of political assertiveness was characteristic of Germans throughout New Mexico. Political apathy in the north, for instance, particularly in land issues in the Hispanic counties, is evident in the activities of Las Gorras Blancas. An extensive and detailed study of the "white hats," whose stronghold was in Las Vegas and San Miguel County, indicates that this group attacked or sabotaged no German or German American. None of the several wealthy German merchants of Las Vegas like Ilfeld and Staab, and the German ranchers in San Miguel County like Solomon Floersheim and Gerhardt, suffered from Las Gorras Blancas.[78]

Still, economic demands led to some political involvement and in a few instances fostered civic-minded action. Political involvement was more visible in towns and cities than in rural New Mexico. Like the Pragers of Roswell and W. F. Kuchenbecker, a hardware merchant who became mayor of Gallup,[79] people with economic interests accepted political posts or nominations to political and civic boards. For example, Franz Huning, who invested heavily in the future of New Albuquerque, chaired or sat on various political committees. In 1878, he was a member of the Board of County Commissioners, when relocation of the county seat from Albuquerque to Bernalillo was under consideration. Realizing that this change would mean the loss of jobs, money, and trade, Huning allowed his store to be used for a petition drive to oppose the move of the county seat.[80] During the 1890s, despite a recession, railroad activities and business in New Albuquerque prospered and Huning became a member of the Board of Trade, which was influential in municipal politics, as did Henry Jaffa and Melchior Werner.[81]

A political refugee from the aborted German revolution in 1848, Melchior Werner came to New Mexico with the U.S. Army prior to 1850. He was civic oriented and became an executive member of the Republican Party in New Albuquerque. In 1882, as a candidate for Probate Clerk, he switched to the People's Party which, at least on the local level, had some economic and political impact.[82] In 1885 Henry Jaffa, who eventually became Albuquerque's first mayor, was president of the Board of Trade and also a major member of the People's Party.[83] Even though Jacob Korber was twice elected alderman on the Democratic ticket for the second ward in Albuquerque (1893–1895), once with Herman Brockmeyer, a second-generation German plumber, Korber's activities centered around German immigrants and their children.[84]

Although much of this political involvement was economically motivated, a certain civic sense cannot be discounted. Franz Huning, for example, combined economic and urban political interests. Described as having "a predominating interest in matters of personal business, a dislike of controversy, particularly in a political nature," he offered free land in New Albuquerque to build hotels, churches, and other enterprises to develop the town.[85] Visionary in promoting Greater Albuquerque and engaged in the coexistence of American Hispanics and other American ethnic groups, he worked toward the judicial and political unity of the two towns through economic and political projects. He also encouraged the construction of bridges and tramway lines between the communities and suggested the county courthouse be built in Old Town to unify the Hispanic town and the new area. Perhaps as a symbolic gesture, he situated his famed "Huning Castle" half in Old Town and half in New Town of Albuquerque.[86]

A few Germans were interested beyond local issues. Statehood, for instance, was a matter that dominated territorial politics for more than half a century. Although delays over statehood had many causes, the issue sheds further light on Germans' and German Americans' political activities in New Mexico. Germans with strong economic interests voiced their opinions to influence the outcome of statehood.

The controversy over statehood erupted instantaneously in 1850 after New Mexico became a United States territory. The most popular arguments against statehood were twofold: that the territory had a small population and that the majority of its residents were Spanish-speaking. These arguments surfaced within and outside New Mexico.[87] Like many others in New Mexico, Germans were divided on the issues surrounding statehood.

Early German opinions on the issue are scarce, with Charles Blumner the earliest German indicating his opinion: Already, during the Mexican period, he had closely associated himself with Manuel Alvarez, the American Consul in Santa Fe, who favored statehood immediately after New Mexico became a part of the United States. In the 1860s Charles Clever's speeches also suggest that he favored statehood, a rare political issue on which he agreed with the *Santa Fe New Mexican*, an ardent supporter of statehood.

German opinions are more readily available after 1880. Generally, Republicans pushed for statehood based on the assumption that statehood would bring more immigrants and capital from the East to the territory. Melchior Werner, for instance, represented these ideas in the county Republican Party in Albuquerque.[88] Democrats, on the other hand, feared that the legislation for statehood would benefit special interest groups such as large landowners and mine owners with patents.[89] In Albuquerque younger German and German American artisans and merchants met at Democratic party meetings. Jacob Schwarz, L. P. Krawinkle, Jacob Toepfer, Ernest Kreigelsteiner, H. Hahn, Otto Mann, and Sam Neustadt joined the Young Democrats.[90] Although some Germans voted according to party line, the available opinions of Germans suggest that they were divided by personal interest rather than by party affiliation, religion, or ethnicity.

A few ethnic Germans of New Albuquerque seemed more reluctant than their fellow Germans in Santa Fe to favor statehood. In a petition to the U.S. Congress in 1890, Ernest Meyers, Simon Neustadt, Jacob Weinmann, Solomon Weiler, F. Lowenthal, and members of the Mandell family, all merchants and artisans, gave reasons for their indignation. They resisted higher taxes and were angry about the power Santa Fe continued to exert over new commercial centers like Albuquerque. The emphasis on "Americanization" and "English Language Only" in the petition to Congress revealed the signatories' vision of the future New Mexico. Obviously they were fearful that a small group of politicians in Santa Fe could dominate a Hispanic population and take over the new state government.[91] An early scholar concluded that the Albuquerque Germans' attempt to prevent statehood was a Jewish effort, as many of the signers were Germans of Jewish faith in fear of higher taxes. A more obvious point, however, was neglected: All those German and other signatories were residing in New Town Albuquerque, a community with few Hispanics and Catholics.[92]

Over the years hostility developed between Santa Fe and Albuquerque. Part of this competition arose from demographic changes altering economic and political activities in New Mexico. On the one hand, the railroad passed by Santa Fe to go directly to Albuquerque. This action brought more new immigrants from European and Asian countries and eastern regions, Germans and German Americans among them, to Albuquerque and lured Germans merchants like Benjamin Schuster, Edward Spitz, and Charles Ilfeld from Santa Fe and Las Vegas to Albuquerque. On the other hand, a conservative establishment of the pre-railroad days still controlled Santa Fe. The growing rivalry between the two towns sparked disputes over political power, the location of the territorial government, and several other issues. As a part of these changes, the German merchants in Santa Fe, considered part of older immigration, lost economic leadership to Albuquerque, Belen, Las Cruces, and other expanding towns. As the Santa Fe Trail lost its importance in transportation to the railroad, Santa Feans also felt increased efforts by citizens of Albuquerque to secure the capital seat as well as opposition in statehood matters. Santa Fe's citizens had to be reminded "that carrying Santa Fe is not carrying the Territory."[93] Franz Huning's view of statehood seems to confirm that perception, when he scribbled down on a handwritten, undated note that a statehood movement was once again under way, but a majority of New Mexicans was against it.[94]

Not surprisingly, the issue of statehood not only divided Anglo-Americans from Hispanics but Germans from one another as well. By the end of the century, when, among other issues, the statehood issue polarized Republicans Miguel A. Otero and Thomas B. Catron,[95] established German Santa Feans like Abraham Staab and Frederick Muller sided with Catron.[96] Staab even traveled as far as Socorro to solicit funds for Catron's statehood agenda.[97] Catron and his ring members continued to represented special interest groups. Besides mining and land interests, Catron, Mariano S. Otero (cousin of Miguel Otero), Staab, and others held military warrants that, it was alleged, would be paid once New Mexico gained statehood.[98]

Miguel Otero, Hispanic on his father's side and Anglo-American from his mother's family, tried to combine American and Hispanic business interests with Hispanic traditional values; but his authoritarian leadership and the persistent rumors about graft, particularly from Albuquerque, made many strong enemies. Those who did not want to be associated with the infamous Santa Fe Ring aided Otero in the hope that he could narrow the American-Hispanic gap and help to achieve statehood. Among the many Otero proponents were Nathan Jaffa, a supporter of former Governor Edmund Ross, and Max Frost, owner of the influential *Santa Fe New Mexican*. The Spiegelbergs, often in conflict with Catron over banking ventures, and other German merchants in Santa Fe and Albuquerque, also championed Otero.[99]

Paul A. F. Walter, another educated and rather apolitical German, came to New Mexico at the turn of the century for health reasons. Nevertheless, Walter, concerned about New Mexico's future, entered statehood politics as an aid to New Mexico's Republican delegate William H. Andrew. Whereas Andrew participated in mining and railroad enterprises, Walter sought civic improvement for Santa Fe and New Mexico and became involved in the affairs of the Museum of New Mexico and the School of American Research.[100] In fact, when in 1913 Bronson Cutting's *New Mexican* debated the merits of Edgar Hewett, the director of the School of American Research, and suggested the need for a new director, Paul A. F. Walter and others stood up to denounce the *New Mexican* and its writer, H. H. Dorman.[101] Like Huning, Korber, and other Germans, Walter became involved in politics that revolved around specific civic and cultural issues, including lobbying in the legislature for cultural programs. In his pursuit for statehood, he was driven by the hope of improving cultural institutions through additional federal funding.

The struggle for statehood finally paid off, and in 1910 an assembly convened and adopted a conservative constitution devoid of progressive ideas.[102] Not surprisingly, few Germans were present at the convention. Of the one hundred members of the constitutional convention, only four Germans, no second-generation German, and no prominent third-generation German participated. Moses L. Stern for Bernalillo, Charles E. Miller for Doña Ana, Charles H. Kohn for Quay, and John Becker for Valencia, more or less political novices, voted for the constitution. Conversely, Nathan Jaffa, who as secretary of the territory organized the ceremony, was experienced in public service and was even considered by some Republicans as their nominee for governor for the state. Typically, however, Jaffa, who managed the mercantile store of the Jaffa Brothers in Las Vegas and later founded the mercantile business of Jaffa-Prager

Company in Roswell, was not interested in the demanding position of governor and declined to have his name go before the convention.[103]

The history of the State of New Mexico did not see a change in Germans' political activism, even though Arthur Seligman emerged in the 1920s and 1930s as a capable leader in state politics and eventually became governor. German men and increasingly more women continued to accept appointments to civic-political positions. In 1914 Governor William McDonald, for instance, appointed several German women from across the state to the Woman's Auxiliary Exposition Commission.[104] Shortly after New Mexico's statehood, however, came the clouds of war in Europe, and the outbreak of World War I diminished German participation in politics.

Except for World War I, which posed a dilemma for many ethnic Germans, New Mexico in the nineteenth and early twentieth centuries was devoid of issues that affected them as an ethnic group. Even some xenophobic and anti-Semitic anxieties within the Populist movement had little impact on Germans and German Americans in New Mexico. Robert Larson, who conducted an extensive study of Populism in New Mexico, could not detect any anti-German or anti-Jewish remarks directed toward Germans and German Americans.[105] To be sure, occasional anti-Semitic statements occurred like those aimed at Solomon and Simon Bibo and Bernhard Seligman, but they were rare and unrelated to a Populist philosophy.[106] Even a few Germans participated in the Populist movement, including Sigmund Lindauer, a Jewish German from Grant County, and Ben Meyer from Albuquerque. Neither the movement itself nor any German Populists in New Mexico, however, gained political prominence.[107]

Both Germanophobic expressions and Germanophile emotions rarely surfaced until World War I. Never were feelings friendlier toward Germans in New Mexico than during the Franco-Prussian War of 1871 when New Mexicans and other Americans cheered the defeat of France. The *Santa Fe New Mexican* even printed special bulletins on the course of the war,[108] with other Santa Fe newspapers and territorial politicians being outspokenly pro-German. At the end of the war, Charles Clever headed a group of grateful Germans who thanked the *New Mexican* and Governor William A. Pile for their strong support. But the support Germans received during the Franco-Prussian War was not repeated. Instead, when World War I threatened, pro-German opinions turned quickly to animosity against Germans and German Americans in New Mexico.

Overall, then, Germans and German Americans in New Mexico, like their fellow Germans in other states and territories, did not act as a political bloc. The prerequisites for an ethnic political behavior were not present. Too few Germans and German Americans lived in New Mexico to sway New Mexico politics, and none of the major issues from 1850 to 1920, except for World War I, concerned Germans as an ethnic group. Those who voted cast their votes for an agenda or a candidate that safeguarded their individual interests.

Controversial issues, however, like statehood stimulated German reactions. On this topic, Germans and German Americans were frequently divided by geography and arrival date. For instance, well-to-do ethnic Germans in New Albuquerque, arriving in New Mexico with the railroad in the 1880s, resisted statehood dictated by the Santa Fe elite. Conversely, wealthy Germans in Santa Fe, who came to New Mexico in the 1850s and 1860s via the Santa Fe Trail, joined those in Santa Fe who favored homerule.[109]

In the end, not many politicians emerged from among the ethnic German population in New Mexico. In the early stages of territorial New Mexico, some Germans received federal appointments, and after 1880 some ethnic Germans were elected to territorial offices. Two of the few who stood out were Charles Clever and Bernhard Seligman. Clever's intentions were to exploit and Americanize New Mexico as quickly as possible, and Seligman's perspective was, within limits, to find common grounds among Anglo-American, Native American, and Hispanic ideas. In either case, they were not concerned with promoting ethnic German issues.

Germans in New Mexico, then, generally resembled Fritz Stern's description of the apolitical German. They tended to their businesses to achieve their goal: the betterment of their lives. Most of all, they promoted Kultur. If they moved into politics they did so most often as covert financial backers. That politics for Germans in New Mexico was not essential to protect or promote their lifestyle is best exemplified in Nathan Jaffa, who turned down a Republican nomination for governor of New Mexico and instead enhanced his position in the social and business life of New Mexico. Thomas Mann's conviction, that Germans disliked "Politik" is reflected in the German immigrants to New Mexico:[110] Their political influence was minimal compared to their social and financial position.

—⟊⟊—

Capitalistic Beginnings:
A Reformation of
New Mexico's Economy

New Mexico's isolated villages and towns, traditionally located along the Rio Grande and other year-round rivers and creeks, were remotely situated far from any large economic center. The villages "incorporated the elements of skill which lent themselves to economic self-sufficiency, [and their] commercial enterprise was rudimentary or nonexistent."[1]

Farming and ranching were the main sources of income for New Mexicans. The handful of the Germans, who arrived in the territory between the 1840s and 1860s, settled in northern New Mexico. John Subert began farming with his wife, Francisca Tafolla, in Bernalillo County prior to 1850 and continued into the 1870s. Christino Dennis, too, began farming with his wife, Solidad Gomez, in Taos prior to 1850. Daniel Fritze, who arrived in 1856, represented an exception to the trend of Germans settling in the northern half of New Mexico. He farmed land in Doña Ana County in the 1880s.

German farmers did well. Despite modest living conditions, Dennis listed small improvements worth a few hundred dollars for his farm. Subert worked 80 acres of his 160-acre farm, obtained under the Homestead Act of 1862, with $150 worth of farm equipment and a few farm animals. By 1870 he reduced the improved acreage of his homestead to 20 acres, but maintained a net worth of about $3,000 in personal and real estate.[2] Fritz Eggert and Charles Wengert, who arrived in the 1860s, also owned a debt-free farm.

Farmers with larger holdings, like Georg Berg or Frank Weber, who each maintained 200 acres, invested heavily in farm buildings and farm equipment, owned livestock, and planted Indian corn, oats, and wheat. Over a ten-year period they retained the size of their farms, improved farm buildings and equipment, and raised the traditional crops. In 1880 the two farmers each sold approximately $3,500 worth of farm products.[3]

Generally, German farmers in northern New Mexico cultivated between 10 and 40 acres of land, raised Indian corn, hay, wheat, and occasionally potatoes. In addition, they often owned cattle, horses, and sometimes a few goats.[4] In 1870, Eggert, with the help of farm labor, planted mostly Indian corn on his farm. Later he raised livestock and wheat. In the 1870s Wengert of Taos primarily planted Indian corn and wheat in addition to barley and oats on his 12-acre farm.[5] He also raised large flocks of sheep for their wool. Farm work was hard and tedious labor. In the 1870s, August Cline tilled 100 acres with his New Mexico wife, Dolores, to raise Indian corn and oats and to cultivate an apple orchard. In 1894, they reduced their farming operation and sold 40 acres of their land for $2,200.[6]

William Kronig arrived in New Mexico in 1849. After working at odd jobs and serving in the U.S. Army, Kronig turned to farming. On a piece of land loaned to him, he planted corn with makeshift tools. His harvesting methods were crude, using goats, horses, and sheep to separate the grain from the chaff. Because local labor was cheap and easily available, Kronig hired a native laborer to help plant additional staples such as oats, hops, and wheat. Eventually Kronig earned enough money to acquire a store, and over the years, he accumulated land and stock and invested in other enterprises. By 1880 he owned 865 acres of land to which he added yet another 2000 acres over the next ten years, employed farm labor year-round, and invested heavily in improving his farm.[7]

As New Mexico's population slowly increased, profits became possible. In Santa Fe a bushel of wheat sold for $2.00, and hay, scarce at any

price, sold for $60 a ton in the 1850s and 1860s. Prices for agricultural prod-
ucts remained high in the 1880s: potatoes sold from $12.00 to $15.00 per
bushel; eggs, $.75 per dozen; and flour, $15.00 to $18.00 per hundred
pounds.[8] Emil Fritz derived much of his income from selling flour. In 1869
he offered to sell 15,000 pounds of flour in Mesilla.[9] Flour was in such
high demand that it kept mills, like those owned by German immigrants
Franz Huning in Albuquerque and Louis Huning in Los Lunas, busy.[10]
When possible, farmers directly peddled their products on the market,
through their own mercantile stores or through nearby distributors, who
were quite often German merchants.

By the 1880s increasing numbers of farmers and ranchers, including a
few Germans, arrived in New Mexico. With their children, Charles and
Catherine Fritz began farming near Lincoln, New Mexico. After nearly twenty
years in Pennsylvania, the Fritzes, born in southern Germany, took over brother
Emil's established farm business.[11] The Fritz family maintained large tracts
of lands. Their well-equipped ranch totaled more than 1,000 acres. Similar
to German farmers in northern New Mexico, they diversified their crops and
raised Indian corn, oats, and wheat and cultivated an apple orchard and a
small vineyard. The family also managed milk cows and poultry. Catherine
Fritz may have advanced the production of dairy products through new methods brought along from Pennsylvania. When Catherine Fritz died in early
1884, the editor of the Las Cruces *Rio Grande Republican* praised her achievements in the fields of dairy farming and fruit growing.[12] Combined, their properties and assets were valued in 1880 at $24,000. Their children continued
the farming enterprise and the family still owned the ranch in the 1910s.

After 1880 increasing numbers of ranchers and farmers, including
Germans and German Americans, joined the Fritz family in settling the
southeastern counties of the territory. This growth increased tensions
among homesteaders and ranchers because of competition over land and
water resources. In this period the Fritz family directed their farming and
ranching efforts toward a growing commercial agricultural market, particularly cattle and sheep. The Fritzes participated in a transitional period
of economic and cultural changes in New Mexico, changes that were generated beyond the local market. As Gerald Nash noted, farmers like the
Fritz family "witnessed a confluence of the old agrarian economy of the
nineteenth century with the beginnings of industry and service industries more characteristic of the years after 1900."[13]

Despite the idealism of many newcomers, farming and ranching was difficult. New Mexico's economic makeup combined with the challenging climate, restricted water resources, and unique Hispanic traditions, frustrated German farmers and ranchers. Occasionally they ended up in court over water usage. Alexander Gusdorf of Taos and Louis Huning of Belen were among the many Germans who appealed to courts for additional irrigation water in order to increase profits.[14] The case of La Mesa Community Ditch Co. and Nicholas Appenzoeller went all the way to the territorial supreme court before the dispute over water appropriation was settled.[15]

Farmers borrowed cash, when possible, or entered barter agreements, repaying loans with lumber, bran, corn, wheat, hay, and oats. A few better-known Germans who financed farms by borrowing from merchants were William Kronig of Watrous and Henry Goke of Las Vegas. Diversifying into other entrepreneurial ventures, Kronig owned 400 acres in Mora County and operated a wool mill near Fort Union, whereas Goke directed a general store and flour mill in Sapello and engaged in sheep raising.[16] But not all farmers were successful. Increasingly, cash-starved farmers, German, Anglo-American, and Hispanic alike, borrowed seed to produce cash crops or accepted monetary advances to see them through crop failures and unprofitable seasons. As elsewhere, escalating debts were followed by an increasingly irrational confidence that "nature will fix it."[17]

In sheep ranching, however, the century-old *partido* contract for the raising of sheep and the production of wool remained an important tool.[18] A form of peonage, the system prevailed over barter or monetary loans and was well established by the end of the nineteenth century. It funded many smaller ranchers' debts and secured beneficial investments for merchants and large ranchers who gave *partidarios* little chance for reasonable profit.[19] All the risk rested with the partidarios. If they were unable to meet their obligations, they would lose their stock and land. Partido agreements occasionally ended up in court. August Kirchner, a butcher of more than twenty years in Santa Fe and part-time rancher, sued a partidario over breach of contract, and Ilfeld lost a case concerning a flock of sheep.[20]

In few instances was a partido relationship beneficial to the partidario as a means of getting started in agriculture. A Ms. Lutz, a German woman who resided with her husband in Lincoln County, entered into a partido agreement in 1895 with stock rancher Jose Analla of San Patricio. In this agreement she took over 2,000 ewes on the promise to return the same number of ewes when the contract expired and to deliver two pounds of wool per sheep to Analla each fall.[21] In general, the partido system was a risky option: Few partidarios demonstrated an ability to free themselves from debts without outside aid.[22] The result was often the loss of the homestead to larger ranchers or to merchants with vested interests.

Other agricultural options in New Mexico were limited. As in Germany, less successful farmers tended to leave farming altogether and work for wages.[23] The Gschwind family, for instance, took up a homestead in Oscuro, New Mexico.[24] Initially, the family farmed for decades with reasonable success. The presence of a local blacksmith, a second-generation German himself, suggesting the use of more advanced tools better suited for a market-oriented farm system, adds to the notion of some wealth.[25] Because money was scarce and farmhands were not easily available, all of the children had to participate in the farm chores. Nearby Mescalero Apaches, Herman Gschwind remembered, "did not work for, nor with, white people." He recalled that when water was abundant, cattle and grain did well. Unfortunately, in 1915 a drought destroyed the family's small cattle and goat business and the family moved to El Paso, Texas, to look for economic relief. Ironically, the land of opportunity was across the Rio Grande in Mexico where labor payments were in real silver.[26] When families could hold on to their farms, wives and children, regardless of ethnic background, often maintained the farms while the husbands sought wage-paying jobs.[27]

Statistically, German farmers were likely to own their farm or their house mortgage free. Those who initially rented, like Paul DeWitz of Germany or Georg Stiefel of New Jersey, improved their economic situation over the decade and eventually owned farms. These statistics, however, are deceptive as many Germans and German Americans stayed only a short period of time in New Mexico. For instance, of nearly two hundred ethnic German farmers and ranchers listed in the 1900 census only forty-four appear again in the 1910 census. Of those who stayed in New Mexico, most remained in the same place and continued farming. After 1880, the farmers were second-generation Germans, moving to New Mexico from Midwestern states and Texas.

Few Germans became ranchers. Among the few Germans who succeeded at ranching was Solomon Floersheim. A very successful sheep rancher in northern New Mexico, Floersheim arrived in the relatively poor area of Las Vegas and Mora in the 1870s. He did not immediately become wealthy. Living in a cash-starved region, Floersheim sold his sheep "for about all the cash" he could get his hands on. Indeed, Hugo Seaberg, in a credit report, felt that Floersheim was reliable but that his wealth was limited. Still by 1895, his assessed value was reported as $7,660.[28]

At the end of the nineteenth century and on into the 1910s, sheep and wool became a major New Mexican export. During this period, Floersheim accumulated enough land and sheep to become one of the largest sheep ranchers in northern New Mexico. For Floersheim and his contemporaries, competition in the sheep and cattle business was keen, and profits depended on a variety of circumstances such as railroad rates, market prices, water and land rights, and labor conditions. As elsewhere in the nation, farmers and ranchers viewed railroad companies as "the arrogant manipulator" of their profits.[29] Like others, Floersheim bitterly complained about harsh railroad rates; in his case rates to and from Springer were higher than those in Clayton, eighty miles to the east. As a result, he was "fairly disgusted with the treatment of the R.R.Co."[30]

The market also depended on tariff conditions. Ranchers like Frederick Gerhardt and Floersheim faced setbacks during President Grover Cleveland's free trade administration in the early 1890s, when cheaper foreign wool entered the market.[31] By the end of the century, however, prospects for sheep ranching were improving, and Floersheim's profits increased. The market showed again "extraordinary demand" for sheep and wool throughout the West.[32] At his peak (1897), Floersheim had 70,000 sheep grazing on private and public lands, and these numbers remained high until after World War I, when the sheep and wool market declined. The family sold its last 3,500 sheep in 1945.[33]

Successful ranching and farming in northern New Mexico often depended upon a suitable labor market. Although urban entrepreneurs complained about the high wages they had to pay, farmers and ranchers like Kronig and Floersheim could hire workers at low wages since laborers were available among the native population. These low wages retarded the economic development of New Mexico.[34] In 1910 Floersheim paid local, mostly Hispanic, laborers 20 cents an hour and sometimes less than 50 cents a day. Paying wages in vouchers, redeemable at the local mercantile stores, further eased the entrepreneurs' cash expenditure at the workers' expense.[35] Yet, the local Hispanic population, unacculturated and traditional, made a living on "cheap" wages and refrained from serious wage disputes.[36]

Increasing numbers of homesteaders arrived in New Mexico after 1880 and heightened tensions over water resources.[37] German cattle rancher Gerhardt, who controlled access to water on his homestead near Fort Sumner, warned newcomers that water would be scarce and that 160-acre plots were not large enough to dry-farm and to support a family. Likewise, Floersheim was apprehensive about homesteaders infringing on the open range that was so important for his sheep operation.[38]

The expanded need for water also affected the general population. The discovery of a new water hole raised the hopes for more water and the improvement of business. Increased water use and new farming techniques proved the *arroyo* system (stream channels) insufficient for the agricultural demands. Newcomers encouraged the development of irrigation projects, particularly in the southern regions of New Mexico.[39] Few immigrants to the Southwest understood the balance between justice and equity in water distribution; rather, they viewed water and the connected land "as chattels to be bought and sold at will."[40]

Water as "merchandise," which could be bought and sold, encouraged a more affluent and often nonagrarian German elite in New Mexico to invest in the "American import" of irrigation companies. The separate control of water and land resulted in monopolies that were not necessarily of benefit to the farmers. Water was a commodity, controlled by a "power elite based on the ownership of capital and expertise."[41] Several Germans brokered and profited from this scarce commodity. For instance, Jacob Korber invested in the Albuquerque Land and Irrigation Company; Lehman Spiegelberg, joining like-minded businessmen, organized the Santa Fe Irrigation and Colonization Company; Adolph Guttmann became president of the Arroyo Hondo Mining and Ditch Company in Taos; and Nathan Jaffa of Roswell became "an enterprising proponent of irrigation."[42]

The issue of irrigation was only one of many novelties with which immigrants had to cope. Some traditions were discarded easily. A German farmhouse, for example, where family and animals lived together during long winter months, served no purpose in the New Mexican landscape and open ranges. Farmers also quickly accepted windmills, an unusual sight in Germany.[43]

Figure 5:
Grocer Herbert Blueher, one-time partner of Jacob Korber in an irrigation venture, exhibits his vegetables at the New Mexico Territorial Fair. Cobb Memorial Photography Collection. Courtesy Center for Southwest Research, University of New Mexico, neg. #000-119-0737

Other adaptations did not come easily. Unfamiliar with desert conditions, Jacob Korber and Herman Blueher pursued a rare experiment and operated—however unsuccessfully—a dry-farming venture in Doña Ana County.[44] Justus Schmidt of Wagon Mound promoted the cultivation of flax with little success, despite "having had much practical experience in the cultivation of that plant in Germany." Flax, obviously, was not suited for New Mexico's dry climate.[45]

Still, German and German American farmers and ranchers made a living beyond subsistence; some even became wealthy. In northern New Mexico, often marrying Hispanic women, they more easily acculturated and successfully maintained their farms. However, in the developing farm areas in eastern and southeastern New Mexico, German farm families were less successful. Many, who were attracted by free land, did not know farming; they came only to meet their homestead requirements and sell out. Some simply failed because they underestimated the financial burden and environmental conditions.

Conditions for laborers were not unlike those of farmers. Miners, in particular, experienced difficulties. Although New Mexico had a much longer history in small-scale mining operations than did most other places in the West, its mines were too isolated to attract a "run." Miners and mine operators complained early about the lack of capital and infrastructure to exploit mineral resources. An early spokesperson for extensive exploitation, Charles Clever pled with the members of the U.S. House of Representatives in the 1860s for appropriations and investments for wagon roads and railroad tracks.[46] His political career as delegate from New Mexico, however, was too short-lived to exercise any substantial influence.

Often with little capital, German miners set out for mining placers to prospect. Few were as successful as Sofia Henkel. Henkel of Hanover operated the Hanover Copper Mine in the Pinos Altos Mountains, invested in a steam smelter, and gained considerable wealth.[47] Typically, German men such as Charles Claussen of Doña Ana or Fred Snyder of Colfax worked in the placers and mines. They were first-generation Germans, single, highly mobile, and owning little. Few stayed for more than a short time in New Mexico. Even fewer prospectors, placer miners, and mine laborers were financially successful. Although some may have sold their claims for a profit, the general picture suggests that they sold their claims to make ends meet and turned instead to wage-earning.[48] One longtime Anglo-American miner spoke for many miners, German and otherwise, when he recalled his brother saying: "Hell, this is too slow for me. . . . I'm goin' to work for wages."[49] But more than anything else, world prices and technical limits decided the fate of prospectors, and the trend toward wage-earning mining increased during the early twentieth century.

Many Germans prospected in New Mexico in addition to their primary occupations. Clever reported that in 1866 Jacob Amberg, a successful merchant in Santa Fe, reopened mines in the Pinos Altos area, and by installing a steam mill, he operated the Pinos Altos Mining Company day and night. Near the Moreno mines in present-day Colfax County, William Kronig, farmer and rancher of Watrous, with Lucien Maxwell and others, ran a copper mine trying to strike the main vein.[50] Albert Henry Pfeiffer, Indian Agent at Abiquiu and former member of the U.S. Army, organized several expeditions to the Chama River, San Juan River, and into Colorado looking for minerals. Pfeiffer and his companions did not find enough minerals to strike it rich; but by inflating the news of "gold" in the northwest corner of New Mexico, they opened the area to subsequent settlements and profited in other avenues.[51]

Germans' indifference to mining may have derived from the proximity to Mexico with its cheap labor, unusual mining methods, and unsafe working conditions. Like Chinese immigrants in California and elsewhere, the local labor market helped employers exploit the labor situation in the Southwest and maintain unsatisfactory work conditions for miners.[52] Mine regulations were particularly negligent in New Mexico, resulting repeatedly in fatal accidents, most notably in Dawson, near Raton, in 1913, 1920, and again in 1924.[53] In addition, newly arriving immigrant groups met the mining needs in New Mexico. The censuses of 1900 and 1910 listed thousands of Swedish, Austro-Bohemian, and Italian miners laboring in the mines, particularly in the coal mines near Gallup and Raton. When open pit mines became popular in the early twentieth century, German *Bergleute* and *Steiger* (miners and master miners) saw less and less need for their expertise.[54]

While Germans were disinterested in mine work, they were always engaged in mine ownership. They considered the acquisition of mining claims more promising. Organizations and entrepreneurs were often willing to purchase mineral rights and mine titles from exiting miners. German entrepreneurs, like Lehman Spiegelberg and Jacob Korber, acquired mining claims.[55] In the late 1860s, Henry Lesinsky and Julius Freudenthal of Las Cruces, likewise, accepted mining claims and organized the Longfellow Mining Company in the southwestern corner of the territory. They held on to their claims until the railroad reached Lordsburg, when they sold their shares in the Longfellow, Coronado, Metcalf, and Queen mines for $1.2 million.[56]

Anglo-American labor developed an edge over native competition, however, in the domestic service industry. German men and women were often preferred over Hispanic servants. Servants, particularly women, could always find employment and were frequently mentioned in letters to their relatives in Germany. Hugo Treschwitz of Fort Stanton and August Müller of Monte Vista, Colorado, on the border to New Mexico, described in letters the opportunities for women in the domestic service. They acknowledged that pay and respect were much better in the Southwest than in Germany.[57]

German-born servants appeared in New Mexico as early as the 1840s. Canadian Ceran St. Vrain, one of the first foreign large landholders in New Mexico, employed German Charles Adams as a servant. In the 1870s, the

Springer family hired Anna Rabe of Prussia for their household. Often, domestics were hired before their trip west, like Babette Weindel of Bavaria who arrived in Taos with the Gusdorf family.[58]

Ethnocentric bias against Hispanics also benefited Germans seeking prospective jobs in Anglo- and German-owned hotels and restaurants, which opened in increasing numbers after the arrival of the railroad. According to the *Las Vegas Daily Optic* some businesses preferred Anglo-American waiters and waitress over "Mexican" personnel,[59] and secured German migrants as waitresses in a Las Vegas hotel. The Alvarado Hotel in Albuquerque, for example, employed at least five waitresses of German descent. Although wages of perhaps $40 a month with board granted only a minimal living, it "provided independence . . . generally lacking as a live-in domestic."[60] By 1910 hotel and restaurant owners and managers around the territory from Clovis to Raton, and from Tucumcari to Gallup, employed many German and German American waitresses and waiters.

In the underdeveloped industrial Southwest, skilled laborers were difficult to attract. One obstacle was the difference in craft labor in the Southwest and in Germany. In the United States a craftsworker had to be a Jack-of-all-trades to succeed. For a traditional German or German-trained artisan specialization was more the rule. August Müller, a shoemaker, for instance, had worked as a laborer, farmhand, machinist, and miner after he arrived in the United States. He complained in a letter to his father in Germany that "my craft doesn't do me any good here. Now I'm learning . . . how to shoe horses and how to forge." Eventually, after another occupational change to the bicycling business, he established himself in an automobile repair shop in Denver.[61]

In addition, the traditional work culture of New Mexico could be an impediment to German and other European artisans. The territory's economy was cash-starved and predominantly based on subsistence and self-help. Few Anglo-American clients existed to employ their services. The Hispanic tradition of carpentry and masonry was distinct. Adobe construction required little carpentry or masonry as practiced in Germany. Bakers faced different diets and cash shortages and traditional families who baked their own bread.[62] Similar difficulties plagued dressmakers and tailors. Although some Hispanic women and men may have admired American fashion, the majority kept to their traditional clothes; and these clothes were often sewn or mended in family circles at home.

German artisans who did arrive between 1850 and 1880 gravitated toward the few urban centers of New Mexico. Las Vegas, Santa Fe, Albuquerque, and Las Cruces met Max Weber's definition of an artisan locality or market hamlet.[63] The towns had a sufficiently urbanized population to afford these few craftspersons to service their Hispanic and Anglo clientele.

To make a living in New Mexico, skilled and unskilled workers often had no choice but to adapt their skills and products. As the geographer Carl Sauer has pointed out, every human landscape, at any moment, is an accumulation of practical experience.[64] If a German carpenter could not make a living on German or Anglo-American style carpentry alone, he could make tables and chairs with traditional Hispanic designs, a mason could adapt to adobe-style constructions. Unfortunately, not many of the immigrant artisans who came in the second half of the nineteenth century remained in New Mexico. Although prices were high in the Southwest, and blacksmiths like Peter Zehner of Santa Fe could make $4 to $6 for shoeing a horse in the 1850s and 1860s in Santa Fe, few artisans stayed.[65] If artisans accumulated any wealth, it was modest.

Occasionally German craftsworkers achieved the goal of traditional journeymen and established their own master crafts shops like blacksmith John Ruff of Los Lunas and carpenter Henry Ruhe of Santa Fe. But few German shops were opened during the early territorial period. Among the few who advertised their services were Georg Huth, who operated a bakery next to the Santa Fe Hotel on the plaza,[66] and Henry Ruhe, who established himself in Santa Fe prior to 1850 and operated a carpentry shop. In the 1860 census Ruhe was listed as a "master carpenter."

By the beginning of the twentieth century, more ethnic Germans operated shops. Increased mining activities and continuous railroad operations resulted in increased Anglo-American migration, and the demand for skilled and unskilled labor soared. Many German and even more German American artisans arrived in the territory and established shops in the urban areas and in railroad settlements. More and more milliners and dressmakers like Frances Poppenhager, a second-generation German widow, or Louise Reuteman, a divorced German, had opened shops. Others found employment in the millinery industry. These skilled jobs afforded women economic freedom and financial independence.

The increase in population likewise influenced the construction business. Prior to the arrival of the railroad, German immigrants like Frederick

Gerhardt complained that it was impossible to obtain building material (suggesting his inability to utilize indigenous material); since the railroad's arrival, however, milled lumber was easily available. Furniture makers found employment by making American-style furniture, and carpenters and contractors developed new American-style buildings. German artisans participated in the transformation of Hispanic adobe tradition into the architecture of clapboard and frame houses and false-front commercial buildings.[67]

The demand for new, American-style housing and commercial buildings at the turn of the century clearly benefited many Germans. E. A. Gertig, a carpenter of German descent from Ohio, and Edward Lembke, a German mason in New Mexico for over twenty years, operated construction companies in Albuquerque and "added to the dynamism of the building boom of these years."[68] The construction business was brisk. In a grievance, C. W. Kunz of Albuquerque complained that he could not find carpenters to rebuild his beer storage warehouse that fire destroyed.[69]

The construction boom was not limited to Albuquerque. Philip Hersch, the son of German immigrants to New Mexico, constructed many buildings in Santa Fe between West Alameda Street and Cerillos Road. Otto Leupold operated a contracting business in Deming and participated in that town's building boom.[70]

At the same time, other professions benefited from economic growth. John and Adam Kern, for example, established themselves as butchers in Las Vegas. Although their credit was poor, they were the only butchers in town suggesting at least some financial means.[71]

Bakers offered their goods in small, yet increasing, numbers all over New Mexico. Minnie Steward, a second-generation German, maintained a bakery at her home in Roswell to supplement the family income. In 1870, Joseph Pohmer of Baden, and his Hispanic wife began operating a bakery and general grocery in Old Albuquerque. They derived supplemental income from a small, four-acre vineyard in Albuquerque and were listed in 1870 with $9,000 in property and cash.[72]

In the 1870s, William Baasch came to Las Vegas and worked for the Leon Brothers' bakery. Baasch worked probably just long enough for the brothers to learn Hispanic bakery traditions and to serve Hispanic and Anglo customers. Like other German bakers in New Mexico, he and his second-generation German wife, Clara Maier of Las Vegas, operated an additional income-producing enterprise when they purchased the Farmers' Hotel in Las Vegas.[73]

Gradually New Mexico's increasing population fostered other occupations such as those of brewing and distilling. Since alcoholic beverages were rooted in Hispanic and German traditions, it is not surprising that German beer was available early in Santa Fe and Albuquerque. It was offered first by Charles Deus of Santa Fe, the lone German brewer listed in the territory in 1860. Along with his brother John Peter (who was not listed in the census), he founded Deus and Company in the capital where he sold glasses of beer for 25 cents each. Business was successful enough that he later added a billiard hall.[74] In 1864, George Schneider opened the Pacific Brewery. To make his brew widely known among Santa Feans, he deposited samples of his product with fellow German Charles Eckhardt, owner of a tavern. John May brewed beer in Las Cruces in the 1860s before he went into partnership with Vincente St. Vrain to produced beer for the Mora Distillery and Brewery. In Sapello, Louis Bieler founded the Union Brewery.[75]

Other brewers like Jacob and Henry Loebs found ready employment in the Albuquerque breweries. In the 1890s, Henry was appointed director of the Southwest Brewery and Ice Company. When a power struggle broke out between him and company stockholders, who cut his salary by $50 to $125 per month in 1893, he was able to purchase enough stock to influence future decisions by the stockholders.[76]

The population of New Mexico grew sufficiently thirsty to entice Alfred Katzenberg, son of German and French immigrants, to operate a soda and water plant in Socorro. In the same town Jacob Hammel and his son William operated a branch of the Illinois Brewery, catering to the mining clientele. By 1886 it had the largest beer production in the territory, and the next year William and Jacob Hammel were the sole owners.[77] Arriving late in the nineteenth century, German Joseph Epple easily found employment as "Assistant Brewer" in the Hammels' German brewery.

Other artisans were attracted by New Mexico's economic development. Jacob Korber's blacksmith and wagon business sold and repaired wagons for the miners in the region. Since most wagons were manufactured in the East and ill-suited for the New Mexico climate and terrain, Korber and his blacksmiths modified them to meet mining needs in New Mexico.[78]

The mining industry supported other industries as well. Sufficient ore was found in the mountains west of Socorro for Gustav Billing and his mining engineer, Alfred Schneider, both Germans, to relocate from Leadville, Colorado, to Socorro, New Mexico, and to operate a large-scale smelter. With a good reputation and a near-monopoly on smelter business in the Southwest, Billing's operation received workloads not only from New Mexico, but from Arizona and Utah.[79] The smelter was successful for eleven years until market conditions plummeted and the operation closed.

Wages for skilled and unskilled laborers varied from town to town. In Socorro at the height of the mining boom in the late nineteenth century, masons and carpenters could make $5.00 a day, wagon makers earned $3.50, and unskilled laborers $1.00 to $2.00.[80] Wages in Albuquerque and Santa Fe remained high and did not differ much from those in Socorro. By the end of the nineteenth century Jacob Korber, the Albuquerque blacksmith-entrepreneur employing German wagon makers, blacksmiths, and unskilled laborers, paid $3.50 for skilled and up to $1.50 per day for unskilled labor.

Companies in the East where skilled labor was readily available often complained about the expensive labor costs in the towns and cities of New Mexico. When a wagon manufacturer in the East complained about a 50-cent charge for setting a tire, Korber responded that "it cannot be done here for [less than] that as everything is higher, wages and all out in this country and it cannot be compared with the east."[81]

In the northern part of the territory, however, wages were lower. Charles Ilfeld, a leading merchant in Las Vegas, paid lower wages than did his counterparts in Albuquerque. As his biographer points out, Ilfeld had no constructive labor policy; he considered employees as a mere commodity.[82] In the mid-1880s Ilfeld paid masons $1.50 and carpenters $2.00 a day.[83]

Part of the wage discrepancy is explained by the composition of the respective towns. Whereas Albuquerque (New Town) and Socorro were predominantly settled by Anglo-Americans, Las Vegas and its environs hosted a large Hispanic labor force that allowed employers like Ilfeld, Floersheim, and others to keep wages low. Unfortunately, ethnicity often determined wages. In northern New Mexico, Germans involved in the mercantile business paid their Hispanic laborers less.[84]

The most notable industry in New Mexico during most of the nineteenth and early twentieth century was the trade or mercantile business, which had been conducted on a regular basis since the early nineteenth century. German merchants registered with Mexican authorities in

Santa Fe to do business in Chihuahua and farther south as early as 1824. Men with German-sounding surnames like Rennick, Storrs, and Belcher appeared in Mexican records planning to take trips south on the Camino Real.[85] In 1833, Alonso Bast, Mortiz Franck, and Marcos Feldmann; in 1835, Juan Kaskendolf; and in 1836, Juan Adolfo Gustavo Schmidt, William Kellenvoll, Francisco Tahuffu [sp.?], and Anton Gold received permission to trade in Mexico south of the Rio Grande.[86] In the 1840s German merchant Albert Speyer and Anglo-American merchants Josiah Gregg and James Webb undertook the annual trips from St. Louis, Missouri, to Santa Fe and points south.[87]

These successes of trade across the Santa Fe Trail during the Mexican and early American period offered promising opportunities and served as economic incentives for later German immigration to New Mexico. Mercantile prospects attracted German entrepreneurs to New Mexico and the Southwest. By the time the territory became American, German merchants and peddlers were already situated at "every crossroads."[88]

In the 1850s nearly half of all German immigrants were businesspeople in smaller communities away from large population centers in the United States.[89] They offered their goods in mercantile stores on the plazas of Taos, Santa Fe, and Las Vegas,[90] and traveled to distant settlements to sell their merchandise. In fact, so many German merchants had successfully settled in these towns turning plazas into mercantile centers, that observers sometimes thought Germans controlled the economies of these areas. In the 1860s a medical officer with the U.S. Army observed that "the commercial interests [of the area] were conducted by so-called foreigners: Americans, Germans, and Jews, the latter predominating."[91] Mrs. [Walter] Marmon, a Native American and descendant of one of the large mercantile business owners in the state, recalled that Germans were great traders who often visited Laguna. These visits, not only in New Mexico, but across the Southwest, also constituted a significant social interaction between Germans and the native population in the period prior to the arrival of the railroad.[92]

Many Germans who sold merchandise appeared to have done well, a handful extremely well.[93] These few highly prosperous mercantile families helped form the image of the successful German entrepreneur. Kronig, Spiegelberg, Staab, Huning, and, toward the end of the nineteenth century, Becker and Ilfeld, appeared repeatedly in newspapers and records.

Taking the commercial lead, these merchants profited primarily from the initial boom in government contracts related to forts and reservations.[94]

Government contracts provided the largest profit for merchants. Revenues from the Santa Fe trade were estimated to be $450,000 in 1843 and $2,108,000 in 1876.[95] Several German merchant firms competed for contracts. Large-volume dealers like Zadoc Staab and Co., the Seligman brothers, and the Spiegelberg brothers competed against one another and against merchants such as Romolo Martinez, James J. Webb, and the Marmon brothers. Although Abraham Staab, the Seligmans, and the Zeckendorfs also received government contracts, the Spiegelbergs reaped many of the most lucrative contracts. They were awarded contracts in New York and St. Louis, rather than in Santa Fe, involving delivery of nearly everything that was in demand in New Mexico: from 5,000 pounds of beans at $5.95 per 100 pounds, to more than 40,000 pounds of hay at $1.88 per 100 pounds, to 125,000 pounds of beef at $2.93 per 100 pounds.[96]

The near monopolistic power in the hands of a few merchants in Santa Fe raised protests. People complained that "they each and all think that they are entitled to a share of all monies spent by the Government, whether for the Indians or any other purpose."[97] It appears that German merchants were awarded a major share of the large government contracts available in New Mexico.

These merchants' retail businesses, though mostly profitable, experienced an occasional recession. In 1853, a correspondent of James J. Webb, one of the Anglo-American Santa Fe merchants, observed that the Germans "Hersh and the Speigelbergs [sic] are the only persons who sell anything at retail and they do not much." Other firms were even less fortunate. In one instance, Eugene Leitensdorfer of Taos filed for bankruptcy, and creditors had to go to court to settle their affairs with him.[98]

Business was occasionally so poor that newly arrived merchants sold out to established merchants at a loss. G. Hersh bought merchandise at cost plus freight from a merchant, and another "sold out all his groceries to Levi Spiegelberg and Beuthner at cost and 10c freight, $6000 worth."[99] Assuming that ten cents' freight denoted the usual 100 pounds, this meant a grand profit for the buyer. In comparison, the Spiegelbergs generally charged up to $15.00 per 100 pounds for transportation.[100]

Entrepreneurs sometimes sold out for other reasons. Ludwig Ilfeld handed over his merchandise to Julius Appel and Max Karlsruher to return to Germany. Appel and Karlsruher in turn established themselves and by 1910 owned individual, successful businesses. Carl Huning, brother of Franz and Louis Huning, also sold out to his brother Franz in 1874 and returned to Germany.[101] Others like the Zeckendorf brothers sold their Santa Fe store, and Dittenhoefer, Homberger, and Co. put up their goods for sale because they decided to leave the territory.[102]

With so much of the mercantile power in the hands of a few Germans, complaints and suspicions of improprieties against the leading merchants surfaced. Many merchants were accused of government fraud and land grabbing. Abraham Staab was suspected of mishandling several thousand dollars' worth of militia warrants.[103] Charles Ilfeld and Lehman Spiegelberg were litigants in land claims and land fraud cases.[104] Cecilio Rosenwald and two fellow citizens were accused of improprieties in San Miguel County concerning the sale of government land that resulted in profits of almost $100,000.[105] Few cases, however, were brought to trial; even fewer resulted in a guilty verdict. Complaints "that convictions were almost impossible to secure in New Mexico" were common, and among Germans, only Charles Ilfeld was indicted of land fraud.[106] Otherwise, little evidence could be produced in courts that Germans engaged in land fraud.[107]

Contracts to supply goods were not the only source of income. Appointments as post trader on tribal lands also proved lucrative. These frequently monopolistic trading posts benefited traders not only in sales to Native Americans but also in matters of export. Sheep raising, for instance, dominated the economy of the Navajos, and represented an attractive commodity for merchants and wool dealers. At one time or another German merchants administered many of these trading posts. Willi Spiegelberg worked at the Navajo trading post, the Bibos received commissions for Acoma and other nearby pueblos, the Seligmans administered the Bernalillo post, and the Ilfeld brothers worked at Zuni.[108] While Native Americans often remonstrated against unfair prices, a trustworthy post trader could be beneficial for the merchants in Santa Fe, Albuquerque, or Las Vegas.[109] In the twentieth century when mercantile business declined and federal Indian policies were changing, involvement of German merchants lessened. Their mercantile firms were replaced by individuals such as Emmett Wirt, who managed the post in Dulce at the Mescalero-Apache reservation into the 1930s.[110]

The sutler position at army stations was another sought-after post. And typical of frontier entrepreneurs, Germans took advantage of those economic opportunities when they came along.[111] In the 1860s, Solomon Spiegelberg received the commission for Fort Marcy, Marcus Brunswick was sutler at Fort Stanton, and William Gellermann secured the post at Fort Bascom. Willi Spiegelberg was appointed post trader at Fort Wingate but invited Nathan Bibo to manage the fort. John Weber was awarded the post at Fort Defiance (in Arizona after 1863) in the 1850s.[112] Until geopolitical changes forced the reduction of forts, sutlers found their positions financially rewarding and invested the profits in other commercial enterprises.[113]

These operations by German merchants restricted their mobility to sell goods and merchandise in remote areas. To deal with far-flung markets most Germans established country stores. Unlike earlier peddlers in the northeastern United States, who penetrated the backcountry, and unlike Hispanic merchants, who came with wagons to New Mexican settlements, German merchants tried to find a place to set up shop.[114] Members of the Laguna pueblo, for instance, recollect that early pioneers who set up posts in their vicinity were mostly of German descent.[115]

Quite often the leading merchants set up branch stores. For instance, Julius Freudenthal and Henry Lesinsky of Las Cruces opened stores in Belen, Sapinal, Parajo, and Las Cruces, while the Spiegelbergs established a branch store in Fort Wingate. Abraham Staab and Co. operated a branch retail store at Rincon.[116] Freudenthal and Lesinsky, whose mining operations were in relative isolation in the southwestern corner of New Mexico, established a company store, giving them a substantial control over mine laborers' purchases.[117]

Charles Ilfeld's company maintained branch stores throughout the northern half of the New Mexico territory. When Ilfeld tried to set up a branch store in Willard, however, he crossed into the terrain of another German, John Becker, of Belen. Becker already operated a branch store in Willard. Since the town was not a large enough market to support two stores, Becker accepted an offer by Max Nordhaus, manager of the Charles Ilfeld Company, and sold out. At the turn of the century, Ilfeld opened his last branch store on one of Huning's properties in Albuquerque, anticipating a permanent move to that city.[118]

Generally, branch stores were controlled outlets for merchants and represented a monopoly in a region. The stores frequently returned high profits by preventing customers from buying at less expensive outlets. Stores often forced individual customers into permanent debts and created a dependency that gave merchants control over individual miners, farmers, or small merchants.[119] Lesinsky and Freudenthal, for instance, limited miners in their employ to purchasing supplies from their Las Cruces store or their branch store in Silver City.[120]

Smaller merchants, indebted to larger merchants, felt pressured to purchase at the larger stores. Only a few like William Gellermann refused to do so. A fellow countryman, Gellermann, although contractually obligated to purchase at Ilfeld's stores, procured his supplies elsewhere. As he argued, "goods have to be bought where they are cheapest."[121] Likewise, Prudencia Hoehne, owner of a small store in Las Colonias and wife of German farmer William Hoehne, felt the pressure and complained to Ilfeld that he was always "pricking" her for money.[122]

This web of dependency occasionally divided along racial lines. Ilfeld, for instance, furnished some of his customers with different types of checkbooks: nonnegotiable and negotiable ones. The nonnegotiable checks were printed in Spanish and were good only for the purchase of merchandise at branch stores or at designated stores like Rosenthal's in Las Vegas. Luciano Ulibari, for instance, was repeatedly paid with a draft for merchandise on Rosenthal's store. The negotiable checks, on the other hand, were printed in English and exchangeable for cash.[123]

The branch system declined rapidly in the 1910s. By then local competition increased, mail order companies became popular, and rail and automobile transportation improved, so that merchants lost their control over customers.

Few German nonmercantile entrepreneurs achieved economic success equal to the well-known merchants. Of this group Jacob Korber was perhaps the most prominent. He began his successful career in Albuquerque repairing and selling wagons, continuously expanding his market from Albuquerque to Las Cruces in the South, Gallup in the West, and Santa Fe in the North. Flexible in his approach, Korber began to modify the poorly designed wagons. He even thought about producing his own model, but "the area's economic limitation did not permit this." Always emphasizing his blacksmith shop, Korber nevertheless began to diversify and to invest in properties in Albuquerque and in an automobile franchise and bowling alley. He eventually incorporated. After his death in a car accident in 1921, Korber's children continued their father's work. Today, Korber Electric is still a family-owned enterprise.[124]

The majority of German entrepreneurs, however, although not as successful, prospered, even in remote locations. In 1850 Henry and Maren Birnbaum established their first store in Taos. Ten years later they had relocated in Mora and had a net worth of $12,000. Another German, Moses Sachs, arriving in Valencia County in the late 1840s, initially owned land worth $500. A decade later, through his and his wife's efforts as merchants and government agents, they had accumulated assets worth $4,000.[125] Still another newcomer, Frederick Mueller, initially worked with his wife Theodora Beaubien in Taos. They maintained a store in Taos and another one nearby and their efforts over the years paid off handsomely. By 1860 they had accumulated $14,000 worth of personal and real estate.

Many smaller German entrepreneurs supplemented their incomes through farming. In addition to being Indian agent for the Acoma Pueblo, Nathan Bibo of Bernalillo maintained eleven acres of farmland and five acres of vineyard in 1880. Henry Goke maintained a farm, and a mercantile operation and sawmill in Sapello. In 1880 he planted Indian corn, oats, and wheat and held 2,350 head of cattle and sheep on his 100 acres and the surrounding public land. In 1870, Ferdinand Knauer, a dry-goods merchant in Las Vegas, listed $7,000 worth of property and savings. Ten years later he claimed 17,000 sheep worth $25,000.[126]

It is surprising that the market in New Mexico was sufficiently large to absorb so many merchants and entrepreneurs. Unlike the intense competition among Jewish German merchants elsewhere, German merchants in New Mexico did not experience divisive competition.[127] Reaching out to one another for support and help, the German merchants experienced little intra-ethnic pressure in their economic areas.[128] Instead, they referred business to each other, tried to avoid duplications, and served as references for each other on potential government contracts. In general, German merchants and entrepreneurs coexisted and worked together peacefully.

Jacob Korber of Albuquerque illustrates this theme. He was unwilling to add one type of carriage to his line of merchandise because Gross, Blackwell, and Company of Las Vegas carried that brand. He also tried to involve other German merchants in the carriage business and offered Fred Scholle, Edward Mertz, Charles Ilfeld, and Isedor Freudenburg commissions if they sent customers to him. Moreover, Charles Ilfeld shipped items to the mercantile store of Jaffa and Prager in Roswell so they could profit from a specific exchange. In turn, Charles Ilfeld found financial support

Figure 6:
Prager brothers and Nathan Jaffa pose with Pat Garret in front of their store in Roswell. General Photo Collection. Courtesy Center for Southwest Research, University of New Mexico, neg. #990-026-0002

among the Spiegelbergs. Clearly, in the business sector, Germans, and particularly wealthy Germans, looked out for each other.[129]

Business and employment policies, too, were similar among Germans and typical of those among most ethnic groups. Hiring from within an ethnic group was a preferred practice. Employment policies among German entrepreneurs in New Mexico reflect a supportive attitude toward fellow Germans. Obviously, the ethnic German labor force in New Mexico was much smaller than the one in the Midwest or in cities like Milwaukee and San Francisco, so German employers in Santa Fe, Las Vegas, and Albuquerque could not—and did not want to—rely exclusively on German employees. More often than not, however, Germans took in other Germans as apprentices, craftspersons, clerks, or partners.

Immigrant merchants in New Mexico realized that they were not sufficiently prepared for a cash-starved economy. They often spent time as clerk or bookkeeper in a mercantile firm or went into partnership with more experienced merchants before attempting to set up their own businesses. The unfamiliarity of newcomers with the practice of dealing in exchange of goods rather than in cash was initially confusing and needed adjustment.[130]

Franz Huning clerked in Simon Rosenstein's store, and Huning later employed John Becker. Herman Heinrich worked for his uncles Franz and Louis Huning when he first arrived in Albuquerque.[131] Solomon Floersheim worked for the Rosenwald store in Trinidad, Colorado, and then in the 1880s briefly worked for Charles Ilfeld in Las Vegas.[132] Nathan Bibo employed his sister Lina Weiss as manager of his farm enterprise; Jaffa & Prager Co. hired J. J. Rheiner away from St. Louis for their harness and saddle department in Roswell; John May employed Dirk Seligman in his store in Las Cruces; and Solomon Jacob Spiegelberg, in addition to teaching his brothers, employed Jacob Nusbaum to clerk in his stores.[133] John Staerkel was employed at Herman Blueher's produce store on the plaza in Albuquerque. After several years of clerking in German-owned stores in Trinidad and Albuquerque, Emil Uhlfelder opened his own store, "The White House," in Santa Fe on the Plaza in the early twentieth century.[134] That operation remains today on the city plaza.

Connections among German merchants were also expressed in partnerships. Newspapers in the early 1850s are full of such announcements of partnerships. A partnership existed between Beuthner and Spiegelberg, and Seligman and Clever briefly joined forces in 1852. Cancellations of German partnerships appeared equally often in the newspapers. Two merchants in Doña Ana County, Louis Geck and John Zoeller, dissolved their partnership, the firm of Loeb and Weinheim split, and Amberg, Elsberg, and Ilfeld also ended their partnership.[135] Some partnerships broke down because of financial or personal differences; others dissolved because the partners wished to go into business for themselves.

However, Germans did not limit their partnerships and employees to only Germans. Ilfeld and Huning hired Hispanic clerks; Freudenthal and Lesinsky went into partnership with Nicolas Armijo; John Dold joined forces with Charles Parker, Stephen Brice, and C. G. McClure; and the firm of Guttman and Friedman included John Santistevan as a partner.[136] Yet, top positions in these firms were usually reserved for Germans, often family members.[137]

Despite generally harmonious business relationships among Germans, a few tensions and hostilities erupted. One German, Max Nordhaus, reported

Figure 7:
The Seligman-Clever mercantile store on the southeast corner of the Plaza, was one of the oldest Anglo-American businesses in Santa Fe. The Exchange Hotel (La Fonda) is in the center of this 1855 photo. Courtesy Museum of New Mexico, neg. #10685

to the manufacturer unfair price-cutting practices by the German merchant Rosenthal.[138] Members of the firm of Elsberg, Amberg, and Ilfeld also went to court with each other over alleged mismanagement of funds. In this conflict, Gustave Elsberg claimed the loss of several thousand dollars' worth of merchandise to Jacob Amberg, Charles and Herman Ilfeld, and Arthur Letcher.[139] Lawsuits among German entrepreneurs, although not common, occasionally even reached the New Mexico Supreme Court. Usually these cases pertained to alleged breaches of contract, involving disputes over as little as $100.[140] During the early twentieth century, newspapers were occasionally used to air tensions. In a letter to the editor, for instance, Simon Stern complained about the "poor collections [of bills]" and requested that the many "millionaire" merchants and businessmen pay their local bills instantly instead of delaying payment to the smaller merchants.[141]

During the early territorial period the predominantly agricultural regions of New Mexico provided little incentive for bankers to establish

Figure 8:
Group of German merchants in Albuquerque poses for the camera (left to right): David Weinman, Mike Mandell, Louis Kornberg, (Dr. Z. B. Sawyer), Louis Neustadt. Cobb Memorial Collection. Courtesy Center for Southwest Research, University of New Mexico, neg. #000-119-0384

financial institutions. As a result, merchants established in-house credit systems to meet the needs of the population. Population increase and expanding business transactions between New Mexico and eastern states eventually required the formation of a banking system. A group of influential Santa Fe citizens in 1863 requested a charter for a bank. Two of the petitioners had banking experience: Levi Spiegelberg was exposed to banking operations through his family's bank house in New York, and Sigmund Seligman worked for the bank house of Rothschild in Frankfurt, Germany, before immigrating to the United States. Despite the consortium's banking experience, however, U.S. Congress denied approval of their charter.

Not until 1870 was the first bank opened in Santa Fe by Lucien Maxwell. Soon Maxwell, president of the First National Bank of Santa Fe, sold out to Thomas B. Catron and Stephen B. Elkins, two prominent lawyers with political ambitions. Then the Spiegelberg brothers, with the support of Clever, Guttman, and several influential American Hispanics, followed two years later and opened their own bank. In 1872 they received the charter for the Second National Bank of Santa Fe, which was connected with Park National Bank of New York.[142] Yet even as banks began to appear on the scene, most merchants retained their own informal banking and credit system. For example, Ilfeld, with few connections to eastern bankers, maintained his system into the twentieth century. Abraham Staab, Jacob Korber, and the Spiegelbergs, as well, personally lent money or carried debtors in addition to their banking ventures.[143]

The demand for banking institutions gradually increased. Over time other banks opened and a fair number of bankers formed partnerships with Hispanic and Anglo-American bankers. In the late 1870s Joseph Rosenwald became one of the founders and directors of the San Miguel National Bank in Las Vegas. Another German, George J. Dinkle, served as cashier. Other Germans became active in banking ventures. Joseph J. Jaffa participated in the founding of the Citizens National Bank of Roswell and served as its cashier in the 1910s, and Alexander Gusdorf of Taos was listed in the 1920 New Mexico census as a banker.[144] In Old Albuquerque, the First National Bank was organized in Melchior Werner's hotel. In 1884 Louis Huning was appointed president of the Albuquerque National Bank. In 1902 John Becker established the First National Bank of Belen with Paul Dalies as cashier.[145]

In the truly German tradition of *Borge nicht* (don't borrow),[146] Jacob Korber created his own company bank and opened the Korber-Lamparter firm to act as bank for his many other enterprises. Korber contributed to banking enterprises in the 1910s and 1920s by investing in State National Bank, American Trust and Savings Bank, Capital City Bank of Santa Fe, Sierra County Bank of Hillsboro, Gallup State Bank, and the First State Bank of Bernalillo.[147]

Bankers concerned themselves to a degree with local financial needs, but they kept a keen eye on eastern and European markets. The Capital City Bank maintained exclusive business relations with the bank house of Knauth, Machod & Kuhne in Leipzig, Germany. The Spiegelberg brothers' Second National Bank, in addition to its connections to New York, maintained foreign correspondents in Paris, London, and Berlin.[148] Occasionally, the bankers' actions were not in the best interest of New Mexico. Lehman Spiegelberg, instead of depositing federal monies in New Mexico as initially planned, advised the agency to transfer the money to

New York. He reasoned that the cost to transport the money to New Mexico was prohibitive. The effect was that the currency did not circulate in New Mexico, but remained in the East where lending money was more profitable.[149] Consequently, bankers and large merchant-bankers controlled the flow of money into the territory and influenced investments.[150] Only after the railroad arrived in New Mexico did the financial and economic situation change.

Demographic and infrastructural changes altered the shape of mercantile businesses from retail to wholesale and pushed merchants out of Santa Fe and Las Vegas. For the larger merchants with bigger investments, the era of retail business began to decline.[151] Franz Huning's family divested after his death; Johanna Uhlfelder Blatt, who continued the family business after her husband's death in 1916, cut down on merchandise, and eventually specialized in women's clothing and shoes; and Charles Ilfeld resettled in Albuquerque, handing his business affairs over to Max Nordhaus, his son-in-law. A symbolic sign of the end of this era was the 1914 collapse of one of the first territorial mercantile buildings, the Clever-Seligman building, on the plaza in Santa Fe.[152]

The economic experiences of Germans in pursuit of financial stability and occupational success during the territorial and early statehood period were complex. Financial successes or failures, as Carey McWilliams pointed out in his study of Hispanics in the United States, are "always [experiences] relative to historical and social circumstances."[153] Clearly, terms like "success" and "failure" or "wealth" and "poverty" could then have different meanings. Immigrants became successful, made a reasonable living, owned a home and often a piece of land with farm animals. Unskilled laborers also appear to have improved their economic situation. Aided by industrial developments after the 1880s, many moved from unskilled to skilled occupations. After years of renting a farm or a house, they bought homes. In the major towns Germans steadily maintained or improved their economic situation without being considered "economic outsiders" by their Hispanic and American Anglo neighbors. Few achieved the American dream of "rags to riches," but many found respectability in New Mexico.

Occupational flexibility helped bring economic success to Germans settling in New Mexico. They went from baker to butcher, from miner to brewer, or from farmer to lawyer before they finally established themselves.

Merchants occasionally turned into farmers or maintained another venture on the side. The efforts of many German immigrants and their children paid dividends in long-term prosperity.

For German mercantile families, New Mexico and its towns provided opportunities for profits. If one examines the *Standortproblem*, a town's geopolitical location and its relation to economic growth, it is clear German merchants sought out the most promising business centers.[154] Santa Fe and Las Vegas, and later Albuquerque, formed large economic and social centers for New Mexico's hinterland, and German merchants aggressively capitalized on that circumstance.[155]

Merchants also benefited from the population composition in New Mexico. In mining towns the initial population was always on the move and business was conducted on a cash-and-carry basis. As New Mexico's population became more established, the Germans used a credit or partido system to their advantage. Profitable credit ventures were not beyond a normal risk: New Mexico customers were rooted to the land and were not likely to move elsewhere. The money that circulated was not saved to send for relatives as was often the case with the Irish or Chinese population.[156] Instead, New Mexicans' savings were spent in the stores of local barkeepers and merchants.

Obviously, these factors aided merchants in their drive for financial affluence, but the larger profits lay elsewhere. Large-volume merchants, and particularly German merchants in New Mexico profited from the Santa Fe trade and government contracts. Some profits are astonishing: In the 1860 census, Andres and John Dolds reported their worth as $153,000 and the Spiegelberg family made about $200,000 alone in 1867.[157]

Germans rarely invested their surplus capital in New Mexico's economy. German investors placed their surplus capital elsewhere in the country. To many, "New Mexico [was] good only to earn money,"[158] and one cannot fault Germans for this attitude. Rather, like true Weberian entrepreneurs, they came to the Southwest seeking "profit rationally and systematically."[159] In a way, German entrepreneurs, farmers, miners, and merchants, along with other Anglo-American newcomers, brought to New Mexico an extractive economic system expected to produce profit-making surpluses "that were alien to the mexicano world.[160] Once those profits disappeared, many affluent Germans left the region again. After economic reverses, the Spiegelbergs, one by one, returned to New York and Germany; Zadoc Staab moved to California, paying his "usual [annual] visit" to Santa Fe; and Charles Ilfeld, after his retirement from the firm, spent six months of the year in New York with its metropolitan attractions.[161] They left behind a New Mexico that had just begun to develop its industrial potential.

Others, like the Hunings in Albuquerque, Ganderts in Mora, Rosenwalds in Las Vegas, Freudenthals in Las Cruces, and Gusdorfs in Taos tried to blend into the economic-cultural landscape of New Mexico. Those who stayed beyond the 1920s continued to participate in the transformation of New Mexico's economy to Anglo-American standards and sought their way to prosperity that seemed as much American as German.

CHAPTER five

The Preservation of Kultur in a Multicultural Environment

G erman immigrants to the United States maintained identity and cultural values through ethnic organizations. The presence of ethnic organizations such as churches, newspapers, schools, saloons, and *Vereine* (clubs) eased cultural integration into the new society. Ethnic organizations for foreign-born immigrants also promoted economic advancement and cultural preservation.[1]

The Hispanic Southwest, with its nucleus in New Mexico, was one place in the United States where "the contest for property and profits has been accompanied by a contest for cultural dominance."[2] Yet Germans made only infrequent efforts to preserve or promote German culture in New Mexico. These efforts did not begin until late in the nineteenth century. Public demonstration of German ethnicity was negligible in the predominantly Hispanic culture and developed only gradually as a result of Anglo-American immigration to New Mexico. Still "Germanic" evocations such as "not Latin or Slavic, but Germanic will be and must remain the head and heart of America," occasionally articulated in German immigrant circles in the East, were unheard of in the Southwest.[3]

Immigrants to New Mexico had to cope with a cultural landscape different from that experienced in other parts of the United States. Spanish settlers and Native Americans formed the landscape. For centuries the Catholic Church played a decisive role in New Mexico, thus supporting preservation of Hispanic culture and later postponement of Anglo-American domination. Unlike regions in Texas where denominations settled separately to reinforce their respective religious beliefs, New Mexico Germans settled among Catholics with little concern for the church's influence.[4] Religion providing "spiritual continuity in a world otherwise disrupted," played, publicly at least, only a small part in German immigrants' lives in New Mexico.[5]

Generally, religious Germans were few, and circumstantial evidence suggests there were even fewer Germans who were Catholic. Many Germans in New Mexico, like Franz Huning or Arthur Seligman, were tolerant of religious differences and did not practice religion.[6] If non-Catholics worshipped in the early territorial period, it was done privately as houses of worship did not exist. The Vorenberg family, for instance, held services in their home near Mora, where Emma Vorenberg Wertheim was amazed "that we remained Jewish in this isolated little community."[7] The first registered celebration of Yom Kippur was in Santa Fe at the Spiegelbergs' home in 1860 where many of the Jewish Germans of Santa Fe gathered. Only occasionally did Germans like Frederick Gerhardt sing German hymns in a church choir.[8] Few Germans made any commitments beyond the observance of the high holidays. Germans, Gentiles and Jews alike, came West "to start a new life, not to repeat [the] patterns of the past."[9]

Despite the absence of religious fervor among Germans, many supported church causes. On numerous occasions Germans contributed to church building funds. The Seligman and Staab families contributed to the cathedral in Santa Fe, and Germans in Albuquerque, Carlsbad, Roswell, and other towns donated money or property to support local denominations in New Mexico.[10]

In schools the curriculum was devoid of any reinforcement of the German cultural identity. Catholic priests and nuns provided almost all the teaching; and in the early twentieth century a growing number of these educators were German. Whether Catholic clergy was of German origin or descent, their educational methods and training showed little concern for the preservation of German culture.

German Father Peter Küppers, for instance, who operated schools in the Chaperito and Peñasco-Dixon areas in northern New Mexico in the early twentieth century, wasted little time on Germanic values. However, he went to some lengths to promote Spanish-language education.[11] Especially in smaller New Mexico villages, Catholic orders either resisted the public school system or controlled it well into the 1950s.[12] Generally, Germans in New Mexico never vied for control over education, as did Germans in the Midwest.[13]

New Mexico's German children received their ethnic education, if any, at home. Families relied on their own family members. As Frederick Gerhardt's daughter reminisced, "in father's family, an older sister held daily school for the younger children. She taught German, reading and writing along with English lessons."[14] In Mora, the Vorenbergs employed a governess who taught their children the basic school curriculum in addition to German.[15]

If Germans could afford to do so, they sent their children to private schools or hired tutors. Franz and Ernestine Huning's daughter Clara recalls what was, perhaps, a typical educational situation in Albuquerque: "My first teacher was a Mexican who taught me to...write—Spanish—. The only school was taught—by priests—and for boys only—girls were not supposed to need an education." The Hunings thought, however, that their daughter Clara needed further education. Despite Franz Huning's reputation as a freethinker, the parents took her to the Sisters of Loretto in Santa Fe for schooling.[16]

Under other circumstances, if the family network, through marriage, was non-German, German culture was quickly discarded. This was the case in many New Mexico families where German men married into Hispanic families. Charles and Felicita Alarid Blumner's son Carlos, for instance, attended school "where he learn[ed] English and Spanish."[17] Charles Blumner intended to teach him German personally, yet never found the opportunity to do so.

The children of another German, Alois Scheurich, who emigrated from the Duchy of Baden to Taos, also acquiesced to the Hispanic culture of their mother, Teresina. All Scheurich children attended school in Taos where they learned basic English and Spanish. There is no indication that they ever learned German. The children and their father adopted much of the Hispanic tradition. Once, when a visitor to the Scheurichs was disturbed to find the ears of their six-month-old daughter pierced, Scheurich, showing signs of acculturation, commented, "in this country, the first thing [was to] get the baby baptized—then pierce its ears."[18]

Some immigrants felt the need for more and broader education. Mostly wealthy Germans and German Americans sought Bildung (humanistic education) for their children in the East. As historian George Mosse maintains, "Bildung and respectability were two important aspects of the triumph of the middle class, exemplified by the spread of decent and correct manners and morals."[19] Sending their children to the East for additional education, New Mexico's wealthy Germans produced ambiguous results. They achieved Bildung without interference in the traditional education of Hispanic children; however, acquiring Bildung elsewhere meant wealthy Germans insulated their children from contact with native youth. Subsequently, Germans saw no need to participate in improving the educational possibilities in the territory.[20] As a result, the educational opportunities remained inadequate, particularly for Hispanics, who knew little about Anglo-American culture or its capitalistic system.[21]

Henry Lesinsky sent his children to be educated in New York, for "nothing of this could be had in New Mexico."[22] The Nordhaus and Grunsfeld children of Albuquerque, the Vorenberg children of Mora, and the son of the Prager family of Roswell attended secondary and postsecondary schools in the East.[23] The Huning children were sent to high schools in St. Louis and Germany. Clara Huning's "experience in a convent, in a Presbyterian school, and later the Lutheran Pension, decided [her] not to conform to any set religion."[24]

The preservation of the German language itself was not a public issue in New Mexico. Although "language change, often bitterly fought...was a key indicator" of ethnicity elsewhere, Germans did not use the public arena to fight for the survival of their native language. Even though they lacked numerical dominance, often seen as a necessary precondition, their representation as a sociopolitical and economic force gave Germans the option to pursue German or bilingual education should they have desired it.[25] Yet during the nineteenth century, there were no German schools, and no German classes were offered in New Mexico. German literature was not even accessible in Santa Fe bookstores. The works of well-known Germans such as Wilhelm Schiller and Alexander Humboldt were available only in translation. To read German literature, one had to order the books from the East or Europe.[26] If the German language was to be maintained among Germans, it had to be done at home. The Floersheim family, for instance, who lived near Ocate, taught their children primarily Spanish and German.[27] Helene Billings of Socorro acquired her German from family members and friends, and eventually in schools in Cleveland.[28]

In general, the German language was not an important issue in New Mexico. Germans, particularly those in business, realized that English and Spanish were a necessity and German a cultural luxury. Some German traders even became knowledgeable in Native American languages. For instance, Samuel Dittenhofer, a German American, had enough language skills to serve as scout for Apache chief Victorio; Solomon Bibo knew Keres, the language of Acoma; and Samuel Eldodt, as Adolph Bandelier attested, knew "their [San Juan Pueblo] habits well and something of their language."[29] Moreover, since the native language is often cited as "the single most characteristic feature of a separate ethnic identity,"[30] it is amazing how little correspondence among Germans in New Mexico was done in German. Even intimate letters among Germans were written in English.[31]

Much of the correspondence among Germans within New Mexico was conducted in English. Immigrants not in command of the language still tried to impress with their linguistic progress. August Ehrich tried to use his limited English vocabulary in his letters. His letters reflected what sociolinguists refer to as "code-switching," combining two languages. In one of his letters to Charles Ilfeld, Ehrich continuously interspersed German sentences with English words: "wir haben das *Lumber* und die *Stovepipes* heute bekommen." His letter ended with a Germanized American sentence: "So bitte lassen Sie mich wissen bei *next mail*."[32]

Code-switching signaled partial acculturation. But more importantly, this "code-switching" may have "sprung from the semi-conscious desire to gain control of the symbols of a new culture." In Ehrich's case it could be seen as an attempt to show Ilfeld his progress in mastering the technical English of his job.[33] Clearly, English, Spanish, and Native American languages were the languages to know; Germans in New Mexico never disputed that. Those who felt German was important for their children, primarily middle- and upper-class Germans, gave their children the opportunity to learn German in eastern schools. Those who left the German language behind, the step of cultural assimilation, acquiesced to the Hispanic cultural tradition in northern New Mexico, and later to Anglo-American conformity.[34]

Other ethnic issues, important to Germans elsewhere, were neglected in New Mexico. A native German press was never an issue. Perhaps the German contingent was too small to warrant a German newspaper. Germans represented one of the strongest Euro-American ethnic groups in New Mexico but it is surprising that the leading newspapers were devoid of ethnic German issues. Even when Germans owned and published New Mexico newspapers, German issues were absent. For instance, Charles Clever, who published the Santa Fe newspapers *Gazette* and then the *New Mexican* during the 1850s and 1860s, rarely published any news from Germany or information relevant to Germans in New Mexico. Instead, highly Democratic partisan issues dominated his papers.

Another German, Louis Hommel, publisher of the *Red River Chronicle* and *El Cronica*, did not include German-related issues in his publications, either. Rarely did news from Germany appear in these papers. There was neither a reminder of the Kaiser's birthday nor information concerning economic or political situations in the homeland. Only once was it mentioned that Germany's chancellor Otto Bismarck was ill.[35] Instead, newspapers criticized territorial Republican politicians, big ranchers and landholders, and railroad magnates.[36] During the nineteenth century, German churches, newspapers, and schools, often important institutions for cultural preservation elsewhere,[37] played no role in maintaining German culture in New Mexico. Any reservations Germans had about New Mexico and its multicultural landscape were usually voiced in private.

Despite the disrespect and doubts German and German American writers like Balduin Möllhausen and Robert Schlagintweit expressed in their publications about Hispanic culture in New Mexico, it was precisely that society and culture that eased Germans into the Hispanic Southwest. Society in small German towns was similar to that in New Mexico towns. In fact, Germanness promoting ethnicity in the Midwest and the East to gain social and cultural freedom was not necessary in the Hispanic Southwest.[38] In New Mexico, the few Anglo-Americans did

Figure 9:
Kaffeekränzchen with Lena Bell Huning (2nd from left), ca. 1905.
Cobb Memorial Photography Collection. Courtesy Center for
Southwest Research, University of New Mexico, neg. #000-119-0365

not endanger Germans' lifestyles, nor were Hispanics perceived as a cultural threat. In addition, Hispanics had no sense of mission, equivalent to that of Anglo-Americans in the East or Far West, that drove Germans into ethnic organizations. Instead, because of the absence of an exclusionary Anglo-American society, most of the intraethnic communication among Germans occurred informally.[39]

In the absence of organized and formal ethnic gatherings, Germans met in the houses of fellow immigrants. Flora Langermann Spiegelberg received visitors for weekly entertainment "which abounded with German cuisine."[40] Another German, Josephine Bandelier, wife of German Swiss Adolph Bandelier, regularly attended her traditional *Kaffeekränzchen*, an informal gathering of friends for coffee or tea and pastries.[41]

The initial lack of German proverbial tendency to organize was a consequence of the historical makeup of southwestern towns. In the absence of a continuing, large in-migration, Hispanic settlements developed a

Figure 10 and 11:
Despite different architecture, the villages of Waldkirchen, Germany
(above), and Santa Fe, New Mexico (below), in the early twentieth
century appear similar: unimproved streets from the *Marktplatz* or
the *plaza* lead toward the church along buildings in disrepair.
Courtesy Bildarchiv Schiller Nationalmuseum, Marbach, Germany,
and Museum of New Mexico, neg. #40296

strong sense of community.[42] Towns like Santa Fe and Taos had long-established traditions for insuring social order and community.[43] Because of the established sense of community, settlements in New Mexico and the Hispanic Southwest did not need "to forge some form of community, sometimes by importing women or families, sometimes by interethnic marriage and family formation that led to new ethnic groupings within frontier society."[44] Instead, the existing social and cultural order of New Mexico Hispanics paralleled German societal values. From European descent to Christian religious roots, the varied ethnic groups in New Mexico shared conceptions. For Germans less committed "to the glories of German Kultur," New Mexico's cultural environment offered an unrestricted social life.[45]

Josiah Gregg's castigation of New Mexico's cultural life was in fact an asset for Germans: "the population of New Mexico [was] almost exclusively confined to towns and villages."[46] This was a familiar and home-like situation. New Mexico's towns resembled German communities more than metropolitan German travel writers from Berlin or St. Louis admitted. The settlement patterns in Hispanic towns were familiar enough to Germans that they felt no need for ethnic isolation. Santa Fe and Taos illustrate this similarity. These communities were small villas or ranchos and in many ways as *kleinbürgerlich* or bourgeois as any German *Dorf* (village) comprised of farmers, artisans, storekeepers, and merchants. The design of these communities lacked the grid pattern of Anglo-American towns. Instead winding lanes, resembling German designs of villages such as Rundlingsdörfer, were irregularly shaped and developed from a center out.[47]

Historically, the *rundling* formation, buildings radiating from a central core, developed to prevent possible attack by enemies. The dwellings offered a small garden in the back, often ending in a wall. The streets, frequently dead ends, all led to the center of the village. As a result, the organization and structures of many sites in German or New Mexico communities were distinct only in name: Marktplatz and plaza or the nearby *Gasthaus* and *fonda* (inn). Government buildings, homes, an inn, the obligatory church, and occasionally a few small businesses often surrounded both *Marktplätze* and plazas.[48] Farmers in New Mexico, like their German counterparts, often lived in or near town and journeyed to their nearby fields whereas merchants and craftsworkers clustered near

the center of town where their businesses were located.[49] German artisans and merchants found a similar urban arrangement in New Mexico.

Other conditions were also similar. Pigs or oxen in the streets of small
German towns like Dürbheim, Württemberg, were echoed in pigs or bur-
ros in the streets of communities like Santa Fe, Taos, or Albuquerque. The
streets themselves were unimproved and gaslights were as uncommon in
New Mexico as in rural Germany. Occasionally, New Mexico towns (frequently through the initiative or help of Germans) appeared further
improved than German *Dörfer* at the time. In the 1880s gas lights arrived
in Santa Fe, and Willi Spiegelberg's house was the first to have artificial
light. Las Vegas, through the help of Emanuel Rosenwald, received a street-
car system and an electric light plant.[50] Because the physical conditions
in New Mexico's towns were similar to those in many German villages,
one wonders if German immigrants found the situation as dreadful as
writers at the time assumed.

Although similar settlement patterns eased German and German
American transition, the immigrants seldom approved of the unique architecture of New Mexico. If money and opportunity allowed, they moved
quickly from adobe houses into European-style houses. Seen as "improvement," clapboard or frame houses replaced adobes.[51] Especially after the
1880s, ethnic Germans moved rapidly into non-adobe houses. With the
arrival of the railroad in New Mexico, Germans and German Americans
in Las Vegas, Santa Fe, Albuquerque, and points south took advantage of
the new means of transportation and imported more familiar building
material. Willi and Flora Spiegelberg, for instance, resided on Palace Avenue
in Santa Fe in a European-style house designed to reflect their European
upbringing and tastes.[52] Franz Huning had windows and other material
shipped from Chicago. Barbara Huning, recalling her brother-in-law
Franz's European-style home in Albuquerque, remembered that "the beau-
tiful castle [was] the fulfillment of a boyish dream."[53]

The Hunings' residence exhibited amenities such as a ballroom, library,
two kitchens, and the first bathroom with indoor plumbing.[54] This architectural preference of multilevel, European-style houses coincided with a
similar development in Germany, where it was a sign of merchants and man-
ufacturers adopting a more aristocratic lifestyle.[55] The growing number of
European-style houses in Santa Fe and parts of Albuquerque was so apparent that a Royal Prussian architect visiting New Mexico was surprised that

there was no architect "who supervise[d] the construction of buildings and enforce[d] adherence to architectural ideals."[56]

Lifestyle, too, eased German integration into their new setting. New Mexico's Hispanic cultural landscape paralleled German culture more than German immigrants ever acknowledged or perhaps consciously realized. In fact, Germans took advantage of cultural similarities even while remaining largely aloof from Hispanics. The Hispanic traditions of gathering in plazas, in stores, on the streets, and in cantinas resembled the German *Gemütlichkeit*. Yet, both German and Hispanic traditions of visiting saloons after work, in the evening, or on Sunday were often at odds with traditional Anglo-American values. Conversely, in Milwaukee and other northern cities, Germans were uncomfortable in Yankee taverns since the American tradition meant drinking quickly while standing. Moreover, the custom of buying drinks by the round did not appeal to Germans.[57] In heavily Hispanic New Mexico, however, no uneasiness over drinking and socializing occurred. The Anglo-American influence was not strong enough to change the prevailing drinking patterns.

Social sanctioning of alcoholic beverages in the Southwest had other parallels to Germany: Water was often unsanitary, refrigeration for milk was not yet available, and coffee and tea were expensive luxuries.[58] On the other hand, wine had been locally produced around Socorro and in some of the pueblos since the seventeenth century and was well liked by even the most critical Germans.[59] German and Irish immigrant brewers, in addition, provided locally brewed beer.

Echoing native New Mexicans' fondness for cantinas and fandangos, Germans presumably socialized in Hispanic and Anglo-American bars. There are no indications that exclusively German bars existed. Since no formal segregation was in place, Germans and Hispanics, if they did not drink together, at least visited the same establishments. Louis Felsenthal and M. Kayser, for instance, frequented La Fonda at the Santa Fe plaza for games of billiards.[60] Despite harsh reviews of Hispanic taverns in the German literature, Germans seemed to have enjoyed Hispanic cantinas.

Informal social contacts among Germans were not limited to bars. Musical entertainment on the plazas in the Hispanic communities provided excellent opportunities for Germans to meet. When members of military bands were German, as was quite often the case, Germans had ample opportunities to listen to familiar tunes from home. Franz Huning, for instance, recalled that in the early days in Albuquerque the members of the military band "were all German with one or two exceptions." And Robert Schlagintweit observed during his visit in Santa Fe that the military band that performed three times a week at the plaza was led by a conductor who was "as almost everywhere in the United States...a German."[61]

Dances offered additional opportunities to socialize. In the early territorial period, Germans were more drawn to the Hispanic fandangos than casual and highly moralistic travel writers at the time conceded. Germans who spent more than a few days in New Mexico developed an affinity for these events. Fandangos and German folk dances were more similar than generally acknowledged:

> Unlike the constrained etiquette of other ball rooms, the
> German custom authorizes any gent present to ask a lady
> to dance, the lady of course assenting or declining at her
> option.... An unsophisticated gent observes the freedom
> of the dance, and the charming liberty of asking
> whomever he pleases to take a hop.... She says nothing
> but "yaw," takes off her hat, hands her parasol to the near-
> est bystander, modestly stuffs her handkerchief down her
> neck, and complies.[62]

In 1841, Charles Blumner, who by then had lived for nearly a decade in New Mexico described the joyful fandango and remarked "that in no other country have I found such a great passion for dancing regardless among all classes."[63]

Another German assigned to Fort Marcy near Santa Fe, Lt. Christian Kribben, had problems adjusting to the alien culture of New Mexico and with the fandango in particular, but relaxed his assessment as time progressed. Once better acquainted with the new culture, he conceded in a report to the St. Louis newspaper *Anzeiger des Westens* that not only was the local fandango enjoyable, but that it was "admirable how everything remain[ed] within the limits of decency."[64]

Germans seeking additional socializing beyond homes, bars, ballrooms, and plazas had another choice open to them: Freemasonry. In the absence of German cultural and social centers, a few German men gravitated toward secular associations such as the Free Mason's Lodges.[65] Over the years, Germans in New Mexico joined lodges and took prominent roles in their activities. In the 1850s Solomon J. Spiegelberg and Charles Blumner joined the Montezuma Lodge in Santa Fe and in the 1860s and 1870s, in Las Vegas, Louis Sulzbacher, Emanuel Rosenwald, and Charles Ilfeld were among that lodge's masters. Charles and Henry Lesinsky and Aaron Schultz attended the Aztec Lodge in Las Cruces, while Hyman Abraham and Aaron Schultz were members of the lodge in Silver City.[66] By the end of World War I numerous Germans and German Americans throughout New Mexico were thirty-second-degree Masons in the Ancient and Accepted Scottish Rite of Freemasonry.[67] Socioeconomic factors played a role in limiting membership in Masonic lodges to the well-to-do. Most German members in New Mexico's lodges were important and successful businessmen and community leaders.[68]

The Freemason organizations in New Mexico with their affluent and prominent membership were designed to be a "mechanism by which ruling or dominant elements establish, solidify, and perpetuate their hold on social leadership."[69] Besides social conversations at casual gathering of friends in a pub, German Masons took part in decisions that originated in the lodges' chambers and affected all New Mexicans.[70]

Through Masonic lodges Germans helped introduce Anglo-American (rather than German) cultural aspects into civic life in New Mexico towns. The Las Vegas Lodge No. 4, I.O.O.F., where Louis Sulzbacher and Nappelius L. Rosenthal were founding members, existed "for the benefit of benevolent, charitable and educational institutions and to do and perform all other matters and things connected with said object."[71] "Working for the good of civic life" in New Mexico was a theme that never disappeared. In a letter to Charles Ilfeld in 1915, Richard H. Hanna maintained that "the Rite [could] ... be a very valuable agency for good in our state."[72] Yet since few, if any, members in the lodges were of Hispanic origin, the lodges' civic activities showed strong Anglo-American cultural influences. Displaying patriotic sentiments, German and Anglo-American Masons alike took part in organizing parades that reflected Anglo-American values.[73]

The Spiegelbergs, for instance, played a key role in planning Archbishop Lamy's ordination in Santa Fe in 1875.[74] Leading members of the Scottish Rite in Santa Fe, such as German American James Seligman, dominated fiesta-organizing committees. Other Germans could be found in leading roles in public ceremonies. Frederick Muller was commander of President Roosevelt's mounted escort in 1913 and one of De Vargas's captains in the fiesta in 1920.[75] In short, Germans did participate in regular community life.

During the approximately three decades between the 1840s and 1860s, however, there was little public ethnic activity among Germans. Cultural freedom was possible without ethnic defense organizations against the Hispanic culture. Only when the stream of Anglo-American settlers began to increase slowly during the 1870s, and expand after the arrival of the railroad in the 1880s, did Germans organize formal ethnic activities and celebrations.

An early indication of changes due to Anglo-American dominance is the U.S. military in New Mexico. The military is a revealing study in ethnocultural tensions between Anglo-Americans and Germans. Here, as elsewhere in the United States, many German enlisted men displayed a distinct attitude of superiority, promoted German culture, and defended German language in an American setting.[76] Germans in the U.S. Army brought this "Germanness" to New Mexico. The most ethnically oriented entity in New Mexico during the nineteenth century, they observed German holidays, promoted German music, and emphasized German precision in military drills.

German soldiers even maintained their own theater group. To glorify Kultur and Bildung, Germans stationed in New Mexico opened an amateur theater in Santa Fe and performed plays including August von Kotzebue's *Sonnenjungfrauen* and *Dorfbarbier*.[77] Although Germans living in Santa Fe may have attended performances, the theater group's activities were largely directed toward Anglo-Americans in New Mexico. The German soldiers stationed in New Mexico, surrounded by Anglo-American values and standards, displayed an ethnic bias comparable only to that of German and German American travel writers. Most German immigrants making a home in New Mexico did not share the ethnic awareness of these German soldiers.

The increasing stream of Anglo-Americans, including Germans, into New Mexico in the 1880s resulted in increased pressures to become "American." Lured by the economic benefits of Anglo-American influences, Germans soon endorsed separation from the Hispanic population—a group that had allowed Germans to exercise cultural freedom for the past three decades.[78] Conversely, proximity to Anglo-Americans in the economic centers constricted the cultural freedom that Germans had enjoyed earlier among Hispanics.

As a result of swift socioeconomic changes in the late nineteenth century, northern New Mexico increasingly felt the assault of the capitalistic Anglo-American force of economic development and industrial progress. But areas such as Santa Fe, Las Vegas, and Taos, with their strong communal traditions, were so successful in resisting foreign cultural control that Germans and Anglo-Americans alike sought alternative ways to circumvent the Hispanic strongholds.[79] In the 1880s, the newcomers launched "New Towns" next to "Old Towns" in Albuquerque and Las Vegas or gravitated toward new up-and-coming towns along the railroad tracks. In 1883 visiting a friend in the railroad town of Belen, Adolph Bandelier commented that "he is a German; in fact, nearly all foreigners [here] are Germans."[80]

The expanding numbers of Anglo-Americans arriving in New Mexico led Germans to organize ethnic associations as a defense against "Americanization." The simultaneous growth in numbers of German and German American working-class immigrants created new possibilities for German organizations. Old-timers connected with more recent German and German American immigrants and joined cultural clubs that emerged in the decades before World War I. Like clubs in Germany and in other places in the United States, these organizations drew heavily from the ranks of skilled and unskilled laborers and clerical workers for their membership.[81]

The early 1870s marked the first German ethnic organization. According to a brief announcement in a Santa Fe newspaper, an informal meeting of a German singing group in Santa Fe turned into a formally organized *Liedertafel*, headed by Bernhard Seligman, and provided "a sort of social cement" for the German community in Santa Fe.[82] In the same decade, Santa Fe boasted two other German organizations. In 1871, the German Aid Society was founded, whose mission was to help German immigrants in need. The Germania Club was also founded in the early 1870s and by 1875 claimed about forty members. According to a news brief in *The New Mexican*, this club was planning to erect "amicable club rooms including an assembly hall, billiard rooms, parlors, reading and card rooms" for its members to offer an alternative to saloons, green rooms, and "more questionable institutions."[83]

The growing ethnic awareness found in Germans indicated a cultural reservation about Anglo-American culture and a desire to preserve German cultural traditions and independence. In Albuquerque, with a growing Anglo-American population, several ethnic German organizations formed. Their establishment was less a result of exclusion from the Anglo-American society, but rather from a desire to preserve cultural identity and freedom in this multicultural region.[84] In that sense, Germans in Albuquerque continued a long-established tradition in founding the *Deutsche Gesangsverein*. In 1894 another singing organization, the German "Glee" club, began, and its members Georg Weinert, Henry Loebs, Fritz Meier, and five more German and German American members announced their first public concert.[85]

Another organization that provided cultural renewal for German immigrants was Albuquerque's "Germania" club. At the time the club was founded in 1883, with its clubrooms on Gold Avenue, the club officers were William Borchert, Charles Zeiger, F. A. Fritsch, and Maurice Trauer. The club attracted young, single, and less affluent Germans and German Americans. One of Germania's most active members, Jacob Korber, was young, single, and at the beginning of his successful career. His social interests centered on German immigrants and German organizations that promoted German culture and ethnicity. Catering to people of German descent, Korber and "Germania hoped to attract more German immigrants to New Mexico and to promote sociability among German-speaking Americans."[86]

With a Gesangsverein and a social club in place, it was only a matter of time before a *Turnverein* was organized. The founding date of the club is unclear, but planning for the gymnasium began as early as 1892. On 5 March, the German women and men of Albuquerque organized a grand masquerade ball with part of the proceeds going to the Turnverein's building fund. The next month sealed bids for the building were opened at the office of Otto Dieckman, a real estate agent and former president of Southwestern Brewing and Ice Company of Albuquerque. In August, in the *Albuquerque Morning Democrat* secretary William Koenig called for the first meeting of the club in the new gymnasium on Third Street. The Turnverein's announcement was in German and catered to the German community in Albuquerque:

Gut Heil! Naechsten Samstag, den 6. August Versammlung
des Albuquer. Turn-Vereins in der neuen Turnhalle. Wm.
Koenig, Schriftwart.[87]

In the 1890s the organization became the center of activities. The club
held meetings and offered general balls, *Faschings* (carnivals), and *Silvester*
(New Year's Eve) parties for the ethnic German population and presumably offered such activities as team sports, theater, board games, and gym-
nastics since the organization elected a *Zeugwart* to maintain the club's
sports equipment.[88]

The locale of the Turnhalle attracted other German entertainment
into the neighborhood on Gold Avenue. Fritz Lummitzch, also a member of the Turnverein, advertised his liquor store signing jovially as
"Unser Fritz"; Charles Heisch, still another member and owner of the
Tivoli Bar, operated a popular gathering place for other members; and
Jacob Korber kept a bowling alley nearby. Georg Schneider and his partner advertised bowling and billiard tables in their nearby Atlantic Beer
Hall, while Melchior Werner's hotel in Old Town catered to a more
upscale patronage.[89]

By the end of the century German ethnicity was also visible outside
Albuquerque. Long-time residents of Silver City recalled stories that in
the 1880s the greatest asset in town was to know German in order to please
the local saloon owner, Louie Timmer. Mr. Leopold, another German, was
described as a "bigshot, big mining man, and whatever he wanted the town
[Silver City] wanted him to have."[90] Stores in Carlsbad and other places
likewise offered ethnic food such as Sauerkraut or Kraut and Wienies.[91]

Despite sporadic participation in community activities, ethnic activities to maintain German Kultur remained largely out of the public view.
When a rare public showing of ethnicity occurred, it was often at char-
ity concerts. There, a costumed "German Fräulein" presented a musical
solo next to "the Highlander" from Ireland or the Spanish Don; or
Germans might recite German poems and songs such as "Heidenröslein"
and "Du liegst mir im Herzen."[92] In 1892, the German Turnverein participated in a Fourth of July parade. However, the extensive 1892 post-parade
coverage by the *Albuquerque Morning Democrat* neglected to mention
Germans' participation in the parade.[93] Still, in the next year, the
Turnverein had sixty-seven members and was financially sound.

Enough interest existed among Germans and German Americans to establish German lodges. In 1908, John Flaming was the *Oberbarde*, August Klein secretary, and Henry Westerfeld treasurer of the German Einigkeit Lodge, D.O.H. No. 471. They met every second and fourth Tuesday at Red Men's Hall until the end of World War I.[94] For a brief period in 1915, another lodge opened when German women, increasingly active in social and ethnic matters after the 1890s, established the Harugary-Friendship Lodge, D.O.H. No. 145. In general they were dedicated to their fraternal ideals and the promotion of German language, culture, unity, freedom, and community solidarity.[95]

The Jews of Albuquerque, many of whom were of German origin, also felt the need for a place of stability in a changing environment. In 1883, Lodge No. 336 of the Independent Order of B'nai's B'rith was founded. Like its Gentile counterparts, B'nai B'rith was also concerned with charitable functions caring for underprivileged, poor, or sick members of society.[96]

The continuing growth of the Anglo-American population in New Mexico towns was keenly felt among religious Germans. In the late 1880s they began to establish German churches. Contrary to national trends, in which German Jewish communities had built combined networks of religious and secular organizations, the largely German Jewish population of Las Vegas in 1884 was strong enough to form a separate congregation and support a rabbi.[97] Two years later they offered services in their new Temple Montefiore. Other Jewish congregations soon followed. In 1897, Congregation Albert in Albuquerque opened its doors for services, and in 1903 the Jewish community in Roswell established a short-lived congregation.[98]

Protestant Germans likewise felt the need to organize in Anglo-American population centers. In 1896 in the community of Belen, where Adolph Bandelier thought nearly all foreigners to be Germans, the German Evangelical Lutheran Zion's Church was established. In that same year Germans in Santa Fe founded the German Evangelical Lutheran Trinity Church.[99] In the early 1890s German Lutherans gathered in Albuquerque, but due to the absence of a reliable pastor, services were frequently cancelled.[100] The *Albuquerque Morning Democrat* commented that "Pastor Pistor of the German Lutheran church has been relieved of his charge. He is a brilliant scholar and is his own worst enemy."[101]

Subsequently, German community leaders undertook a more organized approach. In February 1893 Jacob Korber, Herman Escherick, Herman Blueher, and four other Germans incorporated St. Paul's Evangelical Lutheran Church. The church's new pastor, G. A. Neuff, offered services each Sunday, and by 1897 the renamed German Evangelical Lutheran Church provided sermons and baptismal certificates in German.[102] Despite several additional name changes and a switch to English sermons in 1913, the German congregation continued to hold regular services through the war years and was still active in 1919.[103]

German language services, however, were available in some churches. In 1914, Pastor Robert Kretzschmer announced German services in the *Morning Democrat* at the German Lutheran Church on Arno Street and Central Avenue.[104] The following year Pastor Carl Schmid conducted German services at the parish's temporary facility in the public library building at Edith and Central. This parish continued to gather publicly for German services in 1915 even after announcements ceased.[105]

In the late nineteenth century women became increasingly involved in organizing ethnic activities. In fact, the religious activities of German organizations that developed after the 1890s could not have been realized without the strong effort of German women. Their contributions in church affairs were considerably greater in the United States than in Germany where women's roles, especially those of middle-class women, were limited to the home.[106] The most compelling reason among Protestant women to get involved, was that, unlike in Germany, no "state church" supported by federal monies existed in the United States. Instead, churches were "self-help organizations" that depended on the active participation and help of their members.[107]

Women answered that call. In the 1870s, Flora Spiegelberg was a leader in efforts to find funds for the St. Francis Cathedral in Santa Fe. In the early 1900s, the Ladies Benevolent Society in Albuquerque took part in raising badly needed funds for a struggling Congregation Albert in Albuquerque.[108] Other women's organizations affiliated with the St. Paul's Evangelical Lutheran Church, like the Martha Society, the Endeavor Society, and the Ladies' Aid Society, performed similar fund-raising functions.

Little is known about German women's organizations in New Mexico, but they did not receive the respect they deserved in the local church hierarchy. Although women were vital to the survival of their local parishes, pastors rarely acknowledged or encouraged their work, and instead looked on women's activities with suspicion. As Irene Häderle poignantly phrased the problem,

> the pastors' fear that the women wanted to take away world rule from the dear Lord was naturally absurd, yet if one replaces the words "dear Lord" and "world rule" with the words "men" and "local church regiment," then these fears will appear under a different light.[109]

German women were also strongly represented in civic organizations such as the Women's Relief Corps of the Grand Army, the Women's Board of Trade, and the Woman's Auxiliary to the St. Louis Exposition. They donated time, money, and goods to those organizations' goals and objectives.[110] Other German women's organizations such as the Ladies Hebrew Benevolent Association of the B'nai B'rith provided social and financial support to religious and secular projects.

Although, strictly speaking, the Jewish associations were not ethnic but religious, a closer look at their membership indicates that a majority of the women were indeed German. In Albuquerque, well-known and long-time residents of New Mexico appear on the membership roster: Grunsfeld, Ilfeld, Jaffa, Mandell; and in Las Vegas the membership list looked similar: Goldstein, Bacherach, Cohn, Stern, Danziger, Taichert, and Ilfeld. The minutes of the Hebrew Ladies Benevolent Society in Las Vegas show that these women frequently considered German-related matters. They planned the establishment of a new Sunday school and discussed the preparations for an upcoming *Maitanz* (May dance). As events led toward war in Germany, the women were kept informed by guest lecturers and considered requests for donations in Europe.[111]

The oldest and best-known immigrant families, such as the Hunings, Seligmans, and Ilfelds, limited their activities to "high society events," exhibiting class rather than ethnic consciousness. Helene Wurlitzer brought the Cleveland String Quartet to Taos annually for a "by invitation only" concert; Helene Blumenschein, daughter of artists Ernest and Mary Blumenschein, imported armoires from Europe.[112]

New Mexico newspapers were filled with announcements of societal events, which well-known Germans attended. The Hunings, Nordhauses,

Rosenthals, Jaffas, Rathgebers, and Barths, along with several Anglo-Americans, made an appearance at a Valentine's Dance party. Helen Huning, Bertha Ilfeld, and several Anglo-Americans attended a reception given in honor of the U.S. Vice President Thomas Marshall at the Barth residence. The list of parties that a small group of affluent Germans and German Americans repeatedly attended or organized is endless. They participated in events at the Alvarado in Albuquerque, and they took part in New Years costume balls like the one in Santa Fe that Ruth Seligman attended as a Teutonic Knight. Or, like later immigrant and artist Gustave Baumann in the late 1910s, they were active in organizations such as the Santa Fe Community Theater.[113] In short, these established and wealthy German and German American families associated with urban middle and upper-middle classes that claimed social and moral primacy in an expanding industrial society.[114] For class-conscious Germans it was more important to exhibit socioeconomic status than to preserve ethnic identity.

Class-consciousness appears to have been closely aligned with exclusionary tendencies. During the many social events toward the end of the nineteenth century in New Mexico's larger towns, Germans and Anglo-Americans intermingled freely, but Hispanics were conspicuously absent. This absence was equally noticeable in social affairs not limited to upper-class Germans; it can also be observed in membership lists of the Albuquerque bicycle and bowling clubs, as well as in events that lower middle-class and working-class members attended. This exclusion of Hispanics runs contrary to a persistent theme that Germans were well liked among Hispanics. Hispanics were absent in sports clubs and Masonic lodges, and they were equally excluded from German birthdays, funerals, and other social events where friends and acquaintances gathered. At a birthday party for her youngest daughter Jane, Helen Huning invited the wife of Isaac Barth and several Anglo-American women, but no Hispanic women.[115]

Funerals, too, contradict the notion of Hispanic-German harmony. Few Hispanic friends attended the funerals of well-known Germans. Among the five pallbearers at Franz Huning's burial on November 1905, all but one were German: Perfecto Armijo was the only Hispanic representative.[116] Only two men with Hispanic surnames attended Emanuel Rosenwald's funeral, whose obituary was carried by *La Voz del Pueblo* and *El Independiente*.[117] Frederick Muller, too, appears to have had many Anglo-American and

Figure 12:
Gustave Baumann (left), known for his woodcuts and marionettes, and
fellow artist, painter Ernest L. Blumenschein (right), pose with John Gaw
Meem. Courtesy Museum of New Mexico, neg. #20749

German friends, but few Hispanic friends and acquaintances. Of the 130 mourners who attended his funeral, only one was Hispanic. The same pattern holds for Germans of the lower-middle and lower classes.[118] Apparently, Germans had fewer social ties to New Mexico's Hispanic population than their romanticized memoirs indicated.

Even German and German American artists, who began to arrive in northern New Mexico at the turn of century, avoided participation in the local Hispanic society. Yet, they used the Hispanic culture for artistic advancement. Many artists were of German descent or had spent some time in Germany. As art historian Stephen Good remarks, "a great number of Americans who studied in Germany were, like Ufer, of German background themselves."[119] The connection of many of the Taos and Santa Fe art colonies to Germany and Europe, and their disregard for Hispanic and Native American art, artists, and artisans was somewhat paradoxical because their purpose was to seek a place to foster a truly "American" art.[120]

Among the artists in the Taos-Santa Fe colony were Ernest L. Blumenschein, Oscar Berninghaus, and Walter Ufer, all second-generation Germans, and Gustave Baumann, born and raised in Germany.[121] These artists saw in the northern New Mexico landscape "the charm produced by the meeting of the wilderness and the cultivated lands within the shadow of primeval grandeur."[122] For newcomers like Gustave Baumann, who arrived in New Mexico in 1918, the region took such a hold on them that many made Taos or Santa Fe their permanent home.[123] The artists "sensed the virility, the incentive, the impelling force, which the German forcefully calls 'Drang,'" and drove them to create magnificent art works.[124]

These artists "freed themselves from the trappings of civilization" and considered themselves to be the "prime translator" of the Southwest and its cultural landscape.[125] In many ways, they attempted to counter a romanticized Southwest portrayed by earlier artists such as Balduin Möllhausen and Albert Bierstadt. Their styles and artistic influences ranged from the Munich school of dark colors and somber tones and the Jugendstil epoch with its light and color (which Ufer pursued) to cubism and expressionism (the latter preferred by Blumenschein and Berninghaus). Through their art, German artists appropriated the northern New Mexico landscape and made it their own.[126]

Despite clear artistic achievements, these artists as cultural translators showed little sensitivity to the region's cultures. Little evidence exists indicating that Germans and German American artists had an understanding of southwestern cultures. The successful artists so grossly underpaid their Indian and Hispanic models that one observer looked back on the models' "patience and loyalty with disbelief." The artists mimicked Native American dances in the annual Taos Fiestas[127] and seemed to consider Hispanics and Native Americans as part of the quaint scenery rather than as "individuals with purposes, plans, options, and initiatives of their own." Unfortunately, the German and German American artists' reactions often resembled behaviors and attitudes of other German immigrants to New Mexico.[128]

German artists did not resist Anglo-American values and influences. In fact, they frequently promoted the "trappings of civilization" they sought to escape and produced "commercial" paintings for the Atchison, Topeka and Santa Fe Railroad.[129] The AT&SF sought European-trained artists, to the exclusion of Indian and Hispanic artists, to illustrate Native American and Hispanic cultural life and promote the Southwest.[130] As good pragmatists, German artists capitalized on this opportunity.

Berninghaus, Blumenschein, and Ufer catered to Eastern art buyers. Aside from a few local art buyers like the Gusdorf family and other merchants, Ufer and Berninghaus found ethnic German patrons in the Midwest like the Busch family of the Anheuser-Busch brewery.[131] Frequently these patrons, instead of accepting the artists' rendering of the Southwest, requested specific details in paintings. An art dealer in Chicago reminded Ufer that a client was waiting for his painting: "[Y]ou know he wants an Indian in typical Indian costume, [and] you need not be afraid of putting too many feathers in it, that's what he likes."[132]

To bolster their status in the art world, the artists founded the Taos Society of Artists "to preserve and promote the native art" and "to encourage sculpture, architecture, applied arts, music, literature, ethnology and archaeology solely as it pertains to New Mexico and the States adjoining."[133] Similar to Germans elsewhere in New Mexico, the Taos Society of Artists benefited from the Hispanic setting, yet did not include Native American or Hispanic artists. Instead of promoting cultural interaction and the artistic works of native New Mexicans, the society promoted European, if not German, technical skills and cultural perspectives.[134]

In addition to virtually excluding Native Americans and Hispanics from their organization, the society altered its by-laws in 1919 to prevent "foreigners" from joining the organization. Illustrious artists such as Dutch painter Henry Balink, Nikolai Fechin and Leon Gaspard of Russia, and Joseph Fleck of Austria were excluded. Society artists felt "they were developing an American form of art that necessitated freedom from foreign influences." Since the Taos Society did not include Hispanics and Native Americans, the founders' intentions of encouraging cultural interaction, as it reads in their constitution, are questionable.[135] And considering that many of the artists received some of their training in German and French art schools, this exclusion of foreigners is even more curious and paradoxical.

Perhaps the "Red Scare" of the post–World War I era was another reason for the society's decision to exclude foreigners. But Walter Ufer's activities have hardly been scrutinized. Ufer was a member of the IWW and had met Leon Trotsky and other prominent socialists and communists of the day.[136] Still, with the exception of *Hunger*, a painting about World War I and its devastating effects on civilization, Ufer was restrained in imposing his political views on his paintings. He focused his efforts on the Hispanics' and especially Native Americans' "pains of cultural transition"[137] and remained one of the few artists who cast a more realistic eye on the cultural experiences of Taos's native populations.[138]

For the Taos painters, with the possible exception of Walter Ufer, Native Americans and Hispanics provided picturesque and quaint subjects, not models for plain living. Like Germans elsewhere in New Mexico since the 1880s, ethnic German artists benefited from the cultural landscapes of the Southwest. Although, upon occasion, they provided social support for the "unfortunate ones," they remained aloof from the Hispanic culture and their attitudes were essentially elitist and ethnocentric.

In conclusion, during the early territorial period Germans took advantage of Hispanic cultural traditions and tolerance. At that point the need for ethnic organizations was less pronounced, and Germans achieved their goals of cultural and social freedom without overt, ethnocentric conduct. But when Anglo-Americans arrived in New Mexico in spiraling numbers in the 1880s, Germans and German Americans increasingly lost sight of their earlier gains. Neglecting the cultural freedom they enjoyed in predominantly Hispanic towns, and seeking economic and political gains, they gravitated toward larger urban Anglo-American centers.

Figure 13:
Very few works of German painters provided critical perspectives of the New Mexico landscape and population as did Walter Ufer in his painting *In Taos* (ca. 1920). Photo Courtesy, Gerald Peters Gallery, Santa Fe, NM

Then a clear change took place. The proximity of Anglo-Americans threatened Germans' cultural autonomy. To preserve cultural traditions they resorted to social and religious solidarity. Mostly the organizations met privately. They rarely made public appearances at large events such as Fourth of July parades. The oldest and best-known German families in New Mexico tended to associate only with Anglo-Americans of the upper class. When they felt the need for ethnicity and Kultur they went on pilgrimages to the East, as Charles Ilfeld and many of the Taos artists did, or they retired to Germany, as Solomon Jacob Spiegelberg did. As an ethnic group, Germans and German Americans did little to promote genuine cultural understanding. Instead, they chose economic success.

CHAPTER SIX

World War One:
The End of an Era

In the nineteenth and early twentieth centuries, Germans in the United States experienced periodic, if brief, eruptions of nativism and hardships. World War I marked a break from a period void of xenophobia that Germans enjoyed in the prewar era. Indeed, no other issue in New Mexico between 1850 and 1920 concerned Germans more than World War I and its repercussions.

Throughout New Mexico, ethnic Germans encountered suspicion. The state's newspapers remained cautious about German conduct prior to the outbreak and during the early stages of the war. The events of the war soon encouraged editors to drop their "journalistic objectivity."[1] War reports from the European front caused a backlash against ethnic Germans and those favoring the German cause.

Despite voices of reason, ethnic Germans and those related to or connected with them had to endure widespread defamation and denunciation. One notable New Mexican, Charles Springer, chair of the New Mexico Council of Defense and holder of an honorary doctoral degree from the

University of Berlin, cautioned his fellow New Mexicans to be careful of accusations and to refrain from mob activities. Although he accepted anti-German sentiments as normal and laudable, he feared New Mexicans would

> be taken advantage of by ... people who will make false accusations against innocent persons in order to get even with them, or possibly simply to make trouble which will help the Germans instead of aiding the ... Allies.[2]

The State Council of Defense ordered and distributed 200 pamphlets entitled *Amerikanische Bürgertreue* (American Citizenship), hoping "to have the hearty cooperation of these people [of German descent] before very long."[3]

Still, the situation slowly deteriorated. The loss of American life in the Atlantic war zone, especially after the *Lusitania* incident in 1915, escalated Anglo-American suspicion of Germans. Anti-German articles appeared increasingly in New Mexico newspapers, accusing Germans of sabotage: damaging factories and destroying wheat.[4] By the time the United States entered the war in 1917 societal pressure no longer allowed any pro-German attitude.

Perhaps the exception was Flora Spiegelberg, who rose to national fame as a pacifist. Because an antiwar movement was considered anti-American, it is surprising that neither Flora Spiegelberg nor her family experienced repercussions. A possible explanation may be that she was from a highly influential German family in New York and knew most of the influential politicians in Washington.

It was unwise to exhibit pro-German feelings in New Mexico. In one location, the Guadalupe County Council of Defense warned individuals who voiced pro-German sentiments of serious consequences. Violators were also reminded that they would "be kept under surveillance from this time on."[5]

Allegations and actions against ethnic Germans after the United States' entry into World War I increased throughout the state. On at least two occasions Germans and German Americans were relieved of their duties. A German teacher had to resign his position at the University of New Mexico, and another, accused of pro-German speeches, was forced to surrender his position on the Bernalillo County Council of Defense. German and German American merchants were accused of taking advantage of the war situation by speculating in wheat and other commodities.[6] Mail of German sympathizers in New Mexico was commonly intercepted and, occasionally, interrupted. In one case a rattlesnake was placed in a mailbox. Only in rare instances, however, were Germans detained as "a danger to the public peace and safety of the United States."[7]

Collective charges were also filed against Germans. In Las Cruces segments of the local population were concerned that Germans might sabotage the newly erected Elephant Butte dam. They filed charges against Germans and requested federal protection.[8] Even religious organizations were not above suspicion. In Roswell, St. Mary's Hospital, established by the Sisters of the Sorrowful Mother in 1906, was staffed exclusively with German and German American sisters. They were accused of unpatriotic activities. A few citizens of Roswell became annoyed that an institution receiving $2,500 annually in state funds had "never owned or raised the American Flag." Since the daily language among the staff was reportedly German, the suspicion in the community increased. In a letter to Charles Springer, A. J. Nisbet, chair of the Chaves County Council of Defense, voiced his concerns:

> I personally do not feel friendly to people in these times, who
> do not talk English. . . . From the best information I can get
> every person up there is an Alien, and speaks German. I think
> it ought to be taken over by the Alien property custodian.[9]

Charges against individuals were filed more often than group charges. Accusations were made "in order to get even with them [Germans], or possibly to simply make trouble." In some cases personal animosity between the accuser and the accused could be established. When John Young brought charges of disloyal actions against A. Eichwald of Cuba, Max Nordhaus disclosed that Eichwald had fired Young from his job. And when Ed Spitzley accused Arthur Wiedeman of Deming of un-American activities, it came to bear that work-related problems preceded the accusations.[10]

Even Germans who were longtime residents of the state and were established leaders of their communities fell under suspicion. For instance, Frederick Scholle, a sheep merchant in Belen since the 1880s, was accused of pro-German activities "in forwarding communications for German agents in the United States" through Juarez and Tampico. One of Scholle's ranching neighbors, Senator Albert Fall, was unable to confirm these accusations.

Fall replied that his "judgement without further knowledge, would be that Scholle would not be found engaged in any efforts, even passively assisting anyone in opposing the policies of this country."[11]

Letters that reported pro-German activities usually contained additional slanderous information, often difficult to substantiate. Scholle, for instance, was described as "not married, drink[ing] heavily, and [having] several mistresses." Often, accusers revealed more about their own political convictions or ignorance than about any pro-German activities. An unsigned letter—not an uncommon tactic—describing the conditions in Roy was received in El Paso, Texas:

> This place is full of Germans; the leading men are supposed
> to be loyal to the United States, but the other night two flags,
> one on the Spanish-American Hall and one on the Florsheim
> Bldg., were pulled down, torn to shreds, braided and tied to
> the bottom of the flag pole. This was all kept quiet, hoping to
> get parties doing it. Florsheim's are Germans. This is a
> Democratic town, and also wet.[12]

Wesley Way, a lieutenant in the U.S. Army stationed in Lordsburg, was even more indiscriminate in his judgment: Everyone who was a member of the I.W.W., sympathetic toward strikers, a gambler, a bootlegger, a convict, a drug dealer, a "nigger," or a "Chinaman," was guilty of pro-German activities.[13]

Another New Mexican, George Kile of Bluewater, reassured Charles Springer in a letter, that Jews had his greatest confidence and respect, but the German Jew was different and had neither his confidence nor his respect. Kile attacked Jewish families residing in Valencia County. In his letter, Kile insinuated that an Albert Baer, the Block family, and the "Bibo and Seligman tribes" not only conducted shady business deals "doing a half million dollars per year," but also traveled extensively and made pro-German statements. Charles Springer, who investigated the case, was asked by the Bernalillo County Council of Defense to call Mr. Kile "down good and hard" if his statements were untrue. Springer informed Kile that "if there are any persons, Jewish or otherwise . . . who are sowing disloyalty," they should be investigated, but, Springer continued, "we hear so many stories of Pro-Germans and disloyalty these days that we do not believe any of them until they are corroborated." Apparently since no action was taken to reprimand or arrest any of the accused, the charges could not be substantiated.[14]

Suspicions of disloyalty to the United States were by no means limited to those of German origin. Because New Mexico once belonged to Mexico, Mexicans and Hispanic New Mexicans were frequently treated with suspicion. Investigations revolved around their enlisting in the U.S. Army, organizing labor unrest, and promoting sabotage. If accusations were followed by an investigation, inquiries usually turned up little. S. Benavides, for instance, was accused of organizing a "Union among the Mexican laborers," but the case was dropped due to a lack of evidence. Americans, too, were investigated. George Carson, a native of Indiana, aroused suspicion among authorities when he requested large-scale topographical maps of Santa Fe County and the city of Santa Fe, though no investigation was ordered.[15]

Even in this atmosphere of suspicion in New Mexico, most ethnic Germans found ways to communicate their allegiance to the United States. As elsewhere in the West, they made cash contributions to the American Red Cross, contributed money to "the coffers of the government," or sent their sons to the army.[16] Many Germans, particularly those in businesses, recalled the Liberty Bond drives and the societal pressure to purchase bonds. Karl Ludwig Grundman and Lucien Hoch, whose fathers served in the Prussian army, were subject to this coercion. Hoch reminisced about these days in Albuquerque: "He [father] was in business, and every time they [Americans] came down, it was five-hundred dollars or so in Liberty Bonds or else."[17] Most Germans purchased bonds, often under considerable financial strain.

Giving patriotic speeches was another way Germans and German Americans could secure the trust of their fellow citizens. For some individuals, self-conscious of their German heritage, making the speeches was not sufficient; they mailed copies of speeches to the Council of Defense. The Reverend P. Kretzschmar of Optimo in northern New Mexico, for example, sent Charles Springer copies of his speeches in the *Wagon Mound Sentinel* reaffirming his patriotism.[18]

In addition to purchasing Liberty Bonds and performing patriotic speeches, second-generation Germans registered for the United States Army or joined clubs and war-related organizations in New Mexico. Besides associations like the "Lick the Kaiser" Club in Eddy County and the "War Chest"

Club in Colfax County, the most important organization for ethnic Germans was the Council of Defense.[19]

The council, instituted by an act of the state legislature for the patriotic cause, listed the names of many of New Mexico's well-established Germans on its membership roster: Grunsfeld, Nordhaus, Scheurich, Kohn, Eldodt, Seligman, Kinkel, Rosenwald, Gusdorf, Kempenich, Becker, and Huning, to name a few. These men served on committees and subcommittees with other Germans and German Americans. Nordhaus and Kempenich, for instance, utilized their financial talents in the Liberty Bond campaign, on the Jewish Welfare Board, and in the United War Work. In another venue, Becker, a captain in the New Mexico Motor Minute Brigade, drove thousands of miles across the state to deliver brief, four-minute patriotic and propagandistic speeches.[20] In addition, Bertha Nordhaus, Miriam Grunsfeld, and many other women of German families chaired departments like Child Welfare, Patriotic Education, and Americanization.[21]

Despite occasional animosity against ethnic Germans, New Mexicans' reactions were mild compared to repercussions nationwide. No Germans were killed, no major German mercantile business was forced to change its name, nor were any German businesses boycotted. Moreover, no forces assembled to prevent Germans from speaking their language, although some may have voluntarily refrained from speaking German in public.[22] The popular cartoon "Katzenjammer Kids," with its stereotypical German characters, continued in the *Albuquerque Morning Journal* until April 1918, only to be replaced by the conceptually similar "Shenanigan Kids."[23]

Repercussions against ethnic Germans were, to a certain extent, limited in New Mexico because of the large Hispanic population. The political allegiance of Hispanics was of greater concern for Anglo-Americans than the loyalty of Germans and German Americans. Many Anglo-Americans in New Mexico worried more about the Southwest's history, recalling Pancho Villa's activities in southern New Mexico. One German living in Albuquerque at the outbreak of the war, for instance, recalled that if there was any prejudice, "it was against the natives, the poor Mexicans."[24] Anglo-Americans' concerns over whether American Hispanics in New Mexico would follow or fight against the American flag may have diverted attention from the ethnic Germans in New Mexico.[25]

Generally, Germans and German Americans in New Mexico either remained silent or rallied together for the American cause. Because many

Germans never broke contact with their families in Germany, the tensions and worries continued throughout the war.

Through family letters during the war Germans in New Mexico kept informed about the situation in Germany. Once the war was over, many sent care packages overseas. Charles Ilfeld, through the American Relief Administration Warehouse in Manburg, Germany, sent food items to relatives in Berlin.[26] German cities also solicited donations of money from the German population in New Mexico. Mayor W. Gerbaulet of Paderborn, for example, requested help: "I sincerely beg you to solicit donations among the people of German descent in the state of New Mexico for the 'Deutsche Vaterland' and especially for your hometown Paderborn."[27]

The limited ethnic conduct that Germans and German Americans followed in New Mexico over the decades allowed them to be supportive of families in Germany and still maintain the appearances of loyalty in New Mexico. Unlike other parts of the United States, where "the war was the occasion that converted latent tensions into manifest hostility," New Mexico never exhibited these tensions. The occasionally strained relationships between Anglo-Americans and Germans elsewhere were not an issue in New Mexico because, by the early twentieth century, Germans in the Hispanic Southwest were part of the majority Anglo culture.[28] Germans and German Americans of the Southwest came away relatively unscathed by the events of World War I—a result of their entire experience of cultural interaction with the diverse mix of New Mexico's people since the 1840s.

World War I ended an era of German immigration to New Mexico and the Southwest that had begun in the 1840s. Following national trends, the number of German immigrants declined at the turn of the century. The war that engulfed Europe in 1914 and eventually drew the United States into the conflict encouraged immigration restrictions. But the process of decline had already begun in 1911 when the Dillingham Commission, headed by Senator William P. Dillingham of Vermont, released its findings. Subsequently, United States immigration laws of 1917 and 1921 and their later alterations enforced a quota system. European immigration to this country was severely restricted and an era of German cultural interaction came to a close.[29]

Conclusion

Although World War I had an impact on ethnic Germans in the United States, hostilities against them in New Mexico were insignificant. The mild animosities against ethnic Germans reflected eight decades of harmonious German settlement in the Southwest. Although ethnic Germans in New Mexico never reached the numbers of Germans in some of the Midwestern states or Texas, they represented a numerically strong Euro-American group with wealthy and influential individuals.

Adverse landscape, unfamiliar cultures, and remoteness from eastern population centers discouraged immigration to the Southwest, keeping the German population small. The German perception of the West and the Southwest, like many Anglo-Americans' impressions, was ethnocentric and stereotypical.[1] German literature about New Mexico and the Hispanic Southwest ignored the presence of Hispanics and Native Americans and emphasized the limitations of the region. Only New Mexico's prospects for mercantile businesses were advertised positively, so, not surprisingly, mercantile entrepreneurs were attracted to the territory. New Mexico frequently appeared as a place for quick profits, but for Germans it was not a land of opportunity that could compete with other regions elsewhere in the United States.

The German entrepreneurs who were attracted to New Mexico had different expectations from Germans settling elsewhere.[2] Some of the wealthiest merchants left New Mexico after gaining financial rewards while others went east or to California for regular extensive visits. Other merchants who arrived prior to the railroad often lived alongside the Hispanic population without any overt displays of German ethnicity. Many Germans were integrated into the northern Hispanic culture. They married into Hispanic families and their children frequently spoke Spanish as their native language. They concentrated on developing economic fortunes, showed little interest in either Hispanic or Anglo-American cultural affairs beyond learning the languages, and were never put into a position to respond defensively to the values of the host society.[3]

The arrival of the railroad was a watershed in the German experience in New Mexico. The railroad, which "symbolized national capitalism's triumph over local autonomy," altered the ethnic makeup in New Mexico so that Germans were forced to modify their conduct.[4] Germans in increasing numbers gravitated toward new Anglo-American centers, changed marriage patterns from Hispanic to Anglo-American spouses, and more publicly proclaimed their ethnicity. Still, German religious services were few, German schools and German newspapers were nearly nonexistent, the German language was spoken only infrequently, and only a few German social organizations emerged in New Mexico.

Germans' ethnic conduct in New Mexico was quite different from the behavior of Germans in Midwestern states and towns. In the Midwest, Germans and German Americans settled in an Anglo-American cultural landscape that appeared restrictive toward many Germans, leading them to gather in larger numbers and to form ethnic organizations. Sometimes, this resulted in tension with non-German neighbors. Because of the sheer numbers, they were not forced "to abandon their German way of life."[5] Instead, they opened German schools, saloons, and Turnvereine that, in turn, resulted in cultural clashes and provoked nativist reactions against Germans.[6] These latent tensions between Anglo-Americans and Germans contributed to the conflict between ethnic Germans and Anglo-Americans during World War I.[7]

But these tensions were absent in New Mexico. The ethnic German population in New Mexico was small in comparison with Midwestern towns and cities and the numbers never were large enough to result in nativist fears. Still, ethnic Germans represented one of the largest Euro-American groups in New Mexico. More importantly, they controlled a significant portion of New Mexico's economy, influenced New Mexico newspapers, and became important social leaders of the state and, therefore, had ample strength to assert their ethnicity.

This proved unnecessary, however. It was not the liberal notion of Anglo-American life but New Mexico's Hispanic culture that allowed Germans to retain old beliefs. They had unrestricted liberties in pursuing economic gain and in participating in cultural activities such as Gemütlichkeit and festivals. Germans' tolerant attitudes toward *Bier und Schnaps*, for instance, which led to occasional strains with the Anglo-American society, were much more accepted in Hispanic cultural life. These circumstances allowed Germans to adjust and acculturate to this country at their own pace.

When the railroad brought more and more Anglo-American migrants to New Mexico, ethnic Germans began to feel threatened and exhibited behaviors similar to those in the Midwest.[8] Arrivals in the 1880s attended ethnic German organizations. Others were already acculturated enough to live untroubled in the Anglo-American centers of New Mexico where demonstrations of ethnicity were of little significance.

The German experience in the Hispanic Southwest was culturally ambiguous and differed from Germans elsewhere. Without public signs of ethnicity, the German experience in New Mexico was successful. Early German immigrants capitalized on the hospitality Hispanic culture provided and acculturated more easily. Many found a comfortable life, even if life was harder than anticipated. Some became very rich. Few Germans settling in New Mexico appear to have returned to Germany. Since return migration was often related to economic disillusionment and the inability to cope with the host country's new challenges, it can be assumed that most Germans were satisfied with their new home in New Mexico.[9]

Yet despite the proximity of the Hispanic culture, and despite the benefits that it offered, Germans considered Hispanic (and Native American) culture inferior to their own. Although Germans benefited from life in the Hispanic Southwest, they displayed typical ethnocentric attitudes. Henry Lesinsky represented many Germans' and German Americans' views when he wrote to his son after a visit to Germany in 1866: "I longed to be back again even among the ignorant Mexicans. They at least had been friendly to me—I was at home amongst them."[10] Germans, like their Anglo-American neighbors, often ignored the ways of Hispanics and Native Americans, limiting cultural exchange and understanding.

It is difficult to understand the immigrant psychology, but New Mexico's Germans, with their various degrees of economic success, represented what has been called "Per Hansa types." Derived from the protagonist of Ole E. Rölvaag's novel *Giants in the Earth*, a Per Hansa symbolized rapid cultural assimilation, economic success, small-town residence, and urban-type occupation.[11]

When the railroad arrived in New Mexico, Germans and their children had adjusted to growth in Anglo-American population by creating only "recreational" organizations for preservation. Today's ethnic legacy is limited to German street names and to a few ghost towns such as Scholle, Ilfeld, and Blumner. Yet their larger legacy, more difficult to assess, involves a significant role in the economic conversion of pastoral and agricultural New Mexico toward Anglo-American industrialism. Germans, like their Northern European counterparts, were driven by their economic desire and by the notion of "progress."

Appendix
A Note on the Analysis
of Occupational Data

—⁓—

Historians have frequently discussed the difficulties in classifying occupations. The two models from which I have drawn here are Stephan Thernstrom's works on blacks and Irish immigrants and Kenneth L. Kusmer's study of blacks.[12] Both authors group their workforces into similar categories, but Thernstrom distinguishes between High White-Collar, Low White-Collar, Skilled, Semiskilled, and Unskilled in order to search for the upward mobility among these groups.[13]

Kusmer uses slightly different categories. Adopting a modified system developed by Alba M. Edwards for his *An Alphabetical Index of Occupations by Industries and Social-Economic Groups* (Washington, 1937), Kusmer distinguishes between Professionals; Proprietors, Managers, and Officials as Entrepreneurs; Clerical Workers; Skilled Workers; Semiskilled Workers; Unskilled Workers; and Personal and Domestic Servants. To determine occupational status and mobility, Kusmer adopted Edwards's ranking system of these groups. Modified for an urban setting (i.e., Kusmer left out farmers in his urban study), he places Professionals at the top of his socioeconomic ladder (zero), and Domestic Servants at

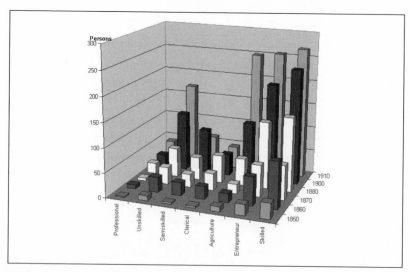

Table 6:
Occupations – 1st Generation Germans

the bottom (seventh and last).[14] Although it is possible to consider professionals socioeconomically more important than unskilled or semi-skilled laborers, it is less acceptable to rank professionals above proprietors and managers, clerks above skilled workers, or unskilled laborers above servants. In the case of Edwards's system, it is difficult to rationalize a ranking of farmers below professionals or above proprietors and skilled workers.

Thernstrom, too, uses occupational categories to trace social inequality. In his search for upward social mobility as a function of economic growth, he regards nonmanual occupations as socially superior to manual labor.[15] Although Thernstrom is more sensitive than Kusmer to the differences between white- and blue-collar groups, he still sees the transition from blue- to white-collar group as progressive (even if he does not find much upward mobility in the groups he studied).

In quantifying upward mobility from servant to professional or from low blue-collar worker to high white-collar worker, both authors apply American cultural values to their research groups. Dealing with Germans requires one to consider German traditional values. Well established and often restrictive, the trade guild system in Germany had its own set of

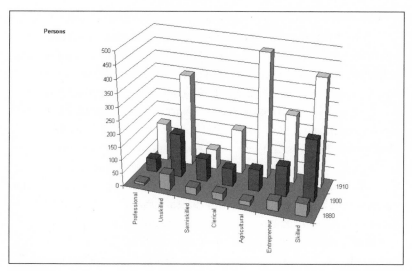

Table 7:
Occupations – 2nd Generation Germans

values regarding upward social mobility. A carpenter or a miner in Germany who spent three years or more in apprenticeship to become a journeyman and who might advance to master carpenter or master miner (Steiger) in another three years, was a respected member of his community. The status of artisanship provided pride, social status, and economic benefits. German sources suggest that despite rapid industrialization in Germany toward the end of the nineteenth century, an average German laborer retained the values of a preindustrial craft worker.[16]

Since the status of labor and artisanship in Germany was unlike that in the United States and in preindustrial New Mexico, I have refrained from making detailed quantitative analyses of upward mobility. Census data alone—without other social variables—cannot position one occupation above another. It is difficult to place, for instance, a carpenter who owns his own shop or a trained nurse who runs her own practice below a merchant who might do business out of a makeshift cabin. Consequently, I have used all but one of Kusmer's categories (servants were placed in the Unskilled group) to identify a general pattern of German and German American occupational types and the changes that occurred.

This placement of occupations into specific categories is far more difficult than Kusmer and Thernstrom suggest and allows for a wide margin of interpretation and for error. Obviously, decisions depend upon the cultural background of the researcher and on the values of the ethnic group under study. W. E. B. DuBois, writing about blacks in urban Philadelphia in 1899, considered black barbers entrepreneurs and black musicians semiskilled. DuBois was more interested in the worker as a proprietor and his economic status, and had valid reasons for categorizing these occupations in this manner.[17] But I consider German barbers, who learn the trade, members of a trade, and musicians, who presumably attended college, as professionals. In general, however, I have placed occupations in groups following Kusmer's model.

In a few situations, I differ from Kusmer's classification of specific professions. Since seamstresses and dressmakers are the female counterparts of tailors, they deserve to be with tailors in the Skilled category rather than in the Semi-skilled group. Further, Kusmer distinguishes between trained nurses (professionals) and other nurses (semi-skilled), a distinction not made in the New Mexico census. Therefore nurses (including midwives) who needed training were placed under Skilled laborers. Other deviations from Kusmer's model are salespersons, whom I placed under unskilled rather than under clerical; chauffeurs whom I listed as semi-skilled rather than unskilled; and laborers, day laborers, janitors, and laundry personnel as unskilled. The largest difference occurs in the interpretation or livery stable keepers and hostlers whom I consider entrepreneurs rather than domestic servants. Other occupations were difficult to fit into any category and thus have not been integrated into these groups: The handful or so of German prostitutes and gamblers who came to New Mexico were omitted; "Employees" and military personnel have also been exempted for the same reasons. Also disregarded were housekeepers, nearly always the wives of family heads and, as such, not gainfully employed. The occupation "own income" I have placed with the entrepreneurs since it seems likely that those persons were retired and lived off their property rentals or income they earned during their working years.

The following list of occupations is arranged by socioeconomic categories; similar occupations, for instance the various types of masons, have been grouped together.

Male Occupational Structure

UNSKILLED
deliveryman
dishwasher
drayman
driller
expressman
iceman
jailer
janitor
laborer
laundryman
liftboy
liveryman
lumberman
lunchman
messenger
packer
porter
pumpman
salesman
servant
tiller
waiter
watchman
yardman

—〰—

SEMISKILLED
bartender
bottler
brakeman
car sealer
cowboy
driver
dyer
herder
gasman
leatherworker
miner
steel polisher
switchman

teamster

—〰—

SKILLED
amalgamator
appraiser
apprentice
artist
assayer
baker
barber
basket maker
boat builder
boilermaker
bookbinder
builder
brewer
butcher
carpenter
cigar maker
cook
cutler
decorator
druggist
electrician
fireman
florist
foreman
gardener
gasfitter
harness maker
jeweler
machinist
mason
masseur
mechanic
miller
millwright
nurse
operator
optician

painter
patternmaker
photographer
piano tuner
plasterer
plumber
policeman
printer
railroad engineer
ranger
roadmaster
roofer
ropemaker
saddler
shoemaker
smith
surveyor
sutler
tailor
taxidermist
typesetter
undertaker
upholsterer
watchmaker
wheelwright

—〰—

AGRICULTURE
dairy farmer
farmer
fruit grower
rancher
stock raiser
winegrower
woolgrower

—〰—

CLERICAL
accountant
agent auctioneer
auditor

bank teller
bookkeeper
broker
cashier
clerk
collector
conductor
dispatcher
inspector
mail carrier
reporter
secretary
solicitor
stenographer
telegrapher
timekeeper,
trainmaster

ENTREPRENEUR
banker

businessman
capitalist
commissioner
contractor
hotelkeeper
Indian agent
landlord
manager
manufacturer
merchant
official
owner
own income
postmaster
president
proprietor
prospector
publisher
restaurateur
saloonkeeper
sheriff

treasurer

PROFESSIONAL
architect
chemist
cleric
dentist
editor
educator
engineer
geologist
lawyer
librarian
musician
pharmacist
physician
Secretary of State
student
veterinarian

Female Occupational Structure

UNSKILLED
attendant
housecleaner
laborer
laundress
saleswoman
servant
waitress

SKILLED
apprentice
artist
baker
cook
dressmaker
midwife
milliner
nurse
operator

shoemaker

AGRICULTURE
dairy farmer
farmer
stock raiser

CLERICAL
agent
bookkeeper
cashier
clerk
stenographer

ENTREPRENEUR
capitalist
hotelkeeper

landlady
merchant
owner
own income
postmaster
restaurateur
saloonkeeper

PROFESSIONAL
cleric
compositor
educator
musician

Notes

—〰—

INTRODUCTION

1.   Jon Gjerde, *The Minds of the West: Ethnocultural Evolution in the Rural Middle West, 1830–1917* (Chapel Hill: University of North Carolina Press, 1997), 2.

2.   Walter D. Kamphoefner, *The Westfalians: From Germany to Missouri* (Princeton, NJ: Princeton University Press, 1987), 11. See also Robert Paul McCaffery, *Islands of Deutschtum: German-Americans in Manchester, New Hampshire, and Lawrence, Massachusetts, 1870–1942* (New York: Peter Lang, 1996), 137.

3.   Elliott Shore, "A New Look at the Nineteenth Century," in *The German-American Encounter: Conflict and Cooperation between Two Cultures, 1800–2000*, ed. Frank Trommler and Elliott Shore (New York: Berghahn Books, 2001), 3.

4.   Russell A. Kazal, *Becoming Old Stock: The Paradox of German-American Identity* (Princeton, NJ: Princeton University Press, 2004), 11–12; Kathleen Neils Conzen, *Making Their Own America: Assimilation Theory and the German Peasant Pioneer* (New York: Berg Publishers, 1990), 33.

5.   Adolph Wislizenus, *Memoir of a Tour to Northern Mexico: Connected with Col. Doniphan's Expedition in 1846 and 1847* (1848; reprint,

Albuquerque, NM: Calvin Horn Publisher, Inc., 1969), 20; Balduin von Möllhausen, *Reisen in die Felsengebirge Nordamerikas* (1861; reprint, München: Lothar Borowsky Verlag, n.d), 2:225; Robert von Schlagintweit, *Die Santa Fe- und Südpacificbahn in Nordamerika* (Köln: Verlag von Eduard Heinrich Mayer, 1884), 233. These and all subsequent translations of German works, newspapers, and manuscripts, indicated by a German title, are by the author.

6. Kathleen Neils Conzen, "Phantom Landscapes of Colonization: Germans in the Making of a Pluralist America," in *The German-American Encounter*, 16.

7. Censuses do not indicate religious preferences, nor do manuscript collections emphasize religious backgrounds of German immigrants.

8. Henry Tobias, *History of the Jews in New Mexico* (Albuquerque: University of New Mexico Press, 1990), 120; Moses Rischin, "Introduction," in *Jews of the American West*, ed. Moses Rischin and John Livingston (Detroit, MI: Wayne State University Press, 1991), 21–22; Raphael Seligmann, "Die Juden Leben," *Der Spiegel* 16 (November 1992): 75.

9. Frederick C. Luebke, *Immigrants and Politics: The Germans of Nebraska, 1880–1900* (Lincoln: University of Nebraska Press, 1969), 16, 28.

10. Kathleen Neils Conzen, *Immigrant Milwaukee, 1836–1860: Accommodation and Community in a Frontier City* (Cambridge, MA: Harvard University Press, 1976), 148; Luebke, *Immigrants and Politics*, 34.

11. "Behavioral assimilation" and "structural assimilation" are terms used by Milton M. Gordon to indicate acculturation to and integration into a host society. Milton M. Gordon, "Assimilation in America: Theory and Reality," *Daedalus* 90 (Spring 1961): 279. See also Luebke, *Immigrants and Politics*, 34–35.

12. In Chapter Two, because census data reveal only first- and second-generation Germans, *German Americans* will represent those Germans who have at least one parent born in Germany. Chapter Two elaborates on the definition of *Germany*.

13. D. W. Meinig, *Southwest: Three Peoples in Geographical Change, 1600–1970* (New York: Oxford University Press, 1971), 28–29;

Richard Francaviglia, "Elusive Land: Changing Geographic
Images of the Southwest," in *Essays on the Changing Images of the
Southwest*, ed. Richard Francaviglia and David Narrett (College
Station: Texas A&M University Press, 1994), 13.

CHAPTER ONE

1. See for example, Paul Wilhelm von Württemberg, *Reise nach dem
nördlichen Amerika in den Jahren 1822 bis 1824* (1835; reprint,
München: Lothar Borowsky Verlag, n.d.), and Maximilian Prinz
zu Wied, *Reise in das Innere Nordamerika in den Jahren 1832 bis
1839–41* (reprint, München: Lothar Borowsky Verlag, n.d.).
Neither man ever moved beyond the Midwest. Gottfried Duden
in *Bericht über eine Reise nach den westlichen Staaten
Nordamerikas* (Elberfeld: S. Lucas, 1829) does not treat New
Mexico, and Friedrich Gerstäcker in *Streif- und Jagdzüge durch die
Vereinigten Staaten* (Jena: H. Costenoble, 1854) never ventured
beyond Arkansas.

2. Gerald D. Nash, "European Images of America: The West in
Historical Perspective," *Montana: The Magazine of Western History*
42 (Spring 1992): 7.

3. See Juliane Mikoletzky, *Die deutsche Amerika-Auswanderung des
19. Jahrhunderts in der zeitgenössischen fiktionalen Literatur*
(Tübingen: Niemeyer, 1988). The author analyzes novels and stories published between 1835 and 1905 for factual information and
usefulness for emigrants.

4. Brent O. Peterson, "How (and Why) to Read German-American
Literature," in *The German American Encounter: Conflict and
Cooperation between Two Cultures, 1800–2000*, ed. Frank
Trommler and Elliott Shore (New York: Berghahn Books, 2001),
88. Carl Wittke, "The American Theme in Continental European
Literature," *Mississippi Valley Historical Review* 28 (June 1941): 3.

5. Ekkehard Koch, *Karl Mays Väter: Die Deutschen Im Wilden Westen*
(Husum: Hansa Verlag, 1982), 81.

6. Nash, "European Images," 8.

7. D. L. Ashliman, "The Image of Utah and the Mormons in
Nineteenth-Century Germany," *Utah Historical Quarterly* 35
(Summer 1967): 210. See also Karlheinz Rossbacher, *Lederstrumpf*

in Deutschland (München: Wilhelm Fink Verlag, 1972), 14, 41. For references to repressive systems and encroachment at the expense of individualism, see, for example, James Fenimore Cooper, *The Last of the Mohicans: A Narrative of 1757* (1826; reprint, New York: Signet Classic, 1962), 137. See also Cooper, *The Pioneers or The Sources of the Susquehanna: A Descriptive Tale* (1823; reprint, New York: Signet Classic, 1964), 153, 318.

8. Susanne Zantop, "Close Encounters: Deutsche and Indianer," in *Germans and Indians: Fantasies, Encounters, Projections,* ed. Colin G. Calloway, et al. (Lincoln: University of Nebraska Press, 2002), 11.

9. Julian Crandall Hollick, "The American West in the European Imagination," *Montana: The Magazine of Western History* 42 (Spring 1992): 17.

10. D. L. Ashliman, "The American Indian in German Travel Narratives and Literature," *Journal of Popular Culture* 10 (Spring 1977): 835. Hartmut Lutz, "German Indianthusiasm: A Socially Constructed German National(ist) Myth," in *Germans and Indians,* 168.

11. Friedrich Gerstäcker, *Georg, der Kleine Goldgräber in Kalifornien* (Berlin: Verlag von Neufeld und Henius, n.d.), 6.

12. Josiah Gregg, *Wanderungen durch die Prärien und das nördliche Mexiko* (Stuttgart: Verlag der Frankh'schen Buchhandlung, 1847).

13. Archibald Hanna, "Introduction," in Josiah Gregg, *Commerce of the Prairies* (1844; reprint, Philadelphia: J. B. Lippincott Company, 1962), 1:x.

14. Gregg, Commerce, 1:70, 75.

15. Robert Schlagintweit, *Die Santa Fe- und Südpacificbahn in Nordamerika* (Köln: Verlag von Eduard Heinrich Mayer, 1884), 233. Before coming to the United States to undertake scientific research, Schlagintweit with his two brothers went on extensive research trips to Asia and South America. His work was acknowledged by Alexander von Humboldt and Kaiser Wilhelm II, and he became a protégé of the renowned chemist Wilhelm Bunsen.

16. Armand W. Reeder, "Introduction," in F. A. Wislizenus, *A Journey to the Rocky Mountains in the Year 1839* (1912; reprint, Glorietta, NM: Rio Grande Press, 1969), n.p.

17. Wislizenus's first book was initially published in German in St. Louis, Missouri, as *Ein Ausflug nach den Felsen-Gebirgen im Jahre 1839* (St. Louis: Wilhelm Weber, 1840). In 1912 it was translated into English with the title *A Journey to the Rocky Mountains in 1839*. Wislizenus's second work, *Memoir of a Tour to Northern Mexico, Connected with Col. Doniphan's Expedition in 1846 and 1847*, was first published as a U.S. Senate document (30th Congress, 1st Session, Miscellaneous No. 26, Washington, DC: Tippin & Streeper, Printers, 1848). In 1850, the translated version, *Denkschrift über eine Reise nach Nord-Mexico, verbunden mit der Expedition des Oberst Doniphan, in den Jahren 1846 und 1847*, appeared in the F. Vieweg und Sohn Verlag in Braunschweig. Like other Germans who went to New Mexico and to Mexico in the period between 1846 and 1848, Wislizenus sent letters to the *Anzeiger des Westens*. Wislizenus's letters arrived in St. Louis during 1847 and dealt primarily with his experiences in El Paso and Mexico. See for example, *Anzeiger des Westens* 12 (June 1847): 26.

18. F. A. Wislizenus, *Memoir of a Tour to Northern Mexico, Connected with Colonel Doniphan's Expedition in 1846–1847* (1848; reprint, Albuquerque, NM: Calvin Horn Publisher, Inc., 1969), 24.

19. Wislizenus, *Memoir*, 26, 160.

20. Wislizenus, *Journey*, 160.

21. Robert Taft, "The Pictorial Record of the Old West: Heinrich Balduin Möllhausen," *Kansas Historical Quarterly* 32 (October 1948): 244.

22. Balduin Möllhausen, *Reisen in die Felsengebirge Nordamerikas* (1861; München: Verlag Lothat Borowsky, n.d.), 1:347.

23. Möllhausen, *Reisen*, 1:114, 2:170.

24. Möllhausen, *Reisen*, 2:155; Möllhausen, *Wanderungen durch die Prärien und Wüsten des westlichen Nordamerika vom Mississippi nach den Küsten der Südsee* (1858; reprint, München: Lothar Borowsky Verlag, n.d.), 260, 262.

25. Möllhausen, *Reisen*, 2:159; Möllhausen, *Wanderungen*, 169.

26. David H. Miller, "Balduin Möllhausen: A Prussian's Image of the American West" (Ph.D. diss., University of New Mexico, 1970), 120–21.

27. Möllhausen, *Reisen*, 1:351.

28. Möllhausen, *Reisen*, 1:354, 2:148–149, 2:153, 2:200, 2:212, 2:225.

29. Horst Dinkelacker, *Amerika zwischen Traum und Desillusionierung im Leben und Werk des Erfolgsschriftstellers Balduin Möllhausen, 1825–1905* (New York: Peter Lang, 1990), 168. For a list of Möllhausen's works, see Dinkelacker, *Amerika zwischen Traum und Desillusionierung*, 74–75, 181–86.

30. Humboldt, "Preface," in Möllhausen, *Wanderungen*, 5–12.

31. Armand [Friedrich Armand Strubberg], *Amerikanische Jagd- und Reiseabenteuer* (1858; reprint, München: Lothar Borowsky Verlag, n.d.), 230, 289, 299.

32. Augustin, "Afterword," in Möllhausen, *Wanderungen*, 531.

33. Karl May visited the eastern United States in 1908. A. T. Haeberle, American Consul General, to Henry L. Stimson, Secretary of State, 29 August 1930. Only Klara May, Karl May's second wife, visited the western parts of the United States in 1930. Klara May to Herbert C. Hoover, 2 August 1930, RG 59, State Department, Decimal File 811.4611, Germany, 25, 26, National Archives, Washington, D.C. An overview of Karl May's life and literary career in Germany is given in Hans Plischke, *Von Cooper bis Karl May: Eine Geschichte des Völkerkundlichen Reise- und Abenteuerromans* (Düsseldorf: Droste-Verlag, 1951), 103–24.

34. "Karl der Deutsche," *Der Spiegel*, 12 September 1962, 72; "Old Shatterhand am Elbestrand," *Zeitmagazin* (28 June 1991): 15. Karl May's popularity and Germans' affinity for Indians led the U.S. State Department as late as the 1960s to recommend to its staff to read May's novels "for a better understanding of the German psyche." Christian F. Feest, "Germany's Indians in a European Perspective," in *Germans and Indians*, 25–26.

35. Nash, "European Images," 12.

36. Karl May, *Winnetou I*, vol. 7 of Karl May's *Gesammelte Werke* (Bamberg: Karl-May Verlag, 1951), 5; Ernst Stadler, "Karl May: The Wild West under the German Umlaut," *Missouri Historical Society Bulletin* 21 (July 1965): 298.

37. Hollick, "The American West," 19.

38. Plischke, *Von Cooper bis Karl May*, 116.

39. For samples of May's descriptions of the Pecos River area, see *Winnetou III*, vol. 9, 78–79, *Die Juweleninsel*, vol. 46, 305–6; for the

Llano Estacado, see *Winnetou III*, 44–46; *Der Ölprinz*, vol. 37, 38–58; for pueblos, see *Der Ölprinz*, 118–20, *Satan und Ischariot*, vol. 32, 98–100, 113.

40. May, *Winnetou I*, 291–92. May is not precise in his terminology and uses both *cliff dwelling* and *pueblo* to describe Winnetou's home. Nevertheless, May was aware that Apaches were historically a nomadic tribe and has Winnetou explain to Old Shatterhand the circumstances of their being semisedentary.

41. May, *Winnetou I*, 288.

42. May, *Krüger Bei*, vol. 21, 147; May, *Der Ölprinz*, 253.

43. Richard H. Cracroft, "The American West of Karl May," *American Quarterly* 19 (Summer 1967): 257.

44. Ray Allen Billington, *Land of Savagery, Land of Promise: The European Image of the American Frontier* (New York: W. W. Norton and Company, 1981), 110.

45. Martin Kuester, "American Indians and German Indians: Perspectives of Doom in Cooper and May," *Western American Literature* 23 (Fall 1988): 220. The "I" narrator, though not to be overrated, certainly had an impact on readers' perceptions of historical accuracy in Karl May's books. Generations of readers like this writer experienced what Peter Handke called "First Reading Adventures." Reading *Schloss Rodriganda*, for instance, through a third-person narrator, is far less exciting than *Winnetou* or *Unter Geier* in "I" form because the latter often puts the reader into the narrator's place and makes him the hero. Peter Handke, "Erste Lese-Erlebnisse," in *Karl May*, ed. Helmut Schmiedt (Frankfurt A.M.: Suhrkamp Verlag, 1983), 35.

46. By July 1929 the Karl-May Verlag sold 5,348,000 authorized copies of Karl May's works in its German edition alone. The bestsellers among his novels were the three volumes of *Winnetou*, each with over 200,000 copies sold. RG 59, 811.4611 Germany, 29, National Archives.

47. Russell Saxton, "Ethnocentrism in the Historical Literature of Territorial New Mexico," Ph.D. diss. (University of New Mexico, 1980), 11.

48. Schlagintweit was admitted as außerordentlicher Professor of Geography to the Ludwigs-Universität in Giessen in 1864. Robert

Schlagintweit Personnel Folder, Phil K 20, University Archives, Ludwig Universität, Giessen, Germany. For biographical data on Schlagintweit, see *Allgemeine Deutsche Biographie* (Leipzig: Dunker und Humblot, 1890), vol. 31, 336–47. In addition to his work on the Santa Fe Railroad, he published monographs on the prairies, the Mormons, California, and the Union Pacific Railroad.

For a list of his speaking engagements in the United States (there were none in New Mexico), see "Robert von Schlagintweit's... Bericht über die 1000...gehaltenen öffentlichen populär-wissentschaftlichen Vorträge" (Leipzig: W. Drugulin, 1878), 53–129, Schlagintweitiana, Bayrische Staatsbibliothek München, Germany. Schlagintweit's public lectures received wide attention and favorable reviews in local newspapers. For example, see the *Cleveland Daily Leader*, 2 March 1869; the *Daily Nonpareil*, Council Bluffs, IA, 4 May 1869; *San Francisco Abend Post*, 7, 8, 23, 26, June 1869; *San Jose Herald*, 28 June 1869.

49. Carl Schurz to Robert von Schlagintweit, 17. April 1880, *Letterbook*, Bd. 31, Schlagintweitiana, Bayrische Staatsbibliothek; Schlagintweit, *Santa Fe und Südpacificbahn*, 247, 253–54.

50. Julius Fröbel, *Aus Amerika: Erfahrungen, Reisen und Studien* (Leipzig: Verlagsbuchhandlung von J. J. Weber, 1857), 2:108, 161. Fröbel's account is very anti-American, criticizing Anglo-American brutality, lack of magnanimity toward weaker Mexicans, rudeness toward women, and ignorance in butchering Indian and Mexican names (Fröbel, *Aus Amerika*, 2:141).

51. Schlagintweit, *Santa Fe und Südpacificbahn*, 218, 229, 245, 258.

52. Schlagintweit, *Santa Fe und Südpacificbahn*, 213, 294.

53. *California Mail Bag*, San Francisco, July 1871, 100.

54. Anne F. Hyde, "Cultural Filters: The Significance of Perception in the History of the American West," *Western Historical Quarterly* 24 (August 1993): 362.

55. Schlagintweit, Santa Fe und Südpacificbahn, 233, 235–36.

56. ibid., 258.

57. ibid., 268.

58. Saxton, "Ethnocentrism in the Historical Literature," 12.

59. Gregg, *Commerce*, 1:120.

60. Wislizenus, *Memoir*, 26.

61. Möllhausen, *Reisen*, 2:237.
62. Schlagintweit, *Santa Fe und Südpacificbahn*, 217.
63. Möllhausen, *Reisen*, 2:211; Wislizenus, *Tour*, 27.
64. David J. Weber, "'Scarce More than Apes': Historical Roots of Anglo American Stereotypes of Mexicans in the Border Region," in *New Spain's Far Northern Frontier: Essays on Spain in the American West, 1540–1821*, ed. David J. Weber (Albuquerque: University of New Mexico Press, 1979), 296.
65. May, *Winnetou I*, 175; May, *Satan und Ischariot*, 84.
66. May, *Die Felsenburg*, vol. 20, 74–75, 77; May, *Satan und Ischariot*, 100.
67. Wislizenus, *Memoir*, 26.
68. Möllhausen, *Reisen*, 2:160–61. Möllhausen used the derogatory word *Pfaffen*, meaning priest or pastor, over the more neutral words *Priester* or *Pfarrer*.
69. Phillip Wayne Powell, cited in Weber, "Historical Roots of Stereotypes," 300.
70. Burl Noggle, "Anglo Observers of the Southwest Borderland, 1825–1890," *Arizona and the West* 1 (Summer 1959): 121.
71. Charles F. Lummis, "The White Indian," *Land of Sunshine* 13 (June 1900): 8–15.
72. Daniela Moneta, "A Tramp across the Continent," *Chas. F. Lummis: The Centennial Exhibition, Commemorating His Tramp across the Continent*, ed. Daniela Moneta (Los Angeles: Southwest Museum, 1985), 17–20.
73. Ramón A. Gutiérrez, "Charles Fletcher Lummis," in *Nuevomexicano—Cultural Legacy: Forms, Agencies, and Discourse*, ed. Francisco A. Lomelí, et al. (Albuquerque: University of New Mexico Press, 2002), 12.
74. Bernard L. Fontana, "A Dedication to the Memory of Adolph Bandelier, 1840–1914," *Arizona and the West* 2 (Spring 1960): 3.
75. *The Delight Makers* was initially written in English, and after no American publisher could be found to print it, Bandelier turned to Germany to find a publisher. Julia Keleher and Elsie Ruth Chant claim that Bandelier published *Die Köshare*, as the novel was titled in German, in Freiburg. Julia Keleher and Elsie Ruth Chant, *The Padre of Isleta* (Santa Fe, NM: Rydal Press, 1940), 35. But this is doubtful. Bandelier sent the manuscript to Friedrich

Ratzel's magazine *Das Ausland,* which published earlier essays by Bandelier, but it appears that the novel was not published by Ratzel. The *Belletristisches Journal* in New York purchased the novel and ran it serially from 1 January to 14 May 1890. Charles H. Lange and Carroll L. Riley, eds., *The Southwestern Journals of Adolph F. Bandelier, 1883–1884* (Albuquerque: University of New Mexico Press, 1970), 402; see also Charles H. Lange, Carroll L. Riley, and Elizabeth M. Lange, eds., *The Southwestern Journals of Adolph F. Bandelier, 1889–1892* (Albuquerque: University of New Mexico Press, 1984), 447 n. 545.

76. Lange, *Southwestern Journals, 1889–1892,* 45–46. For Bandelier's concept of Native Americans and the descendants of the Spanish crown, see ibid., 262, n. 95.

77. *Highland Union,* 1, 8 October 1880.

78. ibid., 8 October 1880.

79. ibid., 18 May 1883.

80. ibid., 5 November 1880; Bandelier reconfirmed these beliefs in a lecture he gave before a German gathering in the Turnhalle in Highland two months later. *Highland Union,* 7 January 1881.

81. Bandelier made these observations during a lecture before the New Mexico Historical Society in Santa Fe, which was reprinted in the *Highland Union* (2 June 1882).

82. *Anzeiger des Westens,* 26 September 1883.

83. Nash, "European Images," 11. In 1908, Zane Grey's novel *The Last of the Plainsmen* (*Der Letzte Präriejäger,* München: Awa, 1908) was his first novel in translation on the German market. Zane Grey's novels began to appear more frequently in Germany in the 1930s.

84. Christoph Hering, "Otto Ruppius, der Amerikafahrer, Flüchtling, Exilschriftsteller, Rückwanderer," in Sigrid Bauschinger et al., *Amerika in der deutschen Literatur* (Stuttgart: Philipp Reclam Jun., 1975), 124.

None of the German writers (none of whom spoke Spanish) cared to include in their works Native American and Hispanic perceptions of the Southwest and New Mexico. What Chicano novelist Rudolfo Anaya criticized at the American Writers' Congress in 1981 was certainly true in the nineteenth century: New Mexico's native populations experienced "the censureship of being completely ignored." Cited in Alexander Ritter, "German-American Literature: Critical Comments on the Current State of Ethnic Writing in German and Its Philological Description," in *America and the Germans: An Assessment of a Three-Hundred-Year History*, ed. Frank Trommler and Joseph Veigh (Pittsburgh: University of Pennsylvania, 1985), 1:344.

85. Hector Lee, "Tales and Legends in Western American Literature," *Western American Literature* 9 (Winter 1975): 247.

CHAPTER TWO

1. Stephan Thernstrom, *Poverty and Progress: Social Mobility in a Nineteenth Century City* (Cambridge, MA: Harvard University Press, 1964), 4.

2. Margo J. Anderson, *The American Census: A Social History* (New Haven, CT: Yale University Press, 1988), 85. Anderson's book is an in-depth work of the history of why and how the census has been taken and what its significance has been in American history.

3. *Population Schedules of the Seventh Census of the United States, 1850: New Mexico; Population Schedules of the Eighth Census of the United States, 1860: New Mexico; Population Schedules of the Ninth Census of the United States, 1870: New Mexico; Population Schedules of the Tenth Census of the United States, 1880: New Mexico; Population Schedules of the Twelfth Census of the United States, 1900: New Mexico; Population Schedules of the Thirteenth Census of the United States, 1910: New Mexico*, New Mexico Territorial Records, microfilm; *Population Schedules of the Fourteenth Census of the United States, 1920: New Mexico*, New Mexico State Records, microfilm, Center for Southwest Research, University of New Mexico (hereafter the Center is cited as CSWR). The Census of 1890 was burned in Washington, D.C. Statistics on German demography in this chapter, unless noted otherwise, are my computations.

4. Anderson, *The American Census*, 19.

5. Sophisticated examinations such as clustering and scale analysis are very time consuming with uncertain improvement of the results. In an essay on quantitative analysis, Allan Bogue details its historical development. Although Bogue is a firm believer in the benefits of quantitative analysis, he admits that it has limitations.

Allan G. Bogue, "The Quest for Numeracy: Data and Methods in American Political History," *Journal of Interdisciplinary History* 21 (Summer 1990): 89–116, esp. 115–16.

6. Frederick C. Luebke discusses the difficulty of defining Germans in several of his books and essays. See, for example, his *Immigrants and Politics: The Germans of Nebraska, 1880–1900* (Lincoln: University of Nebraska Press, 1969), 8–11; and Luebke, *Germans in the New World: Essays in the History of Immigration* (Urbana: University of Illinois Press, 1990), xiii–xiv. See also Christof Mauch and Joseph Salmons, eds., *German-Jewish Identities in America* (Madison, WI: Max Kade Institute for German-American Studies, 2003), 2.

7. Luebke, *Immigrants and Politics*, 10.

8. *Seventh Census of the United States: 1850* (Washington, DC: Robert Armstrong, Public Printer, 1853), 996; Richard R. Greer, "Origins of the Foreign-Born Population of New Mexico during the Territorial Period," *New Mexico Historical Review* (hereafter *NMHR*) 17 (October 1942): 282.

9. *Population of the United States in 1860; compiled from the Original Returns of the Eighth Census* (Washington, DC: Government Printing Office, 1864), 566–67, 572–73. The censuses of 1850 and 1860 include the negligible share of Arizona, which became a separate territory in 1864.

10. *Ninth Census of the United States, 1870* (Washington, DC: Government Printing Office, 1872), 336–42.

11. *Tenth Census of the United States, 1880* (Washington, DC: Government Printing Office, 1883), 492–95.

12. The U.S. Bureau of Census statistics show a steady decrease in German immigrants to the United States after 1890. From 1890, when 1,445,181 Germans migrated to the United States, the numbers dramatically declined by more than 10 percent each decade, until 1920, when only 174,227 Germans entered this country. For detailed statistical information, see N. Carpenter, "Immigrants and Their Children," *U.S. Bureau of the Census Monograph*, No. 7 (Washington, DC: Government Printing Office, 1927), 324–25.

13. The statistical information for the second decade of the twentieth century is from the *Fourteenth Census of the United States Taken*

in the Year 1920, Population (Washington, DC: Government Printing Office, 1922), 2:697–701.

14. David M. Emmons, *The Butte Irish: Class and Ethnicity in an American Mining Town, 1875–1925* (Urbana: University of Illinois Press, 1989), 63. Dino Cinel, *From Italy to San Francisco: The Immigrant Experience* (Stanford, CA: Stanford University Press, 1982), 106.

15. Wilbur Zelinsky, *The Cultural Geography of the United States* (Englewood Cliffs, NJ: Prentice-Hall, Inc., 1973), 22.

16. Chris Wilson, *The Myth of Santa Fe: Creating a Modern Regional Tradition* (Albuquerque: University of New Mexico Press, 1997), 52, 74.

17. Nancy S. Landale and Avery M. Guest, "Generation, Ethnicity, and Occupational Opportunity in Late 19th Century America," *American Sociological Review* 55 (April 1990): 282.

18. Walter Nugent, "The People of the West since 1890," in *The Twentieth-Century West: Historical Interpretations,* ed. Gerald D. Nash and Richard W. Etulain (Albuquerque: University of New Mexico Press, 1989), 46.

19. Nebraska's Siman Act in 1919, for instance, required school instruction in English only but was declared unconstitutional in 1923. See Luebke, *Germans in the New World,* 43–46. Jonathan Zimmerman, "Ethnics against Ethnicity: European Immigrants and Foreign-Language Instructions, 1890–1940," in *The Journal of American History* 88 (March 2002): 1384.

20. See Pearce S. Grove, et al., *New Mexico Newspapers: A Comprehensive Guide to Bibliographical Entries and Locations* (Albuquerque: University of New Mexico Press, 1975). Under the title *Der Sendbote des Göttlichen Herzens Jesu,* Anselm Weber wrote a series of monthly religious accounts in Arizona between 1899 and 1921, but there is no indication that they had any impact on German culture in New Mexico. See Robert L. Wilken, *Anselm Weber, O.F.M.: Missionary to the Navaho, 1898–1921* (Milwaukee, WI: Bruce Publishing Company, 1955), 241.

21. Darlis A. Miller, "Cross-Cultural Marriages in the Southwest: The New Mexico Experience, 1846–1900," *NMHR* 57 (October 1982): 335, 339.

22. Nugent, "The People of the West," 42.

23. F. A. Ehmann, "The Effect of the Railroad on New Mexico," *Password* 8 (Summer 1963): 56.

24. For in-depth explanations and justifications for my occupational model, see the appendix.

25. Elliott West, *Growing Up with the Country: Childhood on the Far Western Frontier* (Albuquerque: University of New Mexico Press, 1989), 184.

26. For the Italian Jesuits' early role in New Mexico, see Frederick G. Bohme, *A History of the Italians in New Mexico* (New York: Arno Press, 1975), 24–65.

27. Wilson, *The Myth of Santa Fe*, 67.

28. Sidney Pollard, *The Genesis of Modern Management* (Baltimore, MD: Penguin Books, 1968), 190.

29. Rodman Wilson Paul, *Mining Frontiers of the Far West, 1848–1880* (Albuquerque: University of New Mexico Press, 1974), 156–59.

30. Norbert Finsch, *Die Goldgräber Kaliforniens: Arbeitsbedingungen, Lebenstandard und politisches System um die Mitte des 19. Jahrhunderts* (Göttingen: Vandenhoeck & Ruprecht, 1982), 135. Disposing of the myth of free labor is not unique to leftist historians; see Earl Pomeroy, *The Pacific Slope: A History of California, Oregon, Washington, Idaho, Utah, and Nevada* (New York: Alfred A. Knopf, 1965), 5.

31. Priscilla Long, *Where the Sun Never Shines: A History of America's Bloody Coal Industry* (New York: Paragon House, 1989), 177.

32. Robert Kern, ed., *Labor in New Mexico: Unions, Strikes, and Social History since 1881* (Albuquerque: University of New Mexico Press, 1983), 4.

33. William J. Parish, *The Charles Ilfeld Company: A Study of the Rise and Decline of Mercantile Capitalism in New Mexico* (Cambridge, MA: Harvard University Press), 1961.

34. William F. Deverell, "To Loosen the Safety Valve: Eastern Workers and Western Lands," *Western Historical Quarterly* 19 (August 1988): 271.

35. Ehmann, "The Effect of the Railroad," 56, 62.

36. Timothy J. Kloberdanz, "Plainsmen of Three Continents: Volga German Adaptation to *Steppe*, Prairie and Pampa," in *Ethnicity*

on the Great Plains, ed. Frederick C. Luebke (Lincoln: University of Nebraska Press, 1980), 54–72.

37. Bureau of Immigration, *Resources of New Mexico: Prepared under the Auspices of the Territorial Bureau of Immigration* (1881; reprint, Santa Fe, NM: William Gannon, 1973), 8.

38. Victor Westphall, *The Public Domain in New Mexico, 1854–1891* (Albuquerque: University of New Mexico Press, 1965), 51. For general statistics on homesteading in the territory through 1896, see Westphall's appendices.

39. Donald Pisani, *From Family Farm to Agribusiness: The Irrigation Crusade in California and the West, 1850–1931* (Berkeley: University of California Press, 1984), 283.

40. Brian Q. Cannon, "Immigrants in American Agriculture," *Agricultural History* 65 (Winter 1991): 23.

41. One example was the Gross, Blackwell & Company in which Jacob Gross and Miguel A. Otero representing the "Company" went into mercantile and banking partnerships in Las Vegas, New Mexico. Parish, *Charles Ilfeld Company*, 49, 379.

42. One of the earliest German entrepreneurs in New Mexico was Charles Blumner, active in Santa Fe since 1836. Thomas Jaehn, "Charles Blumner: Pioneer, Civil Servant, and Merchant," *NMHR* 61 (October 1986): 319–27.

43. Parish, *Charles Ilfeld Company*, 46.

44. Larry Schweikart, "Early Banking in New Mexico from the Civil War to the Roaring Twenties," *NMHR* 63 (January 1988): 5–6.

45. Robert Kern, ed., *Building New Mexico: The Experience of a Carpenter Union in the Southwest* (Albuquerque: New Mexico Humanities Council and the District Council of the United Brotherhood of Carpenters, 1983), 25.

46. I have taken samples of Germans' census data from Mora, Doña Ana, and Santa Fe Counties and checked against county assessment records where available. While the assessed values in the county records and the value listed in the census records never matched, the assessed values roughly followed the data from the census records and the overall impression of individuals' wealth to establish patterns.

47. The Hanover mines earned a reputation a century later, when the town and the mine experienced the most controversial strike in New Mexico's history, resulting in the famous film *Salt of the Earth*. For more details about the strike that lasted from October 1950 until January 1952, see James J. Lorence, *The Suppression of Salt of the Earth: How Hollywood, Big Labor and Politicians Blacklisted a Movie in Cold War America* (Albuquerque: University of New Mexico Press, 1999).

48. Dee Brown, *The Gentle Tamers: Women of the Old Wild West* (1958; reprint, Lincoln: University of Nebraska Press, 1981), 17. For a history of changing views of women's roles in the West, based on Brown's *Gentle Tamers*, see Joan M. Jensen and Darlis A. Miller, "The Gentle Tamers Revisited: New Approaches to the History of Women in the American West," *Pacific Historical Review* 2 (May 1980): 173–213.

49. Kate H. Parker, "'I Brought with Me Many Eastern Ways': Euro-American Income-Earning Women in New Mexico, 1850–1880" (Ph.D. diss., University of New Mexico, 1984), 13.

50. Sarah Deutsch, *No Separate Refuge: Culture, Class, and Gender on an Anglo-Hispanic Frontier in the American Southwest, 1880–1940* (New York: Oxford University Press, 1987), 15. This experience is certainly not exclusively southwestern; for the ordeal of the Malic family in the Pacific Northwest, see Lillian Schlissel, "Family on the Western Frontier," in *Western Women: Their Land, Their Lives*, ed. Lillian Schlissel et al. (Albuquerque: University of New Mexico Press, 1988), 83–84.

51. Parker, "'I Brought with Me Many Eastern Ways,'" 39.

52. Julie Roy Jeffrey, *Frontier Women: The Trans-Mississippi West, 1840–1880* (New York: Hill and Wang, 1979), 90–91. Pay for teachers was low. In 1880, for example, New Mexico's teachers earned the lowest wages in the West, $30.67 per month, whereas Arizona's teachers were paid $76.58 per month; see West, *Growing Up with the Country*, 192–94.

53. Robert L. Griswold, "Anglo Women and Domestic Ideology in the American West in the Nineteenth and Early Twentieth Centuries," in *Western Women*, ed. Schlissel et al., 18.

54. Sandra L. Myres, *Westering Women and the Frontier Experience 1800–1915* (Albuquerque: University of New Mexico Press, 1982), 214.

55. Deutsch, *No Separate Refuge*, 115.

56. For a discussion of Catherine Fritz's activities, see Chapter Four; *Red River Chronicle*, San Lorenzo, 31 May 1882; David Remley, *Bell Ranch: Cattle Ranching in the Southwest, 1824–1947* (Albuquerque: University of New Mexico Press, 1993), 87; Tomas Jaehn, "Institutional History," Inventory File, White House Papers, MS 444, CSWR.

57. Agnes Morley Cleaveland, *No Life for a Lady* (Boston: Houghton Mifflin Company, 1941), 21.

58. Griswold, "Anglo Women and Domestic Ideology," 4.

59. Thernstrom, *Poverty and Progress*, 3.

60. Landale and Guest, "Generation, Ethnicity, and Occupational Opportunity," 293.

CHAPTER THREE

1. Joseph S. Rouck and Bernhard Eisenberg, eds., *America's Ethnic Politics* (Westport, CT.: Greenwood Press, 1982), 7; Nathaniel Weyl, *The Jew in American Politics* (New Rochelle, NY: Arlington, 1968), 63; James M. Bergquist, "The Forty-Eighters: Catalysts of German-American Politics," in *The German-American Encounter*, 33.

2. Dale Baum and Worth Robert Miller, "Ethnic Conflict and Machine Politics in San Antonio, 1892–1899," *Journal of Urban History* 19 (August 1993): 63, 78.

3. Paul Kleppner, "Voters and Parties in the Western States, 1876–1900," *Western Historical Quarterly* 14 (January 1983): 53.

4. Luebke, *Immigrants and Politics*, 6; *Germans in the New World*, 85. In *Ethnic Voters*, edited by Luebke, Charles Wilson Emery, Joseph Schafer, Andreas Dorpalen, Hildegard Binder Johnson, Paul J. Kleppner, and others, came to the same conclusions in studies of Abraham Lincoln's election in 1860.

5. Stanley B. Parsons, *The Populist Context: Rural Versus Urban Power on a Great Plains Frontier* (Westport, CT.: Greenwood Press, 1973), 101–19.

6. Henry J. Tobias, *A History of the Jews in New Mexico* (Albuquerque: University of New Mexico Press, 1990), 44, 88. Of course, the Jewish tendency to integrate into the culture and politics of the host society was not unique to New Mexico, where Jews were among the

first German arrivals prior to and during the territorial period. As Carey McWilliams pointed out in a pioneering essay on social discrimination, "where Jews were present on the scene before the community started to grow—before the status lines were sharply drawn—they were often taken into membership with a naive unawareness of their Jewishness or a marked indifference to the fact." Carey McWilliams, "Does Social Discrimination Really Matter?" in *Sociological Analysis*, ed. Logan Wilson and William L. Kolb (New York: Harcourt, Brace and Co., 1949), 503.

7. Roger Daniels, *Coming to America: A History of Immigration and Ethnicity in American Life* (New York: HarperCollins Publishers, 1990), 156; Tobias, *A History of the Jews*, 28.

8. Walter D. Kamphoefner, "German and Irish Big City Mayors: Comparative Perspective on Ethnic Politics." Paper read at the symposium "New Approaches to Migration Research: Americans in Comparative Perspectives," Texas A&M University, 22–24 April 1997, 2.

9. Daniels, *Coming to America*, 148. Born and educated in Germany, Carl Schurz was elected a senator from Missouri in 1868, and in 1877 President Rutherford B. Hayes appointed him secretary of state; Peter Altgeld, who arrived in this country as an infant, rose to governor of Illinois and received national attention in the aftermath of the Haymarket Square riots of 1886 in Chicago; Moses Alexander of Idaho, a native of Bavaria, was the first Jewish governor (1915 – 1919) in the United States.

10. For example, see Alice Kessler-Harris and Virginia Yans-McLaughlin, "European Immigrant Groups," in *Essays and Data on American Ethnic Groups*, ed. Thomas Sowell (Washington, DC: Urban Institute, 1978), 123.

11. Luebke, *Immigrants and Politics*, vii.

12. Thomas Mann, *Betrachtungen eines Unpolitischen* (Berlin: S. Fischer Verlag, 1918), xxxiii.

13. Fritz Stern, "The Political Consequences of the Unpolitical German" (1960), in *The Failure of Illiberalism: Essays on the Political Culture of Modern Germany* (New York: Alfred A. Knopf, 1972), 6.

14. Jürgen Habermas, "Vorwort," in Victor Faría, *Heidegger und der Nationalsozialismus* (Frankfurt a.M.: S. Fischer, 1989), 16–17.

15. Mann, *Betrachtungen*, 238.
16. Theodore Schieder, *Vom Deutschen Bund zum Deutschen Reich, 1815–1871* (Stuttgart: Klett Verlag, 1970), 75.
17. Stern, "Political Consequences," 10.
18. Franz Huning, *Trader on the Santa Fe Trail: The Memoirs of Franz Huning* (Albuquerque, NM: University of Albuquerque, 1973), 2–3.
19. Johann Friedrich Huning [father] to Franz Huning, 12. Dezember 1846, Erna Fergusson Papers, MSS 45, Box 3, Folder 12, Center for Southwest Research, General Library, University of New Mexico (hereafter the Center is cited as CSWR).
20. Johann Friedrich Huning to Franz Huning, n.d., Fergusson Papers, Box 3, Folder 12.
21. Letters from Hugo Düllens, who occasionally helped out Franz financially, indicate this attitude. Fergusson Papers, Box 3, Folder 12.
22. Testament, Huning-Fergusson Papers, MSS 194, Box 2, Folder 20, CSWR.
23. Stern, "Political Consequences," 6.
24. Mann, *Betrachtungen*, xxxvi, xxxx.
25. Booklists are dated 1882, 1883–1884, and "Germany." The theater and concert list is from 1880–1881, Huning-Fergusson Papers, Box 2, Folder 17. The list reveals that Huning had also read books by Balduin Möllhausen, one of the foremost German writers on the Southwest.
26. Royce Jane Balch, "Jacob Korber, Early Businessman of Albuquerque, New Mexico 1881–1921" (M.B.A. thesis, University of New Mexico, 1955), 6–7.
27. Balch, "Jacob Korber," 27–29.
28. Tobias Brinkmann, "We Are Brothers! Let Us Separate," in Mauch and Salmons, *German-Jewish Identities*, 47. W. G. Ritch, comp., *The Legislative Blue-Book of the Territory of New Mexico* (Santa Fe, NM: Charles W. Greene, Public Printers, 1882), appendix, 39, 45. Also see Henry Tobias and Charles E. Woodhouse, "New York Investment Bankers and New Mexico Merchants: Group Formation and Elite Status among German Jewish Businessmen," *NMHR* 65 (January 1990): 38–39.

29. *Albuquerque Morning Democrat*, 8 March 1892. Translation: "This
year is a leap year/[for which] I bet a thousand *thaler* cash/where
women are actually allowed to vote/even if they are otherwise
generally considered zeros." The entire quatrain was written in
inadequate German (beyond a typesetter's faults), indicating that
by the 1890s some German-speaking men and women were losing
their German.

30. Michael L. Lawson, "Flora Langerman Spiegelberg: Grand Lady
of Santa Fe" (Southern California Jewish Historical Society, 1975,
typescript), 6.

31. Lawson, "Flora Langerman Spiegelberg," 17.

32. In the 1890s a small Swiss colony obtained 4,000 acres of land
near Vaud in the Pecos Valley. The colony may have had plans for
a town, but was not successful. *Albuquerque Morning Democrat*, 17
February 1892.

33. Terry G. Jordan, *German Seed in Texas Soil: Immigrant Farmers in
Nineteenth-Century Texas* (Austin: University of Texas Press,
1966), 43.

34. See David M. Emmons, *The Butte Irish: Class and Ethnicity in an
American Mining Town, 1875–1925* (Urbana: University of Illinois
Press, 1990), 63.

35. F. Chris Garcia and Paul L. Hain, eds., *New Mexico Government*
(Albuquerque: University of New Mexico Press, 1976), 7.

36. Ernest B. Fincher, "Spanish-Americans as a Political Factor in
New Mexico, 1912–1950" (Ph.D. diss., New York University, 1950),
131. The study is Thomas D. Hall, *Social Change in the Southwest,
1350–1880* (Lawrence: University of Kansas Press, 1989), 159. His
findings that eastern newcomers changed the economic and political situation in New Mexico, although correct, are not new. At
the turn of the century writer Mary Austin had complained about
capitalism altering the New Mexico setting. These charges do not,
however, prove that the patron system did not exist prior to the
American arrival.

37. Luebke, *Immigrants and Politics*, 34.

38. The role of immigrant societies in a comparative study of Irish
and Germans is described in Reinhard R. Doerries, *Iren und
Deutsche in der Neuen Welt: Akkulturationsprozesse in der*

Amerikanischen Gesellschaft im Späten Neunzehnten Jahrhundert (Stuttgart: Rudolf Steiner Verlag, 1986), 153–55. Also see Kathleen Conzen, *Immigrant Milwaukee, 1836–1860: Accommodation and Community in a Frontier City* (Cambridge, MA: Harvard University Press, 1976), 154–91.

39. Kleppner, "Voters and Parties," 53, 55.

40. Raymond E. Wolfinger, "The Development and Persistence of Ethnic Voting," *American Political Science Review* 59 (December 1965): 896.

41. Findings of two sociologists suggest that immigrants generally needed some time to become accustomed to the American political system before they participated in the political process. See Peter Tuckel and Richard Maisel, "Voter Turnout among European Immigrants to the United States," *Journal of Interdisciplinary History* 24 (Winter 1994): 407–30.

42. Howard R. Lamar, "Political Patterns in New Mexico and Utah Territories 1850–1900," *Utah Historical Quarterly* 28 (October 1960): 364.

43. Jack E. Holmes, *Politics in New Mexico* (Albuquerque: University of New Mexico Press, 1967), i.

44. Lamar, "Political Patterns," 367.

45. Terry J. Lehmann, "Santa Fe and Albuquerque 1870–1900: Contrast and Conflict in the Development of Two Southwestern Towns" (Ph.D. diss., Indiana University, 1974), 33.

46. Lehmann, "Santa Fe and Albuquerque," 31.

47. Charles Blumner's life in New Mexico is revealed in his letters to his relatives in Germany. Charles Blumner Letters (AC 231), Angélico Chávez History Library, Palace of the Governors, Santa Fe, NM.

48. Thomas E. Chávez, *Manuel Alvarez 1794–1856: A Southwestern Biography* (Niwot: University Press of Colorado, 1990), 60.

49. Through the decades, Blumner also served as marshal, sheriff, and tax collector.

50. Huning, *Trader on the Santa Fe Trail*, 10.

51. *Santa Fe Weekly Gazette*, 25 June 1853. Initially, Clever owned the *Santa Fe New Mexican* but sold it in 1863; later he acquired the *Santa Fe Gazette* to promulgate his ideas of capitalism, statehood, and Americanization.

52. *Santa Fe Gazette*, 2 February 1867; *Santa Fe New Mexican*, 26 May 1868.

53. Charles P. Clever, *New Mexico: Her Resources, Her Necessities for Railroad Communication with the Atlantic and Pacific States; Her Great Future* (Washington, DC: McGill and Witherow, Printers, 1868), 36, 40.

54. Richard White, "Race Relations in the American West," *American Quarterly* 38 (Bibliography 1986): 397.

55. Robert W. Larson, *New Mexico's Quest for Statehood, 1846–1912* (Albuquerque: University of New Mexico Press, 1968), 92.

56. The literature on political corruption is enormous. For instance, see Lincoln Steffens, *The Shame of the Cities* (New York: Hill and Wang, 1957), chapters 2 and 4, on the city government in predominantly German St. Louis.

57. Tobias, *A History of the Jews*, 46–47.

58. Floyd S. Fierman, "The Triangle and the Tetragrammaton: A Note on the Cathedral at Santa Fe," *NMHR* 37 (October 1962): 312–13; Jacqueline D. Meketa, *Louis Felsenthal: Citizen-Soldier of Territorial New Mexico* (Albuquerque: University of New Mexico Press, 1982), 81.

59. Lillie Gerhardt Anderson, "A New Mexico Pioneer of the 1880's," *NMHR* 29 (October 1954): 252.

60. Holmes, *Politics in New Mexico*, 266; see also Richard Lowitt, *Bronson M. Cutting: Progressive Politician* (Albuquerque: University of New Mexico Press, 1992), 281.

61. Henry J. Tobias and Charles E. Woodhouse, *Santa Fe: A Modern History, 1880–1990* (Albuquerque: University of New Mexico Press, 2001), 37.

62. Ritch, *Legislative Blue-Book*, 60–62.

63. Paul A. F. Walter, "Necrology: Arthur Seligman," *NMHR* 8 (October 1933): 306.

64. House Journal, 24th Legislative Assembly, 1880, Territorial Archives of New Mexico (hereafter TANM), 5:689.

65. Council Journal, 28th Legislative Assembly 1888–1889, TANM, 7:10, 7:633–34; *Report of the Secretary of the Territory, 1903–1904, and Legislative Manual, 1905* (Santa Fe, NM: The New Mexican Printing Company, 1905), 162.

66. Bureau of Immigration, *Resources of New Mexico: Prepared under the Auspices of the Territorial Bureau of Immigration* (1881; reprint, Santa Fe, NM: William Gannon, 1973), [53]. Marion Dargan, "New Mexico's Fight for Statehood, 1895–1912," *NMHR* 18 (January 1943): 71.

67. Ritch, *Legislative Blue-Book*, 126; Tobias, *A History of the Jews*, 118.

68. For example, see the Bureau of Immigration's publications *Report of San Miguel County* (Santa Fe: New Mexican Print, 1882); *Report as to Socorro County* (Socorro, NM: Socorro Daily News Office, 1881); *New Mexico*, Winter edition (Las Vegas, NM: J. A. Carruth, Printer, 1889), and *Resources of New Mexico*.

69. Louis Prager Sr., "My Memories of Roswell, 1903–1978" (Roswell, 1978) [interview] (soundcassette). The interview and additional information about the Pragers, second-generation Germans from Pennsylvania, was furnished by Louis Prager Jr. in an interview with the author, Roswell, 29 September 1990.

70. Prager Sr., "My Memories of Roswell"; Tobias, *A History of the Jews*, 126–27.

71. None of the available sources indicates any major German involvement in the Lincoln County dispute. See Howard R. Lamar, *The Far Southwest, 1846–1912: A Territorial History* (New Haven, CT: Yale University Press, 1966), 155–62; Robert M. Utley, *High Noon in Lincoln: Violence on the Western Frontier* (Albuquerque: University of New Mexico Press, 1987).

72. A. A. McSween to J. F. Tunstall, 23 February 1878, Folder "John H. Tunstall, Correspondence 1876–78," Robert N. Mullin Collection, Nita Stewart Haley Memorial Library, Midland, Texas.

73. Joel K. Jacobsen, "An Excess of Law in Lincoln County: Thomas Catron, Samuel Axtell, and the Lincoln County War," *NMHR* 68 (April 1993): 151.

74. Lee Scott Theisen, ed., "Frank Warner Angel's Notes on New Mexico Territory, 1878," *Arizona and the West* 18 (Winter 1976): 355, 361, 365, 366, 368.

75. Robert A. Widenmann to Carl Schurz, 11 March 1878, Folder "John H. Tunstall, Correspondence 1876–78," Mullin Collection. Widenmann certainly was biased in his accounts but understood the larger scope of the events. At a later date, Widenmann

thought about reopening matters but Carl Schurz, with whom
he had extensive discussions, advised him not to do so. Robert A.
Widenmann to Mrs. [R. H.] Kempf, 3 February 1927, Folder
"John H. Tunstall, Correspondence, [n.d.]," Mullin Collection.

76. Howard R. Lamar, "The Santa Fe Ring," in *New Mexico, Past and
Present: A Historical Reader*, ed. Richard N. Ellis (Albuquerque:
University of New Mexico Press, 1971), 156. Also see Lamar, *The
Far Southwest*, 147; Holmes, *Politics in New Mexico*, 49; Robert W.
Larson, *New Mexico Populism: A Study of Radical Protest in a
Western Territory* (Boulder: Colorado Association University
Press, 1974), 30.

77. Tobias, *A History of the Jews*, 84; Lehmann, "Santa Fe and
Albuquerque," 45.

78. Robert J. Rosenbaum, *Mexicano Resistance in the Southwest: "The
Sacred Right of Self-Preservation"* (Austin: University of Texas
Press, 1981), 99–101. A list of the attacks of *Las Gorras Blancas* is in
Appendix E (167–8), while Appendix G lists some of the *politicos*
of Las Vegas (179).

79. *Albuquerque Morning Journal*, 12 February 1892.

80. *Albuquerque Republican Review*, 1 November 1875.

81. Huning, *Trader on the Santa Fe Trail*, 125.

82. *Albuquerque Democrat*, 26 October 1882, cited in Lehmann, "Santa
Fe and Albuquerque," 160, 163; Larson, *New Mexico Populism*, 167.

83. Lehmann, "Santa Fe and Albuquerque," 176.

84. Balch, "Jacob Korber," 28–29.

85. Lehmann, "Santa Fe and Albuquerque," 149.

86. Huning, *Trader on the Santa Fe Trail*, 122; Lehmann, "Santa Fe and
Albuquerque," 181.

87. Dorothy E. Thomas, "The Final Years of New Mexico's Struggle
for Statehood, 1907–1912 (M.A. thesis, University of New Mexico,
1939), 37; Larson, *New Mexico's Quest for Statehood*, 119, 124–25.

88. Lehmann, "Santa Fe and Albuquerque," 160.

89. Frank D. Reeve, *History of New Mexico* (New York: Lewis
Historical Publishing Company, 1961), 2:325.

90. *Albuquerque Morning Journal*, 24 February 1892.

91. *Senate Miscellaneous Documents*, Fiftieth Congress, Second
Session, Vol. 2, Doc. No. 52.

92. Archie Mitchell McDowell, "The Opposition to Statehood within the Albuquerque Territory of New Mexico" (M.A. thesis, University of New Mexico, 1940), 28.

93. *Santa Fe New Mexican*, 15 March 1870.

94. Note, Huning-Fergusson Papers, Box 2, Folder 17. The German note must have been written after 1883, since he mentions the death of his daughter Elli (1881) and the completion of the "Huning Castle" (1883).

95. Larson, *New Mexico's Quest for Statehood*, 195–98.

96. Frederick Muller's role and influence in Santa Fe politics has yet to be determined. Muller set up residence in Santa Fe sometime in the second half of the nineteenth century and served in the Indian Wars and in Teddy Roosevelt's Rough Riders. Muller did not hold any office, but his name appears often in Santa Fe newspapers in conjunction with powerful politicians. He received special attention in a dispute over the New Mexico Rough Riders flag, when he claimed that the flag was given to him, but others argued that it was the property of the people of New Mexico.

97. McDowell, "The Opposition to Statehood," 47–48.

98. Reeve, *History of New Mexico*, 2:326; McDowell, "The Opposition to Statehood," 68.

99. Holmes, *Politics in New Mexico*, 151; Larry Schweikart, "Early Banking in New Mexico from the Civil War to the Roaring Twenties," *NMHR* 63 (January 1988): 5.

100. Beatrice Chauvenet, "Paul A. F. Walter: A Man Who Lived and Wrote Santa Fe History," *El Palacio* 88 (Spring 1982): 31; Larson, *New Mexico's Quest for Statehood*, 213–14.

101. Lowitt, *Bronson M. Cutting*, 47.

102. Dorothy I. Cline, "Constitutional Politics in New Mexico: 1910–1976," in *New Mexico Government*, ed. Garcia and Hain, 221.

103. *Proceedings of the Constitutional Convention of the Proposed State of New Mexico Held At Santa Fe, New Mexico* (Albuquerque: Press of the *Morning Journal*, 1910), 4–7, 8, 252; Ralph E. Twitchell, *Leading Facts of New Mexico History* (Albuquerque, NM: Horn and Wallace, Publishers, 1963), 2:567.

104. *Albuquerque Morning Journal*, 12 January 1914.

105. Larson, *New Mexico Populism*, 108.

notes to pages 70–74

106. In 1886 S. M. Ashenfelter of Las Cruces remarked to Gov. Edmund Ross about his appointment of Bernhard Seligman as treasurer that too many Jews were involved in Santa Fe politics; "Edmund G. Ross, 1885–1889, Letters Received," 22 December 1886, TANM, Roll 101, Folder 518. In a letter to Willi Spiegelberg, Simon and Solomon Bibo of Cebolleta referred to a protest note over a land claim against *"un Ricco israelito"* and felt that this hatred was directed toward the Jewish race. Simon Bibo to Willie Spiegelberg, 31 July 1896, Jewish Families and Congregations in New Mexico and Southern Colorado, microfilm #15, CSWR. Also see, Floyd S. Fierman, "The Impact of the Frontier on a Jewish Family: The Bibos," *American Jewish Historical Quarterly* 59 (June 1970): 496–97.

107. Tobias, *A History of the Jews*, 120; Larson, *New Mexico Populism*, 87.

108. Oliver La Farge, *Santa Fe: The Autobiography of a Southwestern Town* (Norman: University of Oklahoma Press, 1959), 69.

109. Lehman, "Santa Fe and Albuquerque," 57.

110. Mann, *Betrachtungen*, xxxii.

CHAPTER FOUR

1. Jack E. Holmes, *Politics in New Mexico* (Albuquerque: University of New Mexico Press, 1967), 22.

2. Productions of Agriculture, Schedule 2, Territorial Census of New Mexico, Bernalillo County, 1860 and 1870 (hereafter cited as Agricultural Census).

3. Agricultural Census, Mora County, 1870 and 1880.

4. Agricultural Census, Mora County, 1870 and 1880, San Miguel County, 1870 and 1880; Register Book, n.d., 7–34, Thomas B. Catron Collection, MSS 6, Center for Southwest Research, University of New Mexico (hereafter the Center is cited as CSWR).

5. Agricultural Census, San Miguel County, 1870 and 1880, Taos County, 1880.

6. *Contracts and Agreement*, D, 27, Lincoln County Courthouse; Agricultural Census, Lincoln County, 1880.

7. Charles Irving Jones, "William Kronig, New Mexico Pioneer," pt. 2, *New Mexico Historical Review* 19 (October 1944): 274, 280 (hereafter *NMHR*); William J. Parish, *The Charles Ilfeld Company:*

A Study of the Rise and Decline of Mercantile Capitalism in New Mexico (Cambridge, MA: Harvard University Press, 1961), 59; Agricultural Census, Mora County, 1880; Mora Assessment Roll 1, 1884–1892, New Mexico State Record Center & Archives (hereafter the Archives are cited as NMSRC&A).

8.   William A. Keleher, *Turmoil in New Mexico, 1846–1868* (Albuquerque: University of New Mexico Press, 1952), 44; Blandine Segale, *At the End of the Santa Fe Trail* (Milwaukee, WI: Bruce Publishing Company, 1948), 87.

9.   *Santa Fe Gazette*, 15 May 1869.

10.   Nathan Bibo, "Reminiscences of Early New Mexico," *Albuquerque Sunday Herald*, 4 June 1922.

11.   Lily Klasner, *My Girlhood among Outlaws*, ed. Eve Ball (Tucson: University of Arizona Press, 1972), 56–57. For details on the Murphy-Fritz store and the Fritz estate, see Frank D. Reeve, *History of New Mexico* (New York: Lewis Historical Publishing Company, 1961), 2:312–14, and Robert M. Utley, *High Noon in Lincoln: Violence on the Western Frontier* (Albuquerque: University of New Mexico Press, 1987), 38–41.

12.   Agricultural Census, Lincoln County, 1880; Darlis A. Miller, "The Women of Lincoln County, 1860–1900," in *New Mexico Women: Intercultural Perspectives*, ed. Joan M. Jensen and Darlis A. Miller (Albuquerque: University of New Mexico Press, 1986), 182; Joan M. Jensen, "Butter Making and Economic Development in Mid-Atlantic America, 1750–1850," *Signs* 13 (Summer 1988), reprinted in Jensen, *Promise to the Land: Essays on Rural Women* (Albuquerque: University of New Mexico Press, 1991), 173; *Rio Grande Republican*, Las Cruces, 19 January 1884.

13.   Gerald D. Nash, "New Mexico in the Otero Era: Some Historical Perspectives," *NMHR* 67 (January 1992): 4; Thomas R. Wessel, "Agricultural Depression and the West, 1870–1900," in *The American West: As Seen by Europeans and Americans*, ed. Rob Kroes (Amsterdam: Free University Press, 1989), 73; Mark Somma, "Ecological Flight: Explaining the Move from Country to City in Developing Nations," *Environmental History Review* 15 (Fall 1991): 4.

14.   John O. Baxter, *Dividing New Mexico's Waters, 1700–1912* (Albuquerque: University of New Mexico Press, 1997), 87.

15. La Mesa Community Ditch vs. Appenzoeller, 28 April 1914, *Report of Cases Argued and Determined in the Supreme Court of the Territory of New Mexico* (Chicago: Callaghan and Co., 1915), vol. 19, 1914, 75–88 (hereafter cited as *Supreme Court*).

16. Parish, *Charles Ilfeld Company*, 59; Agricultural Census, San Miguel County, 1880.

17. Maria E. Montoya, "The Dual World of Governor Miguel A. Otero: Myth and Reality in Turn-of-the-Century New Mexico," *NMHR* 67 (January 1992): 29; *The Economist*, cited in W. Turrentine Jackson, *The Enterprising Scot: Investors in the American West after 1873* (Edinburgh: Edinburgh University Press, 1968), 246.

18. Parish, *Charles Ilfeld Company*, 45.

19. ibid., 154.

20. Kirchner vs. Laughlin, 18 January 1888, *Supreme Court*, vol. 4, 1887–1888; *Ilfeld vs. Gonzales*, 12 January 1919, *Supreme Court*, vol. 25, 1919–1920, 608–11.

21. *Contracts and Agreements*, D, 67–68, Lincoln County; Miller, "Women of Lincoln County," in *New Mexico Women*, ed. Jensen and Miller, 199.

22. Parish, *Charles Ilfeld Company*, 165.

23. Richard J. Evans and W. R. Lee, eds., *The German Peasantry: Conflict and Community in Rural Society from the Eighteenth to the Twentieth Century* (New York: St. Martin's Press, 1986), 108.

24. Herman Gschwind, telephone interview with author, 24 July 1990; Donald Gschwind, Morton Grove, IL, to author, 1 August 1990, 19 November 1990.

25. Allan G. Bogue, "Pioneer Farmers and Innovation," *Iowa Journal of History* 56 (January 1958): 1–2, 15.

26. Herman and Selma Gschwind, interview with author, El Paso, TX, 29 July 1990.

27. Joan Jensen, "New Mexico Farm Women, 1900–1940," in *Labor in New Mexico: Unions, Strikes and Social History since 1880*, ed. Robert Kern (Albuquerque: University of New Mexico Press, 1983), 69; Lillie Gerhardt Anderson, "New Mexico Pioneer of the 1880's," *NMHR* 29 (October 1954): 255; Sarah Deutsch, *No Separate Refuge: Culture, Class, and Gender on an Anglo-Hispanic*

Frontier in the American Southwest, 1880–1940 (New York: Oxford University Press, 1987), 115.

28. Hugo Seaberg to James H. Walker, n.d., Letterbook #2, 280; Hugo Seaberg to unknown, n.d., Letterbook #2, 272, Hugo Seaberg Papers, MSS 165, CSWR; Mora County Assessment Roll 2, 1892–1897, NMSRC&A.

29. Robert H. Wiebe, *The Search For Order, 1877–1920* (New York: Hill and Wang, 1967), 53.

30. Solomon Floersheim to Messrs. Gross, Blackwell & Co., 21 January 1898; Solomon Floersheim to C. R. Hudson [A.T.&S.F.], 24 January 1898, Gross, Blackwell, and Company Papers, MSS 96–1, Box 1, CSWR. In the 1880s, J. A. Muller, a fellow German and New Mexico legislator, introduced a bill that regulated passenger fares on railroads, but not freight fares. Legislative Assembly, 1882, CB 57, NMSRC&A.

31. Anderson, "New Mexico Pioneer," 252.

32. Arthur Blackwell to Jacob Gross, 10 March 1897, Gross, Blackwell, and Company Papers, Box 2; "New Mexico's Prospects: Past and Future of Her Sheep Industry," *Wool Record*, 9 November 1897, 27.

33. Notes, n.d., Erna Fergusson Papers, MSS 45, Box 7, Folder 5, CSWR.

34. Carey McWilliams, *North of Mexico: The Spanish-Speaking People of the United States* (reprint; New York: Greenwood Press, 1968), 215.

35. The injustice of paying employees in kind rather than wages was recognized in New Mexico. But the New Mexico legislature enacted only a limited law in 1897 that regulated the payment of wages in the nonagricultural sector. Haven Tobias, "New Mexico Labor Legislation, 1912–1949," in *Labor in New Mexico*, ed. Kern, 280.

36. A similar conclusion is drawn in a case study among Chinese laborers in California. Mark A. Johnson, "Capital Accumulation and Wage Rates: The Development of the California Labor Market in the Nineteenth Century," *Review of Radical Political Economics* 21 (Fall 1989): 77.

37. Ernest B. Fincher, "Spanish-Americans as a Political Factor in New Mexico, 1912–1950" (Ph.D. diss., New York University, 1950), 32–33; McWilliams, *North of Mexico*, 76.

38. Anderson, "New Mexico Pioneer," 253–55; Parish, *Charles Ilfeld Company*, 177.

39. Hugo Seaberg to Elizabeth Seaberg, 5 August 1890, Letterbook #2, 400, Seaberg Papers; Nash, "Otero Era," 7.

40. Michael C. Meyer, *Water in the Hispanic Southwest: A Social and Legal History, 1550–1850* (Tucson: University of Arizona Press, 1984), 163; Frances Leon Quintana, "Land, Water, and Pueblo-Hispanic Relations in Northern New Mexico," *Journal of the Southwest* 32 (Autumn 1990): 296.

41. Victor Westphall, *The Public Domain in New Mexico, 1845–1891* (Albuquerque: University of New Mexico Press, 1965), 83. Donald Worster, *Rivers of Empires: Water, Aridity, and the Growth of the American West* (New York: Pantheon Books, 1985), 7, 50.

42. Royce Jane Balch, "Jacob Korber, Early Businessman of Albuquerque, New Mexico, 1881–1921" (M.B.A. thesis, University of New Mexico, 1955), 104; Floyd S. Fierman, *The Spiegelbergs: Pioneer Merchants and Bankers of the Southwest* (Waltham, MA: American Jewish Historical Society, 1967), 386; *Santa Fe Weekly Gazette*, 25 September 1869; *Santa Fe New Mexican*, 8 April 1930.

43. Brian Q. Cannon, "Immigrants in American Agriculture," *Agricultural History* 65 (Winter 1991): 33. Windmills, used exclusively in northern Germany and the Low Countries, have no relation to windmills used in the United States. German windmills, used primarily for milling flour, were built differently.

44. Balch, "Jacob Korber," 105.

45. Bureau of Immigration, *New Mexico*, Winter Edition (Las Vegas, NM: J. A. Carruth, Printer, 1889), 37; Sadie L. George, "Frontier Town," *New Mexico Magazine* 29 (December 1951): 18 (hereafter cited as *NMM*). Justus Schmidt was later murdered by a disgruntled customer; *Albuquerque Morning Democrat*, 3 July 1892.

46. Charles P. Clever, *New Mexico: Her Resources, Her Necessities for Railroad Communication with the Atlantic and Pacific States, Her Great Future* (Washington, DC: McGill & Witherow, Printers, 1868), 36.

47. Clever, *New Mexico*, 14.

48. Norbert Finsch, *Die Goldgräber Kaliforniens: Arbeitsbedingungen, Lebensstandard und Politisches System um die Mitte des 19.*

Jahrhunderts (Göttingen: Vandenhoeck und Ruprecht, 1982), 109; Rodman Wilson Paul, *Mining Frontiers of the Far West, 1848–1880* (1963; reprint, Albuquerque: University of New Mexico Press, 1974), 97.

49. A. L. Owen, interview by Lou Blachly, 20 February 1952, Pioneer Foundation (hereafter PF), tape 222, transcript, CSWR.

50. Clever, *New Mexico*, 22–23, 34; Keleher, *Turmoil*, 348.

51. Robert J. Torrez, "The San Juan Gold Rush of 1860 and Its Effect on the Development of Northern New Mexico," *NMHR* 63 (July 1988): 258–60, 265.

52. Carlos A. Schwantes, "The Concept of the Wageworkers' Frontier: A Framework for Future Research," *Western Historical Quarterly* 18 (January 1987): 53.

53. James Whiteside, "Coal Mining, Safety, and Regulation in New Mexico, 1882–1933," *NMHR* 64 (April 1989): 174; on mining safety in the West, see Priscilla Long, *Where the Sun Never Shines: A History of America's Bloody Coal Industry* (New York: Paragon House, 1989).

54. Michael P. Malone and Richard W. Etulain, *The American West: A Twentieth-Century History* (Lincoln: University of Nebraska Press, 1989), 25–26.

55. Henry J. Tobias, *A History of the Jews in New Mexico* (Albuquerque: University of New Mexico Press, 1990), 69; Balch, "Jacob Korber," 104.

56. Jackson, *The Enterprising Scot*, 166.

57. August Müller to Bertha Müller, 11. November 1899, in "'Wir hatten ein schlechtes Schiff…': Briefe eines Westerwälder Amerika-Auswanders," ed. Thomas A. Bartolosch (Archiv Altenkirchen Veröffentlichung, 1984); Hugo Treschwig to Sophie Treschwig, 16. August 1889, Ft. Stanton. These collections of letters are part of the "German Immigrant Letters" project funded by the Volkswagen Foundation at the University of Bochum, Germany. Copies of letters from the Southwest were made available by Wolfgang Helbich, project leader.

58. Kate H. Parker, "'I Brought With Me Many Eastern Ways': Euro-American Income-Earning Women in New Mexico, 1850–1880" (Ph.D. diss., University of New Mexico, 1984), 72.

59. Parker, "Eastern Ways," 74–75.

60. Mary Lee Spence, "They Also Serve Who Wait," *Western Historical Quarterly* 14 (January 1983): 11, 16. The *Albuquerque Morning Journal* reprinted an *New York Herald* article "No Cash 'Tips' for Women," which pointed out that waitresses are tipped less than waiters or not at all; *Albuquerque Morning Journal*, 11 May 1895.

61. Kathleen Neils Conzen, *Immigrant Milwaukee, 1836–1860: Accommodation and Community in a Frontier City* (Cambridge, MA: Harvard University Press, 1976), 96; Stephan Thernstrom, *Poverty and Progress: Social Mobility in a Nineteenth Century City* (Cambridge, MA: Harvard University Press, 1964), 17. August Müller to Peter Müller, 28. Juni 1898 in "'Wir hatten ein schlechtes Schiff.'"

62. Robert Kern, "Carpenters in New Mexico, to 1910," in *Building New Mexico: The Experience of a Carpenters Union in the Southwest*, ed. Robert Kern (n.p.: New Mexico Humanities Council, 1983), 22. Conzen, *Immigrant Milwaukee*, 97.

63. Max Weber, *Economy and Society: An Outline of Interpretive Sociology*, ed. Guenther Roth and Claus Wittich (New York: Bedminster Press, 1968), 3:1219.

64. John Leighly, *Land and Life: A Selection from the Writings of Carl Ortwin Sauer* (Berkeley: University of California Press, 1965), 360.

65. Keleher, *Turmoil*, 44.

66. *Santa Fe Gazette*, 30 January 1864, 9 September 1865.

67. Anderson, "New Mexico Pioneer," 249; Kern, "Carpenters in New Mexico," 24.

68. Kern, "Carpenters in New Mexico," 29; Nash, "Otero Era," 6.

69. *Albuquerque Morning Journal*, 29 June 1893.

70. Kern, "Carpenters in New Mexico," 23; Arnold Leupold, telephone interview, 24 July 1990, Santa Rita, CA; Arnold K. Leupold, "Reminiscences" (6 January 1990), 2, typescript; copy in possession of the author.

71. Seaberg to Bradstreet, 2 April 1891, Letterbook #2, 196, Seaberg Papers.

72. Agricultural Census, Bernalillo County, 1870 and 1880.

73. S. Omar Barker, "Next Door to Murder," *NMM* 30 (October 1952): 22.

74. Harold A. Wolfinbarger, "Captain Richard Charles Deus, 1822–1904," reprint, in *Denver Westerners Brandbooks*, ed. Milton Callon (Denver: n.p., 1968), [9].

75. *Santa Fe Gazette*, 11 January 1868, 30 July 1864; Terry J. Lehman, "Santa Fe and Albuquerque 1870–1900: Contrast and Conflict in the Development of Two Southwestern Towns" (Ph.D. diss., Indiana University, 1974), 29.

76. *Rankin vs. Southwest Brewery and Ice Co.*, January 1913, *Supreme Court*, vol. 12, 1903–1904, 49–62.

77. Bruce Ashcroft, "Miner and Merchant in Socorro's Boom Town Economy, 1880–1893," *NMHR* 63 (April 1988): 112.

78. Balch, "Jacob Korber," 26, 61.

79. Robert W. Eveleth, "Gustav Billing, the Kelly Mine, and the Great Smelter at Park City, Socorro County, New Mexico," *New Mexico Geological Society Guidebook* (Socorro, NM: n.p., 1983), 93.

80. Ashcroft, "Miner and Merchant," 116.

81. Balch, "Jacob Korber," 35, 64.

82. Parish, *Charles Ilfeld Company*, 87.

83. Ledger, 11 March 1885, Charles Ilfeld Company Papers, MSS 91, Box 294, no folder #, CSWR.

84. Johnson, "Capital Accumulation," 76.

85. "Trade between Missouri and Mexico: Answers of Augustus Storrs to Queries Addressed to Him by the Hon. Thomas H. Benton," *Niles Register* 27 (15 January 1825): 312; Documents 1–3, 7, 1827, Passport Collection, MSS 184, CSWR.

86. Documents 107, 110, 111, 1833; Document 150, 1835; Documents 2, 6, 7, 13, 1836, Passport Collection.

87. Adolph Wislizenus, *Memoir of a Tour to Northern Mexico: Connected with Col. Doniphan's Expedition in 1846 and 1847* (1848; reprint, Albuquerque, NM: Calvin Horn Publisher, 1969), 13–14. Wislizenus noted bones and skulls of about 100 mules that Albert Speyer had lost several years earlier while traveling the plains in a snowstorm.

88. Holmes, *Politics in New Mexico*, 19; William J. Parish, "The German Jew and the Commercial Revolution in Territorial New Mexico, 1850–1900, " Sixth Annual Research Lecture, University of New Mexico, 1 May 1959, 324.

89. Gerald Sorin, *Tradition Transformed: The Jewish Experience in America* (Baltimore: Johns Hopkins University Press, 1997), 92.

90. Many merchants advertised in the leading newspapers in Las Vegas and Santa Fe, the *Optic*, *Gazette*, and *New Mexican*; for example, *Santa Fe Gazette*, 30 July 1864, 1 May 1869.

91. See Chris Wilson, *The Myth of Santa Fe: Creating a Modern Regional Tradition* (Albuquerque: University of New Mexico, 1997), 45, 48. R. H. Kay, *Little Pills* (Pittsburg, KS: *Pittsburg Headlight*, 1918), 20, cited in Tobias, *A History of the Jews*, 73.

92. Mrs. [Walter] Marmon, Laguna, 22 August 1967, Doris Duke Oral History Collection (hereafter DDC), tape 515, transcript, CSWR. Karl A. Hoerig, "The Relationship between German Immigrants and the Native Peoples in Western Texas," *Southwestern Historical Quarterly* 47 (January 1994): 434.

93. The labor market in New Mexico mirrored national trends in the 1850s: The majority of the German workforce in the nation made its living in manufacturing and commerce, which included a small elite of wealthy and influential merchants. Bruce Levine, *The Migration of Ideology*, Occasional Paper No. 7 (Washington, DC: German Historical Institute, 1992), 9.

94. For example, *Santa Fe Gazette*, 24 October 1863.

95. Hubert H. Bancroft, *History of Arizona and New Mexico* (1889; reprint, Albuquerque, NM: Horn and Wallace, 1962), 332; Arnold L. Rodriguez, "New Mexico in Transition," *NMHR* 24 (July 1949): 215. See also Josiah Gregg, *Commerce of the Prairies*, 2 vols. (1844, reprint; Philadelphia, PA: J. A. Lippincott Company, 1962) and "Answers of Augustus Storrs."

96. Fierman, *Spiegelbergs*, 388, 390; Tobias, *A History of the Jews*, 71; Lee Scott Theisen, ed., "Frank Warner Angel's Notes on New Mexico Territory, 1878," *Arizona and the West* 18 (Winter 1976): 356–66.

97. Bureau of Indian Affairs, Letters and Documents Relating to the Bibo and Spiegelberg Families, Record Group 75, 22 December 1873, cited in Tobias, *A History of the Jews*, 87–88.

98. Leitensdorfer and Houghton vs. Webb, January 1853, *Supreme Court*, vol. 1, 1852–1879, 34–74.

99. Ralph Paul Bieber, "The Papers of James J. Webb, Santa Fe Merchant, 1844–1861," *Washington University Studies* 11 (1924): 292, 294.

100. Fierman, *Spiegelbergs*, 390.
101. Parish, *Charles Ilfeld Company*, 207. Note by Franz Huning, n.d. [1884], Huning-Fergusson Papers, MSS 194, Box 2, Folder 17, CSWR.
102. *Santa Fe Gazette*, 1 April 1865; 4 April 1868.
103. Archie M. McDowell, "The Opposition to Statehood Within the Territory of New Mexico, 1888–1903" (M.A. thesis, University of New Mexico, 1940), 68.
104. Fierman, *Spiegelbergs*, 396; Parish, *Charles Ilfeld Company*, 184.
105. *New Mexico State Democrat*, Albuquerque, 22 March 1912.
106. Westphall, *The Public Domain*, 102–5.
107. Fierman, *Spiegelbergs*, 397.
108. Parish, "German Jew," 320–21.
109. Peter Iverson, *The Navajo Nation* (1981; reprint, Albuquerque: University of New Mexico Press, 1984), 168; Ray Yazzie, Navajo, 8 October 1968, DDC, tape 142, transcript.
110. Mary Becenti, Jicarilla, 11 June 1970; Nolan Amarillo, Jicarilla, 9 June 1970, DDC, tape 662, transcript.
111. Darlis A. Miller, "The Perils of a Post Sutler: William H. Moore at Fort Union, New Mexico, 1859–1879," *Journal of the West* 32 (April 1993): 7.
112. Parish, "German Jew," 320–21; Floyd S. Fierman, "The Impact of the Frontier on a Jewish Family: The Bibos," *American Jewish Historical Society* 59 (June 1970): 463.
113. Miller, "The Perils of a Post Sutler," 17.
114. David Jaffee, "Peddlers of Progress and the Transformation of the Rural North, 1760–1860," *Journal of American History* 78 (September 1991): 511; Marmon, DDC, transcript; Henry Tobias and Charles E. Woodhouse, "New York Investment Bankers and New Mexico Merchants: Group Formation and Elite Status among German Jewish Businessmen," *NMHR* 65 (January 1990): 28. Sedentary merchants were the rule, as has been pointed out in major works on mercantile businesses in New Mexico, yet peddlers did not disappear. In the early twentieth century, "modified" peddlers appeared in the form of vendors or "drummers" and were utilized in the backcountry. Charles Ilfeld of Las Vegas, the Ilfeld Brothers of Albuquerque, and John Becker of Belen sent out traveling salesmen to cover the backcountry.

115. Jones, "William Kronig," pt. 2, 289; Marmon, DDC, transcript.

116. *Santa Fe Gazette*, 25 February 1865; Fierman, *Spiegelbergs*, 463; *Mulvey vs. Staab & Co.*, January 1887, *Supreme Court*, vol. 4, 1887–1888, 175.

117. Jackson, *The Enterprising Scot*, 163–66; Tobias, *A History of the Jews*, 69. For further details in labor exploitation, see Mario Barrera, *Race and Class in the Southwest: A Theory of Racial Inequality* (Notre Dame, IN: University of Notre Dame Press, 1979), 41.

118. Beatrice Ilfeld Meyer, *Don Luis Ilfeld* (Albuquerque, NM: Albuquerque Historical Society, 1973), 1, 3; Parish, *Charles Ilfeld Company*, 229, 242.

119. Parish, *Charles Ilfeld Company*, 44, 51. The company store system was used in various forms by miners, ranchers, farmers, and small businesspeople; Barrera, *Race and Class*, 41.

120. Jackson, *Enterprising Scot*, 164.

121. Parish, *Charles Ilfeld Company*, 199.

122. Prudencia Hoehne to Charles Ilfeld, 27 February 1895, Ilfeld Papers, Box 5, Folder 1.

123. Parish, *Charles Ilfeld Company*, 201; ledger entry, 11 March 1885, Ilfeld Papers, Box 294. For further details on dual wage structures between Anglo (including German) and Hispanic laborers in the Southwest, see Barrera, *Race and Class*, 41–45.

124. *Albuquerque Morning Journal*, 19 January 1921; Balch, "Jacob Korber," 37–58, 78, 94–114.

125. Darlis A. Miller, "Foragers, Army Women, and Prostitutes," in *New Mexico Women: Intercultural Perspectives*, ed. Joan M. Jensen and Darlis A. Miller (Albuquerque: University of New Mexico Press, 1986), 144.

126. Agricultural Census, San Miguel County, 1880, and Bernalillo County, 1880.

127. Robert Cherry, "American Jewry and Bonacich's Middleman Minority Theory," *Review of Radical Political Economics* 22 (Summer/Fall, 1990): 162.

128. Tobias and Woodhouse, "New York Investment Bankers," 32.

129. Balch, "Jacob Korber," 46, 53; Parish, *Charles Ilfeld Company*, 73, 219.

130. Conzen, *Immigrant Milwaukee*, 115.

131. Note, n.d. [1884], Huning-Fergusson Papers, Box 2, Folder 17; Anna Nolan Clark, "Pioneer of Progress," *NMM* 15 (January 1937): 21; Genry Keith, "Crossroads," *NMM* 18 (February 1940): 36; Ellen K. Duemling, "German-Americans in the United States (1914–1918): An Oral History Project" (term paper, English 406, University of New Mexico, May 1982), 13.

132. Note, Fergusson Papers, Box 7, Folder 5.

133. Floyd S. Fierman, "The Bibos," 467; *Albuquerque Morning Democrat*, 17 February 1892; *Santa Fe New Mexican*, 1 September 1930. Information on John May was provided by his grandson Gus Seligmann, University of North Texas.

134. *Albuquerque Morning Journal*, 8 July 1895; *Santa Fe New Mexican*, 27 June 1916; Correspondence A–Z, 1912, White House Papers, MSS 444, Box 1, Folder 1, CSWR.

135. *Santa Fe Gazette*, 11 December 1852; 4 July 1857; 29 May 1869.

136. *Santa Fe Gazette*, 8 August 1863, 8 October 1864, 1 April 1865.

137. As far as can be determined, no major enterprises such as those of Huning, Korber, Spiegelberg, Ilfeld, and Becker employed Hispanics in top positions.

138. Parish, *Charles Ilfeld Company*, 218.

139. Gustave Elsberg vs. Jacob Amberg, Receiver's Report, 9 July 1877, Gustave Elsberg Papers, MSS 305, CSWR. The company had already dissolved in 1869, *Santa Fe Gazette*, 29 May 1869.

140. For example, *Spiegelberg vs. Mink*, July 1859, *Supreme Court*, vol. 1, 1852–1879, 308–14; *Dold vs. Dold*, January 1867, *Supreme Court*, vol. 1, 397–400; *Ilfeld vs. Stover*, 5 January 1887, *Supreme Court*, vol. 4, 1887–1888, 1–7.

141. *Albuquerque Morning Journal*, 3 January 1915.

142. Larry Schweikart, "Early Banking in New Mexico from the Civil War to the Roaring Twenties," *NMHR* 63 (January 1988): 2; Fierman, *Spiegelbergs*, 398–99, 417; Paul A. F. Walter, "Necrology: Arthur Seligman," *NMHR* 8 (October 1933): 306–7.

143. Frank Bond, "Memoirs of Forty Years in New Mexico," *NMHR* 21 (October 1946): 346; Fierman, *Spiegelbergs*, 425.

144. Tobias, *A History of the Jews*, 67; advertisement, *Cactus*, Roswell High School Yearbook, 1914.

145. *Albuquerque Morning Journal,* 4 December 1881; Bernice Ann Rebord, "A Social History of Albuquerque, 1880–1885" (M.A. thesis, University of New Mexico, 1947), 11; Keith, "Crossroads," 36.

146. Jacob Korber used the German slogan *BORGE NICHT* (don't borrow) where B represented 1, O represented 2, and so on, as a key for code-marking in one of his inventory and sales record ledgers between 1899–1903. Balch, "Jacob Korber," 75.

147. Balch, "Jacob Korber," 36, 102–3.

148. Roman L. Latimer, "Bankers and Merchants to New Mexico Territory," *Numismatic Scrapbook Magazine* 38 (25 February 1972): 130; Letters of Credit, Foreign, 1881–1903, 26 vols., Capital City Bank Records, First National Bank Collection, MSS 177, CSWR. In the 1920s several banks crashed, among them Capital City Bank. It was then taken over by First National Bank in 1923. See First National Bank Collection, Box 17.

149. Latimer, "Bankers and Merchants," 134; Lynne Pierson Doti and Larry Schweikart, *Banking in the American West: From the Gold Rush to Deregulation* (Norman: University of Oklahoma Press, 1991), 29–30.

150. Doti and Schweikart, *Banking in the American West,* 25.

151. Lehman, "Santa Fe and Albuquerque," 219–20; Tobias and Woodhouse, "New York Investment Bankers," 47. See also Levine, *The Migration of Ideology,* 6.

152. A brief history of the Johanna Uhlfelder Blatt's White House, see Institutional History, White House Papers, Inventory Folder; *Albuquerque Morning Journal,* 6 July 1914.

153. McWilliams, *North of Mexico,* 71.

154. Leighly, *Carl Ortwin Sauer,* 358.

155. Wiebe, *Search for Order,* 2.

156. See David M. Emmons, *The Butte Irish: Class and Ethnicity in an American Mining Town, 1875–1925* (Urbana: University of Illinois Press, 1989), 62–70.

157. Fierman, *Spiegelbergs,* 430.

158. Family Correspondence, 11 July 1869, Freudenthal Family Papers, Rio Grande Historical Society, New Mexico State University, Las Cruces, cited in Tobias, *A History of the Jews,* 30.

159. Max Weber, *The Protestant Ethic and the Spirit of Capitalism,* trans. Talcott Parsons (New York: Charles Scribner's Sons, 1958), 64.

160. Robert J. Rosenbaum, *Mexicano Resistance in the Southwest: "The Sacred Right of Self-Preservation"* (Austin: University of Texas Press, 1981), 12.

161. *Santa Fe Gazette*, 15 May 1869; Parish, *Charles Ilfeld Company*, 210; the 1920 Federal Census for Santa Fe City lists one Abraham Spiegelberg, 69 years old, single, and born in New York, as "Critic [sic], Indian Curios."

CHAPTER FIVE

1. Frederick Luebke, *Bonds of Loyalty: German Americans and World War I* (DeKalb: Northern Illinois University Press, 1974), 28; Earl Pomeroy, "On Becoming a Westerner: Immigrants and Other Migrants," in *Jews of the American West*, ed. Moses Rischin and John Livingston (Detroit: Wayne State University Press, 1991), 191.

2. Patricia Nelson Limerick, *The Legacy of Conquest: The Unbroken Past of the American West* (New York: W. W. Norton and Company, 1987), 27.

3. Kazal, *Becoming Old Stock*, 119.

4. D. Michael Quinn, "Religion in the American West," in *Under an Open Sky: Rethinking America's Western Past*, ed. William Cronon et al. (New York: W. W. Norton and Company, 1992), 154.

5. Kathleen Conzen, *Immigrant Milwaukee, 1836–1860: Accommodation and Community in a Frontier City* (Cambridge, MA: Harvard University Press, 1976), 158.

6. Paul A. F. Walter, "Necrology: Arthur Seligman." New Mexico Historical Review 8 (October 1933): 313 (hereafter NMHR).

7. Emma Vorenberg Wertheim, "Memoirs," Jewish Families and Congregations in New Mexico and Southern Colorado, microfilm, reel 10, Center of Southwest Research, Zimmerman Library, University of New Mexico (hereafter the Center is cited as CSWR). See also Gerald Sorin, *Tradition Transformed: The Jewish Experience in America* (Baltimore: Johns Hopkins University Press, 1997), 1–3.

8. Lillie Gerhardt Anderson, "A New Mexico Pioneer of the 1880's," *NMHR* 29 (October 1954): 253, 257.

9. Marc Lee Raphael, "Beyond New York: The Challenge to Local History," in *Jews of the American West*, ed. Rischin and Livingston, 50.

10. Henry Tobias, *A History of the Jews in New Mexico* (Albuquerque: University of New Mexico Press, 1990), 79–82; Franz Huning, *Trader of the Santa Fe Trail: The Memoirs of Franz Huning* (Albuquerque, NM: University of Albuquerque Press, 1973), 125; Henriette Wertheim Goldberg, "Questionnaire," Jewish Families and Congregations in New Mexico; Ferenc Morton Szasz, *The Protestant Clergy in the Great Plains and Mountain West, 1865–1915* (Albuquerque: University of New Mexico Press, 1988), 25.

11. Peter Küppers, "Ein Deutscher Priester in Neu Mexiko," unpublished manuscript, unpaginated, Historic-Artistic Patrimony and Archives of the Archdiocese of Santa Fe, Santa Fe, N.M. See also Tomas Jaehn, "The Priest Who Made Schools Bloom in the Desert: Peter Küppers, 1911–1957," in *Seeds of Struggle—Harvest of Faith: The Papers of the Archdiocese of Santa Fe Catholic Cuarto Centennial Conference*, ed. Thomas J. Steele et al., (Albuquerque, NM: LPD Press, 1998), 291–310.

12. Carolyn Zeleny, *Relations between the Spanish-Americans and Anglo-Americans in New Mexico* (New York: Arno Press, 1974), 249; Charles D. Biebel, "Cultural Change on the Southwest Frontier: Albuquerque Schooling, 1870–1895," *NMHR* 53 (July 1980): 226.

13. Conzen, *Immigrant Milwaukee*, 181.

14. Anderson, "A New Mexico Pioneer," 249.

15. Laurel Drew, "Henrika (Busch) Huning: A Woman of Early New Mexico," unpublished paper (Albuquerque Public Library, Special Collections, 1963), 7; Vorenberg, "Memoirs," Jewish Families and Congregations in New Mexico.

16. "Memoirs of Clara Huning Fergusson," Huning-Fergusson Collection, MSS 194, Box 1, Folder 6, CSWR.

17. Charles Blumner to his mother, 28 December 1858, Blumner Letters (AC 231).

18. Evaline Throop Alexander, Diary entry for 2 November 1866, Diary, 30 April 1866–17 January 1867, P-E 216, Bancroft Library, University of California, Berkeley, CA.

19. George L. Mosse, "Jewish Emancipation: Between Bildung and Respectability," in *The Jewish Response to German Culture: From the Enlightenment to the Second World War*, ed. Jehuda Reinharz

and Walter Schatzberg (Hanover, NH: University Press of New England, 1985), 16.

20. Jane C. Atkins, "Who Will Educate: The Schooling Question in Territorial New Mexico, 1846–1911" (Ph.D. diss., University of New Mexico, 1982), 33. See also Alejandro Portes and Min Zhou, "Should immigrants assimilate?" *The Public Interest* 116 (Summer 1994): 25.

21. Zeleny, *Relations*, 263, 278; Ernest B. Fincher, "Spanish-Americans as a Political Factor in New Mexico, 1912–1950" (Ph.D. diss., New York University, 1950), 59.

22. Henry Lesinsky, *Letters Written by Henry Lesinsky to His Son* (New York: n.p., 1924), 46.

23. Bernice Ann Rebord, "A Social History of Albuquerque, 1880–1885" (M.A. thesis, University of New Mexico, 1947), 76. After high school in Albuquerque, the Nordhaus children were sent east for their college education; Erna Fergusson Papers, MSS 45, Scrapbook 56, CSWR. The Vorenberg children went to high school and college in Pennsylvania; Wertheim, "Memoirs," Jewish Families and Congregations in New Mexico; Louis Prager enrolled at the University of Pennsylvania; newspaper clip, no date, furnished by Louis Prager Jr., Roswell, 29 September 1990.

24. "Memoirs of Clara Huning," Huning-Fergusson Collection, Box 1, Folder 6; Rebord, "A Social History," 76.

25. Kathleen Neils Conzen et al., "The Invention of Ethnicity: A Perspective from the U.S.A.," *Journal of American Ethnic History* 12 (Fall 1992): 14. See also Paul Fessler, "Grandpa Never Had Bilingual Education: Lessons from the 1890s for the Bilingual Debate of the 1990s." Paper read at the symposium "New Approaches to Migration Research: German-Americans in Comparative Perspectives," Texas A&M University, 22–24 April, 1997, 9.

26. *Santa Fe Weekly Gazette*, 9 April 1864. Most likely, Germans had their German Bible and a few German books. I did not find a single issue of a German journal like the popular *Der Hausfreund* or a German newspaper, nor a receipt for a subscription.

27. Note, Fergusson Papers, Box 7, Folder 5.

28. Among her papers are several German poems by her brothers dated from 1897 to 1904, indicating that German was spoken at

home. Gustave Billings Papers, Wurlitzer Foundation, Taos, NM. See also John Scala, *The Lady of the Casa* (Santa Fe, NM: Rydal Press, 1959), 12.

29. "Ancient Santa Fe, 1883," dictation by Samuel A. Dittenhofer, HHB P-E 5, Bancroft Library; Floyd S. Fierman, "The Impact of the Frontier on a Jewish Family: The Bibos," *American Jewish Historical Quarterly* 59 (June 1970): 475–77; Charles H. Lange and Carroll L. Riley, eds., *The Southwestern Journals of Adolph F. Bandelier, 1883–1884* (Albuquerque: University of New Mexico Press, 1970), 411.

30. George De Vos and Lola Romanucci-Ross, eds., *Ethnic Identity: Cultural Continuities and Change* (Palo Alto, CA: Mayfield Publishing Company, 1975), 15.

31. Louis Sulzbacher to Emanuel Rosenwald, n.d., Emanuel Rosenwald Papers, MSS 220, Box 1, Folder "S,T,W," CSWR. Sulzbacher's letter is written in English and indicates unidentified financial and moral improprieties. Among Charles Ilfeld's business papers are a series of letters from Willi Spiegelberg to him, all written in English. Charles Ilfeld Company Collection, MSS 91, Folder 19, Box 5, CSWR.

32. August Ehrich to Charles Ilfeld, 14 October 1893, Ilfeld Collection, Box 294, no folder number (italics mine).

33. David A. Gerber, "'You See i Speak Wery Well Englisch': Literacy and the Transformed Self as Reflected in Immigrant Correspondence," review essay, *Journal of American Ethnic History* 12 (Winter 1993): 61.

34. Richard H. Thompson, *Theories of Ethnicity: A Critical Appraisal* (Westport, CT: Greenwood Press, 1989), 79–80.

35. *Albuquerque Morning Democrat*, 3 July 1885.

36. *Red River Chronicle*, 29 April, 20 May 1882; David Remley, *Bell Ranch: Cattle Ranching in the Southwest, 1824–1947* (Albuquerque: University of New Mexico Press, 1993), 85, 87.

37. Luebke, *Bonds of Loyalty*, 28; Luebke, *Immigrants and Politics: The Germans in Nebraska, 1880–1900* (Lincoln: University of Nebraska Press, 1969), 34.

38. Luebke, *Bonds of Loyalty*, 61.

39. Conzen, *Immigrant Milwaukee*, 154, 156.

40. Michael L. Lawson, "Flora Langermann Spiegelberg: Grand Lady of Santa Fe," typescript, ([San Diego]: Southern California Jewish Historical Society, 1975), 7. See also Christopher Clausen, "How to Join the Middle Class," *American Scholar* 62 (Summer 1993): 415.

41. Charles H. Lange, Carroll L. Riley, and Elizabeth M. Lange, eds., *The Southwestern Journals of Adolph F. Bandelier, 1889–1892* (Albuquerque: University of New Mexico Press, 1984), 53.

42. John Mack Faragher, "Americans, Mexicans, Métis: A Community Approach to the Comparative Study of North American Frontiers," in *Under an Open Sky: Rethinking America's Western Past*, ed. William Cronon et al. (New York: W. W. Norton and Company, 1992), 103.

43. Quentin Anderson, "A Culture of One's Own," *American Scholar* 61 (Autumn 1992): 534.

44. Faragher, "Americans, Mexicans, Métis," in *Under an Open Sky*, ed. Cronon et al., 95.

45. Jack E. Holmes, *Politics in New Mexico* (Albuquerque: University of New Mexico Press, 1967), 30; Stanley Nadel, *Little Germany: Ethnicity, Religion, and Class in New York City, 1845–1880* (Urbana: University of Illinois Press, 1990), 104.

46. Josiah Gregg, *Commerce of the Prairie* (1844; reprint, Philadelphia: J. B. Lippincott Company, 1962), 1:74.

47. On Santa Fe, see Chris Wilson, *The Myth of Santa Fe: Creating a Modern Regional Tradition* (Albuquerque: University of New Mexico Press, 1997), 33, 65, 123.

48. Marc Simmons, "Settlement Patterns and Village Plans," in *New Spain's Far Northern Frontier: Essays on Spain in the American West, 1540–1821*, ed. David J. Weber (Albuquerque: University of New Mexico Press, 1979), 105. A similar, "less intrusive" settlement pattern is described in Karl A. Hoerig, "The Relationship between German Immigrants and the Native Peoples in Western Texas," *Southwestern Historical Quarterly* 47 (January 1994): 434.

49. Alvar W. Carlson, The Spanish-American Homeland: Four Centuries in New Mexico's Rio Arriba (Baltimore, MD: Johns Hopkins University Press, 1990), 142; Faragher, "Americans, Mexicans, Métis," in *Under an Open Sky*, ed. Cronon et al., 100.

50. Agnesa Lufkin Reeve, *From Hacienda to Bungalow: Northern New Mexico Houses, 1850–1912* (Albuquerque: University of New Mexico Press, 1988), 76; *Las Vegas Daily Optic,* 20 March 1915.

51. Faragher, "Americans, Mexicans, Métis," in *Under an Open Sky,* ed. Cronon et al., 106.

52. Lawson, "Flora Langermann Spiegelberg," 12.

53. Julia Keleher and Elsie Ruth Chant, *Padre of Isleta* (Santa Fe, NM: Rydal Press, 1940), 32.

54. Huning Castle floor plan, Bunting Collection, Box 1, Folder 18a, John Gaw Meem Archives, CSWR.

55. Karl Erich Born, *Von der Reichsgründung bis zum Ersten Weltkrieg* (Stuttgart: Klett Verlag, 1970), 45.

56. *Albuquerque Morning Democrat,* 5 July 1914. Despite many Germans' preference for European-style houses, Isaac Hamilton Rapp, of Austrian descent, and Jesse Nussbaum, of German descent, were instrumental in developing an attractive yet simple and sturdy form of "Spanish Pueblo Revival" to maintain New Mexico's architectural heritage. See Carl D. Sheppard, *Creator of the Santa Fe Style: Isaac Hamilton Rapp, Architect* (Albuquerque: University of New Mexico Press, 1988), 74–76; Carey McWilliams, *North of Mexico: The Spanish-Speaking People of the United States* (1948; reprint, New York: Greenwood Press, 1968), 73.

57. Conzen, *Immigrant Milwaukee,* 157.

58. Lynn Abrams, *Workers' Culture in Imperial Germany: Leisure and Recreation in the Rhineland and Westphalia* (New York: Routledge, 1992), 64.

59. Richard Erdoes, *Saloons of the Old West* (New York: Alfred A. Knopf, 1979), 96; Christian Kribben in *Anzeiger des Westens,* St. Louis, MO, 17. Oktober 1846.

60. *Santa Fe Daily New Mexican,* 9, 10 October 1868.

61. Huning, *Trader on the Santa Fe Trail,* 57–58; Robert Schlagintweit, *Die Santa Fe und Südpacificbahn in Nordamerika* (Köln: Verlag von Eduard Heinrich Mayer, 1884), 238.

62. *New York Herald,* 1857, quoted in Nadel, *Little Germany,* 108–9.

63. Charles Blumner to Hannchen Blumner, 18 March 1841, Blumner Letters (AC 231).

64. *Anzeiger des Westens*, 9 January 1847, 14 November 1847, 21 October 1846.

65. Jon Gjerde, *The Minds of the West: Ethnocultural Evolution in the Rural Middle West, 1830–1917* (Chapel Hill: The University of North Carolina Press, 1997), 108.

66. *Santa Fe Weekly Gazette*, 21 May 1853; *Las Vegas Daily Optic*, 20 March 1915; "1867–1921, Personal Correspondence," William C. Ilfeld Collection, NMSRC&A; Rebord, "Social History of Albuquerque," 114–15; LaMoine "Red" Langston, *A History of Masonry in New Mexico* (Roswell, NM: Hall-Poorbaugh Press, [1977]), 137–38; Tobias, *A History of the Jews*, 82.

67. For a [1918] roster of membership, see Folder "Scottish Rite Freemasonry-Misc. Programs, 1914–1937," Adella Collier Collection, NMSRC&A.

68. Nadel, *Little Germany*, 111.

69. Carey McWilliams, "Does Social Discrimination Really Matter?" in *Sociological Analysis*, ed. Logan Wilson and William L. Kolb (New York: Harcourt, Brace and Company, [1949]), 501.

70. Terry J. Lehmann, "Santa Fe and Albuquerque, 1870–1900: Contrast and Conflict in the Development of Two Southwestern Towns" (Ph.D. diss., Indiana University, 1974), 49; Wilson, *The Myth of Santa Fe*, 185.

71. Certificate of Incorporation of Las Vegas Lodge No. 4, Jewish Families and Congregations in New Mexico.

72. Richard H. Hanna to Charles Ilfeld, 12 January 1915, "1867–1921, Personal Correspondence," William C. Ilfeld Collection.

73. Ronald L. Grimes, *Symbol and Conquest: Public Ritual and Drama in Santa Fe, New Mexico* (Ithaca, NY: Cornell University Press, 1976), 73, 86.

74. Lawson, "Flora Langermann Spiegelberg," 9.

75. For the evolution of the Santa Fe Fiesta and Euro-American influence and decline, see Wilson, *Myth of Santa Fe*, chapter six; see also Folders "Proceedings of the Grand Commandery— Knights Templar of New Mexico" and "Scottish Rite Freemasonry—Misc. Programs, 1914–1037," Adella Collier Collection (Adella Collier was Frederick Muller's daughter).

76. Luebke, *Bonds of Loyalty*, 27–28.

77. *Anzeiger des Westens,* 9 January 1847, 27 February 1847.

78. Zeleny, *Relations,* 309–11.

79. Faragher, "Americans, Mexicans, Métis," in *Under an Open Sky,* ed. Cronon et al., 106.

80. Lange and Riley, *Southwestern Journals, 1883–1884,* 19.

81. Luebke, *Bonds of Loyalty,* 43–44.

82. *Santa Fe Weekly Post,* 11 March 1871; Nadel, *Little Germany,* 114.

83. *Santa Fe Weekly Post,* 6 May 1871; *Santa Fe Weekly New Mexican,* 9 February 1875, 22 February 1876; Tobias, *A History of the Jews,* 83.

84. Conzen, *Immigrant Milwaukee,* 154; see also Faragher, "Americans, Mexicans, Métis," in *Under an Open Sky,* ed. Cronon et al., 103–4.

85. Rebord, "Social History," 92; *Albuquerque Morning Democrat,* 26 June 1894.

86. *Albuquerque Morning Journal,* 23, 27 March 1883; *Albuquerque Daily Democrat,* 10 April 1883; Royce Jane Balch, "Jacob Korber, Early Businessman of Albuquerque, New Mexico, 1881–1921" (M.B.A. thesis, University of New Mexico, 1955), 11; Rebord, "Social History," 92, 115.

87. *Albuquerque Morning Democrat,* 27 February, 29 April, 6 August 1892. Schlagintweit mentioned another Turnverein operating in Santa Fe during the summer of 1881. The existence of that club cannot be verified. Schlagintweit, *Santa Fe und Südpacificbahn,* 243.

88. Balls in the Turnhalle were announced among other dates in the *Albuquerque Morning Democrat* on 31 December 1892 (Silvester), 21 February 1893 (Fasching), 22 April 1893, 24 February 1895 (Fasching); *Albuquerque Morning Democrat,* 4 July 1893.

89. *Albuquerque Morning Democrat,* 23 February, 6 July 1892, 12 September 1893; see also Balch, "Jacob Korber," 79; *Albuquerque Morning Journal,* 4 December 1881.

90. Mrs. Louis Abrahams, interview by Lou Blachly [1952–53], Pioneer Foundation (hereafter PF), tape 1, transcript, CSWR; Ida Burgess, interview by Lou Blachly, PF, tape 111, transcript; Ida Burgess, interview by Lou Blachly, PF, tape 224, transcript.

91. *Carlsbad Argus,* 26 June 1908.

92. *Albuquerque Morning Democrat,* 19 February 1892, 22 July 1893, 30 October 1895, 12 April 1914, 21 February 1892, 3 May 1914.

93. *Albuquerque Morning Democrat,* 3, 6 July 1892.

94. For information on the lodge, see sections on organizations and societies in the various city directories of Albuquerque from 1908 to 1918.

95. Nadel, *Little Germany*, 111–12; inquiries about the two German lodges at Masonic centers in Germany brought negative replies.

96. Tobias, *A History of the Jews*, 107–9.

97. Sorin, *Tradition Transformed*, 30.

98. Tobias, *A History of the Jews*, 110–12, 128, 200.

99. German Evangelical Lutheran Zion's Church of Belen incorporated 2 July 1896, its license expired 2 July 1945; German Evangelical Lutheran Trinity Church in Santa Fe incorporated 16 July 1896, its license expired 16 July 1946; Corporations Classified, Churches and Religious Associations, Records of Incorporation, Book I, 1876–1882, Index 1868–1910, microfilm, NMSRC&A. Tobias, *A History of the Jews*, 106, 140.

100. *Albuquerque Morning Democrat*, 15, 28 February, 4 July, 22 December 1892.

101. *Albuquerque Morning Democrat*, 22, 23 December 1892.

102. St. Paul's Evangelical Lutheran Church of Albuquerque incorporated 28 August 1893; its license expired 28 August 1943; Corporations Classified, Churches and Religious Associations, Records of Incorporation, Book I, 1876–1882, Index 1868–1910, microfilm, NMSRC&A; *Albuquerque Morning Democrat*, 18 February, 23 April 1893; Albuquerque City Directory (n.p.: Hughes and McCreight, 1897), 11; *Albuquerque Morning Democrat*, 31 December 1893, 2 December 1895; Ellen K. Duemling, "German-Americans in the United States (1914–1918): An Oral History Project" (term paper, English 406, University of New Mexico, 1982), 13.

103. *Worley's Directory of Albuquerque, New Mexico* (Dallas, TX: John F. Worley Directory Company, 1920), 21; *Albuquerque Morning Democrat*, 4 July 1914. See also sections on churches in the Albuquerque city directories from 1908 to 1918.

104. Robert Kretzschmer appears again in 1918 as a pastor in Optimo, NM, near Wagon Mound, where the railroad imported Dunkards, a sect of the German-American Baptists, from Pennsylvania to Optimo. T. M. Pearce, ed., *New Mexico Place Names* (Albuquerque: University of New Mexico Press, 1965), 114.

105. *Albuquerque Morning Democrat*, 13 July 1919.

106. Richard J. Evans, *The Feminist Movement in Germany, 1894–1933* (London: Sage Publications, 1976), 11, 22.

107. Irene Häderle, "Vom Nähzirkel zur Institution: Kirchliche Frauenvereine in Deutschland und in den USA, 1870–1930," (Paper delivered at the Annual Convention of the Deutsche Gesellschaft für Amerikakunde, Münster, 23 May 1991), 6.

108. Tobias, *A History of the Jews*, 143.

109. Häderle, "Vom Nähzirkel zur Institution," 7.

110. *Albuquerque Morning Democrat*, 1, 15 February 1914; *Santa Fe New Mexican*, 30 April 1904.

111. Tobias, *A History of the Jews*, 140; Minutes of the Hebrew Ladies Benevolent Society, Las Vegas, reel 12, Jewish Families and Congregations in New Mexico.

112. Interview with Henry Sauerwein, 8 September 1992, Wurlitzer Foundation, Taos, NM; Helene Greene Blumenschein, "Recollections of the Early Artists," *Ayer Y Hoy en Taos: Yesterday and Today in Taos County and Northern New Mexico* (Spring 1990): 6, "Blumenschein Folder," Vertical File, Harwood Foundation.

113. *Albuquerque Morning Democrat*, 24 March 1892, 15 February 1914, 3 January, 21 November 1915. Tobias and Woodhouse, *Santa Fe*, 91.

114. Clausen, "How to Join the Middle Class," 405.

115. *Albuquerque Morning Democrat*, 15 February 1914.

116. Obituary, Huning-Fergusson Papers, Box 1, Folder 8.

117. *Las Vegas Daily Optic*, 23 March 1915; *La Voz del Pueblo*, East Las Vegas, 27 March 1915; *El Independiente*, Las Vegas, 25 March 1915.

118. Funeral attendance list, Folder 69, Collier Collection; for example, see Mrs. Keppler's obituary, *Albuquerque Morning Democrat*, 1 July 1914.

119. Stephen L. Good, "Walter Ufer: Munich to Taos, 1913–1918," in *Pioneer Artists of Taos*, rev. and enl. edition, ed. Laura M. Bickerstaff (Denver: Old West Publishing Co., n.d.), 120–21. Good, of Rosenstock Arts in Denver, wrote extensively on Walter Ufer and quotes repeatedly from Ufer papers in his possession. My request to examine those papers was denied.

120. Paul A. F. Walter, "The Santa Fe—Taos Art Movement," *Art and Archaeology* 4 (December 1916): 333.

121. Vertical Files at the Harwood Foundation, University of New Mexico, Taos, contain a wealth of information on Taos and Santa Fe artists. Regarding Gustave Baumann, Ann Baumann recalled that her father "always identified himself as an American artist [not German or German-American]." Ann Baumann to the author, 5 February 1993.

122. Walter, "The Santa Fe—Taos Art Movement," 337.

123. Juliet Currie, "Gustave Baumann: A Century of Delight," *El Palacio* 87 (Spring 1981): 28.

124. Walter, "The Santa Fe—Taos Art Movement," 337.

125. William H. Goetzmann and William N. Goetzmann, *The West of the Imagination* (New York: W. W. Norton and Company, 1986), 355–57.

126. Charles C. Eldridge, Julie Schimmel, and William H. Truettner, *Art in New Mexico, 1900–1945: Paths to Taos and Santa Fe* (New York: Abbeville Press, Publishers, 1986), 48–49; Arrell Morgan Gibson, *Santa Fe and Taos Colonies: Age of the Muses, 1900–1942* (Norman: University of Oklahoma Press, 1983), 27.

127. Will-Amelia Sterns, "A Memoir of Walter Ufer, N.A.," *Southwest Art* 5 (February 1976): 70. *Adventures in Kit Carson Land* (n.p.: El Toro Film Company, 1917), filmstrip, #87–88, NMSRC&A.

128. Rhoda R. Gilman, "Exploring Multicultural Perspectives in History," *Minnesota History* 53 (Summer 1993): 226. Claire Morrill, *A Taos Mosaic: Portrait of a New Mexico Village* (Albuquerque: University of New Mexico Press, 1973), 97.

129. Keith L. Bryant Jr., "The Atchison, Topeka and Santa Fe Railway and the Development of the Taos and Santa Fe Art Colonies," *Western Historical Quarterly* 9 (October 1978): 445, 449.

130. Marta Weigle, "Exposition and Mediation: Mary Coltor, Erna Fergusson, and the Santa Fe/Harvey Popularization of the Native Southwest, 1902–1940," *Frontiers* 12 (no. 3, 1992): 119.

131. Broder, *Taos: A Painter's Dream*, 123, 222.

132. Good, "Walter Ufer," 124–25, 133–34.

133. Robert R. White, ed., *The Taos Society of Artists* (Albuquerque: University of New Mexico Press, 1983), 17–18. The society's founding date is in dispute. Varying dates are discussed in White, *Taos Society*, 4–5.

134. Bickerstaff, *Pioneer Artists of Taos*, 32.
135. White, *Taos Society*, 115.
136. Broder, *Taos: A Painter's Dream*, 211; Good, "Walter Ufer," 121.
137. Broder, *Taos: A Painter's Dream*, 215.
138. Eldridge et al., *Art in New Mexico*, 83; Broder, *Taos: A Painter's Dream*, 225.

CHAPTER SIX

1. Lansing B. Bloom, ed., *New Mexico in the Great War* (Santa Fe: El Palacio Press, 1927), 74. The segment on the New Mexico press in this volume was prepared by German Paul A. F. Walter. Written about ten years after the war and six years after the peace of Versailles, the piece is remarkable in the absence of personal perspective. The author showed neither bitterness nor fondness for either Germany or the United States.
2. Charles Springer to William J. Eaton, 25 April 1918, Adjutant General Records, World War I: Propaganda (hereafter AGR), New Mexico State Record Center and Archives, Santa Fe, New Mexico (hereafter the Archives are cited as NMSRC&A).
3. Walter M. Danburg to George F. Porter, 29 October 1917, AGR. A copy of *Amerikanische Bürgertreue von Bürgern deutscher Abkunft* (Washington, DC: Government Printing Office, 1917) is among the AGR.
4. *Santa Fe New Mexican*, 18 April 1918.
5. O. A. Hilton, "Public Opinion and Civil Liberties in Wartime 1917–1919," *Southwestern Social Science Quarterly* 28 (December 1947): 203–4.
6. Alonzo McMillen to Charles Springer, 26 April 1918, Folder "Allied Pro-German Activities," AGR; Correspondence of the New Mexico Council of Defense, November 1917–September 1918, AGR; Max Paul Kempenich to Charles Springer, 21 May 1918, Folder "Food Prices and Profiteering," AGR.
7. Ellen K. Duemling, "German-Americans in the United States (1914–1918): An Oral History Project" (term paper, English 406, University of New Mexico, 1982), 9. Supplementary Report, 29 January 1918, #10488–4; statement, 21 May 1918, #10488–24; T. W. Gregory to Summers Burkhart, 3 November 1917, #10488–1; A.

R. Gere to Major Barnes, 1 March 1918, #10488–14; RG 165, Military Intelligence Division, National Archives, Washington, D.C. (hereafter MID).

8. Correspondence of the New Mexico Council of Defense, November 1917–September 1918, AGR.

9. Letter A. J. Nisbet to Charles Springer, 21 August 1918, AGR. Background information about the order's activities in Roswell was given by Sister M. Bona Ney, SSM, in a letter to the author, 21 September 1990.

10. Max Nordhaus to Charles Springer, 17 June 1918, Folder "Allied Pro-German Activities," AGR; A. R. Grere [to the U.S. Attorney, Albuquerque], 21 January 1918, #10488–9, MID.

11. Albert Fall to A. B. Bielaski, 14 January 1918, #10488–13, MID.

12. Statement, Gus T. Jones, 22 April 1918, #10488–16, MID.

13. Wesley M. Way to Director of Military Intelligence, 12 December 1918, #10488–22, MID.

14. Louis McRae to Charles Springer, 3 May 1918; Charles Springer to George L. Kile, 4 May 1918; George L. Kile to Charles Springer, 5 May 1918; Folder "Propaganda-Racial Problems," AGR.

15. P. K. Brice to Harry O. Willard, 3 April 1918, #10488–17; statement, Pearce C. Rodney, 19 January 1918, #10488–10; R. H. Van Deman to Intelligence Officer, Panama Canal Department, 4 February 1918, #10488–5, MID.

16. Jon Gjerde, *The Minds of the West: Ethnocultural Evolution in the Rural Middle West, 1830–1917* (Chapel Hill: University of North Carolina Press, 1997), 321.

17. Duemling, "German-Americans," 9, 14.

18. P. Kretzschmar to Charles Springer, 28 June 1918, AGR. Optimo was a community of Dunkards, a sect of German American Baptists. Kretzschmar is the same person who conducted services at the Lutheran Church in Albuquerque.

19. Bloom, *New Mexico in the Great War*, 44.

20. *The New Mexico Blue Book or State Official Register, 1919* (Santa Fe: n.p., [1919]), 78–90; Bloom, *New Mexico in the Great War*, 40–54. For a brief history of New Mexico's Four Minute Men, see Richard Melzer, "Stage Soldiers of the Southwest: New

Mexico's Four Minute Men of World War I," *Military History of the Southwest* 20 (Spring 1990): 23–42.

21. Bloom, *New Mexico in the Great War*, 55–56.

22. Frederick C. Luebke, *Bonds of Loyalty: German Americans and World War I* (DeKalb: Northern Illinois University Press, 1974), 16, 247, 271–73.

23. On the history of the "Katzenjammer Kids," who were based on Wilhelm Busch's characters Max and Moritz, see August Derleth's "Introduction" in Rudolph Dirks, *The Katzenjammer Kids: Early Strips in Full Color* (New York: Dover Publications, Inc., 1974); Maurice Horn, ed., *The World Encyclopedia of Comics* (New York: Chelsea House Publishers, 1976), 156–57, 209.

24. Duemling, "German-Americans," 12.

25. International diplomacy added an ironic twist to this concern. English espionage intercepted a telegram, often referred to as the Zimmermann telegram, from German Interior Minister Arthur Zimmermann to the German ambassador in the United States, Graf Johann von Bernstorff. In the telegram the minister requested Bernstorff to contact the Mexican government and to offer to return its former possessions, i.e., Texas, New Mexico, Arizona, and California, if Mexico would join Germany's war efforts. The Mexican government was also encouraged to invite Japan into this entente. Although one wonders what kind of a reaction such an act would have had in the Hispanic and German communities in the Southwest, there is no evidence that New Mexicans knew about it. The telegram is reprinted in Barbara W. Tuchman, *The Zimmermann Telegram* (New York: Ballantine Books, 1985), 7. Also see, Reinhard R. Doerries, *Berlin-Washington, 1908/1917* (Düsseldorf: Athenaeum Verlag, 1975).

26. Food draft copy, 15 June 1920, Folder "Personal Correspondence 1867–1921," William C. Ilfeld Collection, NMSRC&A, Santa Fe, NM. See also Folder "Personal Correspondence, n.d.," William C. Ilfeld Collection.

27. W. Gerbaulet to [Charles] Ilfeld, 18 November 1920, Folder "Personal Correspondence, 1903–1921," William C. Ilfeld Collection.

28. Luebke, *Bonds of Loyalty*, xiii.

29. John Higham, *Strangers in the Land: Patterns of American Nativism, 1860–1925* (New York: Athenaeum, 1971), 311, 324; Higham, *Send These to Me: Jews and Other Immigrants in Urban America* (New York: Atheneum, 1975), 52–55. About the "dogmatically misread" data of the commission, see Thomas Kessner, *The Golden Door: Italian and Jewish Immigrant Mobility in New York City, 1880–1915* (New York: Oxford University Press, 1977), 24–26.

CONCLUSION AND APPENDIX

1. Anne F. Hyde, "Cultural Filters: The Significance of Perception in the History of the American West," *Western Historical Quarterly* 24 (August 1993): 353.
2. Stephan Thernstrom, ed., *Harvard Encyclopedia of American Ethnic Groups* (Cambridge, MA: Harvard University Press, 1980), 413.
3. Frederick C. Luebke, *Germans in the New World: Essays in the History of Immigration* (Urbana: University of Illinois Press, 1990), 162.
4. Sarah Deutsch, "Landscape of Enclaves: Race Relations in the West, 1865–1990," in *Under an Open Sky: Rethinking America's Western Past*, ed. William Cronon et al. (New York: W. W. Norton and Company, 1992), 113.
5. Kathleen Neils Conzen, *Immigrant Milwaukee, 1836–1860: Accommodation and Community in a Frontier City* (Cambridge, MA: Harvard University Press, 1976), 225.
6. Frederick C. Luebke, *Immigrants and Politics: The Germans of Nebraska* (Lincoln: University of Nebraska Press, 1969), 182.
7. Frederick C. Luebke, *Bonds of Loyalty: German Americans and World War I* (DeKalb: Northern Illinois University Press, 1974), xiii.
8. See for instance the sections on German residential areas and on organizational tendencies in Conzen's *Immigrant Milwaukee* (126–91), and the section on assimilation in Luebke's *Immigrants and Politics* (33–52).
9. Bruce Levine, *The Migration of Ideology*, Occasional Paper No. 7 (Washington, DC: German Historical Institute, 1992), 11. Günter Moltmann, "American-German Return Migration in the

Nineteenth and Early Twentieth Centuries," *Central European History* 13 (December 1980): 390.

10. Henry Lesinsky, *Letters Written by Henry Lesinsky to His Son* (New York: n.p., 1924), 45.

11. Luebke, *Immigrants and Politics*, 38.

12. Stephan Thernstrom, *The Other Bostonians: Poverty and Progress in the American Metropolis, 1880–1970* (Cambridge, MA: Harvard University Press, 1973); Stephan Thernstrom, *Poverty and Progress: Social Mobility in a Nineteenth Century City* (Cambridge, MA: Harvard University Press, 1964); Kenneth L. Kusmer, *A Ghetto Takes Shape: Black Cleveland, 1870–1930* (Urbana: University of Illinois Press, 1970).

13. Thernstrom, *Poverty and Progress*, 91; *The Other Bostonians*, 47–48.

14. Kusmer, *A Ghetto Takes Shape*, Appendix I, 275–80.

15. Thernstrom, *Poverty and Progress*, 91; *The Other Bostonians*, 46.

16. Peter Brandt, *Preussen: Zur Sozialgeschichte eines Staates* (Hamburg: Rowohlt Taschenbuch Verlag, 1981), 243. The book is one of five accompanying catalog volumes to the most comprehensive exhibition of "Preussen—Versuch einer Bilanz" (Prussia—An Attempt of an Evaluation) in Berlin in 1981.

17. W. E. B. DuBois, *The Philadelphia Negro: A Social Study* (1899; reprint, New York: Schocken Books, 1967), 101, 122.

Bibliography

—⟋⟋—

ABBREVIATIONS:

CSWR: Center for Southwest Research,
               University of New Mexico, Albuquerque, NM
NMSRC&A: New Mexico State Record Center and Archives,
               Santa Fe, NM

MANUSCRIPTS AND UNPUBLISHED SOURCES

Adjutant General Records, World War I: Propaganda. NMSRC&A.

Adventures in Kit Carson Land. n.p.: El Toro Film Company, 1917.
    Filmstrip, #87–88. NMSRC&A.

Alexander, Evaline Throop. Diary. P-E 216. Bancroft Library, University
    of California, Berkeley.

Baumann, Ann. Letter to the author, 5 February 1993.

Billings, Gustave. Papers. Helene Wurlitzer Foundation, Taos, NM.

Blumenschein, Ernest. Vertical Files. Harwood Foundation, University
    of New Mexico, Taos.

Blumner, Charles. Letters (AC 231). Angélico Chávez History Library,
    Palace of the Governors, Santa Fe, NM.

Bunting Collection, John Gaw Meem Archives. CSWR.

Capital City Bank Records, First National Bank Collection, MSS 177. CSWR.

Catron, Thomas B. Papers. MSS 6. CSWR.

Collier, Adella. Collection. NMSRC&A.

Contracts and Agreement. D, 27; D, 67–68. Lincoln County Courthouse, Lincoln, NM.

Corporations Classified: Churches and Religious Associations, Records of Incorporation. Book I, 1876–1882, Index 1868–1910. NMSRC&A.

Council Journal. 28th Legislative Assembly. 1888–1889. Territorial Archives of New Mexico. NMSRC&A.

County Assessment Records (Tax Rolls). Doña Ana, Mora, Santa Fe Counties. Years vary. NMSRC&A.

Dittenhofer, Samuel A. "Ancient Santa Fe, 1883." HHB P-E 5. Bancroft Library, University of California, Berkeley. Dictation.

Drew, Laurel E. "Henrika (Busch) Huning: A Woman of Early New Mexico." Unpublished Paper, Albuquerque Public Library, Special Collections, 1963.

Duemling, Ellen K. "German-Americans in the United States (1914–1918): An Oral History Project." Term paper, English 406, University of New Mexico, May 1982.

Duke, Doris. Recorded Oral Histories. Soundtapes. CSWR.

Elsberg, Gustave. Papers. MSS 305. CSWR.

Fergusson, Erna. Papers. MSS 45. CSWR.

Fessler, Paul. "Grandpa Neer Had Bilingual Education: Lessons from the 1890s for the Bilingual Debate of the 1990s." Unpublished paper, read at the symposium "New Approaches to Migration Research: German-Americans in Comparative Perspectives." Texas A&M University, 22–24 April 1997.

First National Bank Collection. MSS 177. CSWR.

"Germany." Department of State. RG 59. Decimal File, 811.4611. National Archives of the United States, Washington, DC.

Gross, Blackwell, and Company Papers. MSS 96–1. CSWR.

Gschwind, Donald. Letters to author, 1 August, 19 November 1990.

Gschwind, Herman. Telephone interview with author. El Paso, TX, 24 July 1990.

Gschwind, Herman, and Selma. Interview with author. El Paso, TX, 29 July 1990.

Häderle, Irene. "Vom Nähzirkel zur Institution: Kirchliche
  Frauenvereine in Deutschland und in den USA, 1870–1930." Paper,
  delivered at the Annual Convention of the Deutsche Gesellschaft
  für Amerikakunde. Münster, 23 May 1991.
Helbich, Wolfgang. "German Immigrant Letters." Unpublished project.
  University of Bochum, Germany.
House Journal. 24th Legislative Assembly. 1880. Territorial Archives of
  New Mexico. NMRC&A.
Huning-Fergusson Papers. MSS 194. CSWR.
Ilfeld, Charles. Papers. MSS 91. CSWR.
Ilfeld, William C. Papers. NMRC&A.
Jewish Families and Congregations in New Mexico and Southern
  Colorado. 12 reels. Microfilm.
Kamphoefner, Walter D. "German and Irish Big City Mayors:
  Comparative Perspective on Ethnic Politics." Unpublished paper
  read at symposium "New Approaches to Migration Research:
  German-Americans in Comparative Perspectives," Texas A&M
  University, 22–24 April 1997.
Kuppers, Peter. "Ein Deutscher Priester in Neu Mexiko." Unpublished
  manuscript. Historic-Artistic Patrimony and Archives of the
  Archdiocese of Santa Fe, Santa Fe, NM.
Lawson, Michael L. "Flora Langerman Spiegelberg: Grand Lady of
  Santa Fe." Southern California Jewish Historical Society,
  1975. Typescript.
Legislative Assembly, 1882. CB 57. NMSRC&A.
Leupold, Arnold K. "Reminiscences." 6 January 1990. Typescript.
———. Telephone interview with author. Santa Rita, CA, 24 July 1990.
Mullin, Robert N. Papers. Nita Stewart Haley Memorial Library,
  Midland, Texas.
Ney, M. Bona, SSM. Letter to the author, 21 September 1990.
Passport Collection. MSS 184. CSWR.
Pioneer Foundation. Recorded Oral Histories. CSWR.
Prager, Louis M. "My Memories of Roswell, 1903–1978." Chaves County
  Historical Museum, Roswell, NM. Soundcassette.
Prager, Louis, Jr. Interview with the author. Roswell, NM,
  29 September 1990.
Rosenwald, Emanuel. Papers. MSS 220. CSWR.

Sauerwein, Henry. Interview with the author. Taos, NM,
    8 September 1992.
Schlagintweit, Robert. Papers. Bayrische Staatsbibliothek,
    München, Germany.
Schlagintweit, Robert. Personnel Folder, Phil K 20. University Archives,
    Ludwig Universität, Giessen, Germany.
Seaberg, Hugo. Papers. MSS 165. CSWR.
White House Papers. MSS 444. CSWR.
"World War I." Military Intelligence Division. RG 165. National Archives
    of the United States, Washington, DC.

CENSUS DOCUMENTS

Population Schedules of the Seventh Census of the United States, 1850:
    New Mexico. Microfilm.
Population Schedules of the Eighth Census of the United States, 1860:
    New Mexico. Microfilm.
Population Schedules of the Ninth Census of the United States, 1870:
    New Mexico. Microfilm.
Population Schedules of the Tenth Census of the United States, 1880:
    New Mexico. Microfilm.
Population Schedules of the Twelfth Census of the United States, 1900:
    New Mexico. Microfilm.
Population Schedules of the Thirteenth Census of the United States,
    1910: New Mexico. Microfilm.
Population Schedules of the Fourteenth Census of the United States,
    1920: New Mexico. Microfilm.
Seventh Census of the United States: 1850. Washington, DC: Robert
    Armstrong, Public Printer, 1853.
Population of the United States in 1860; compiled from the Original
    Returns of the Eighth Census. Washington, DC: Government
    Printing Office, 1864.
Ninth Census of the United States, 1870. Washington, DC: Government
    Printing Office, 1872.
Tenth Census of the United States, 1880. Washington, D.C.: Government
    Printing Office, 1883.
Fourteenth Census of the United States Taken in the Year 1920,
    Population. Washington, DC: Government Printing Office, 1922.

Carpenter, N. "Immigrants and Their Children." U.S. Bureau of the
    Census Monograph, No. 7. Washington, D.C.: Government
    Printing Office, 1927.
Senate Miscellaneous Documents, 50th Congress, Second Session, vol. 2,
    Doc. 52.
Productions of Agriculture, Schedule 2, Territorial Census of New
    Mexico: Bernalillo County, 1860, 1870, 1880. Microfilm.
Productions of Agriculture, Schedule 2, Territorial Census of New
    Mexico: Lincoln County, 1880. Microfilm.
Productions of Agriculture, Schedule 2, Territorial Census of New
    Mexico: Mora County, 1870 and 1880. Microfilm.
Productions of Agriculture, Schedule 2, Territorial Census of New
    Mexico: San Miguel County, 1870 and 1880. Microfilm.
Productions of Agriculture, Schedule 2, Territorial Census of New
    Mexico: Taos County, 1880. Microfilm.

NEWSPAPERS (SOME TITLES VARY)

Albuquerque Morning Democrat, 1880–1915.
Albuquerque Morning Journal, 1880–1921.
Albuquerque Republican Review, 1 November 1875.
Albuquerque New Mexico State Democrat, 22 March 1912.
Carlsbad Argus, 26 June 1908.
Cleveland Daily Leader, 2 March 1869.
Council Bluffs (IA)Daily Nonpareil, 4 May 1869.
Highland (IL)Union, 1880–1883.
St. Louis Anzeiger des Westens, 1847–1851.
San Francisco Abend Post, June 1869.
San Francisco California Mail Bag, July 1871.
San Jose Herald, 28 June 1869.
San Lorenzo Red River Chronicle, 1882–1883.
Santa Fe New Mexican, 1868–1918.
Santa Fe Weekly Gazette, 1852–1865, 1869–1869.
Santa Fe Weekly Post, March–May 1871.
La Voz del Pueblo (East Las Vegas, NM), 27 March 1915.
Las Cruces Rio Grande Republican, 19 January 1884.
Las Vegas El Independiente, 25 March 1915.
Las Vegas Optic, 1915.

ARTICLES

Anderson, Lillie Gerhardt. "A New Mexico Pioneer of the 1880's." *New Mexico Historical Review* 29 (October 1954): 245–58.

Anderson, Quentin. "A Culture of One's Own." *American Scholar* 61 (Autumn 1992): 533–51.

Ashcroft, Bruce. "Miner and Merchant in Socorro's Boom Town Economy, 1880–1893." *New Mexico Historical Review* 63 (April 1988): 103–18.

Ashliman, D. L. "The American Indian in German Travel Narratives and Literature." *Journal of Popular Culture* 10 (Spring 1977): 833–39.

———. "The Image of Utah and the Mormons in Nineteenth-Century Germany." *Utah Historical Quarterly* 35 (Summer 1967): 209–27.

Barker, S. Omar. "Next Door to Murder." *New Mexico Magazine* 30 (October 1952): 22–23, 54–55.

Baum, Dale, and Worth Robert Miller, "Ethnic conflict and Machine Politics in San Antonio, 1892–1899." *Journal of Urban History* 19 (August 1993): 63–84.

Bergquist, James M. "The Forty-Eighters: Catalysts of German-American Politics." In *The German-American Encounter: Conflict and Cooperation between Two Cultures, 1800–2000,* edited by Frank Trommler and Elliott Shore, 22–36. New York: Berghahn Books, 2001.

Bibo, Nathan. "Reminiscences of Early New Mexico." *Albuquerque Sunday Herald,* 4 June 1922.

Biebel, Charles D. "Cultural Change on the Southwest Frontier: Albuquerque Schooling, 1870–1895." *New Mexico Historical Review* 53 (July 1980): 209–30.

Bieber, Ralph Paul. "The Papers of James J. Webb, Santa Fe Merchant, 1844–1861." *Washington University Studies* 11 (1924): 255–305.

Bogue, Allan G. "Pioneer Farmers and Innovation." *Iowa Journal of History* 56 (January 1958): 1–36.

———. "The Quest for Numeracy: Data and Methods in American Political History." *Journal of Interdisciplinary History* 21 (Summer 1990): 89–116.

Bond, Frank. "Memoirs of Forty Years in New Mexico." *New Mexico Historical Review* 21 (October 1946): 340–49.

Brinkmann, Tobias. "'We Are Brothers! Let Us Separate!': Jewish Immigrants in Chicago between Gemeinde and Network Community before 1880." In *German-Jewish Identities in America*, edited by Cristof Mauch and Joseph Salmons, 40–63. Madison, WI: Max Kade Institute for German-American Studies, 2003.

Bryant, Keith L., Jr. "The Atchison, Topeka and Santa Fe Railway and the Development of the Taos and Santa Fe Art Colonies." *Western Historical Quarterly* 9 (October 1978): 437–53.

Cannon, Brian Q. "Immigrants in American Agriculture." *Agricultural History* 65 (Winter 1991): 17–35.

Chauvenet, Beatrice. "Paul A. F. Walter: A Man Who Lived and Wrote Santa Fe History." *El Palacio* 88 (Spring 1982): 29–34.

Cherry, Robert. "American Jewry and Bonacich's Middleman Minority Theory." *Review of Radical Political Economics* 22 (Summer/Fall, 1990): 158–73.

Clark, Anna Nolan. "Pioneer of Progress." *New Mexico Magazine* 15 (January 1937): 20–21, 47–52.

Clausen, Christopher. "How to Join the Middle Class." *American Scholar* 62 (Summer 1993): 403–18.

Cline, Dorothy I. "Constitutional Politics in New Mexico: 1910–1976." In *New Mexico Government*, edited by F. Chris Garcia and Paul L. Hain, 219–43. Albuquerque: University of New Mexico Press, 1976.

Conzen, Kathleen Neils. "Phantom Landscapes of Colonization: Germans in the Making of a Pluralist America." In *The German-American Encounter: Conflict and Cooperation between Two Cultures, 1800–2000*, edited by Frank Trommler and Elliott Shore, 7–21. New York: Berghahn Books, 2001.

———, David A. Gerber, Ewa Morawska, and George E. Pozzetta. "The Invention of Ethnicity: A Perspective from the U.S.A." *Journal of American Ethnic History* 12 (Fall 1992): 3–41.

Cracroft, Richard H. "The American West of Karl May." *American Quarterly* 19 (Summer 1967): 249–58.

Currie, Juliet. "Gustave Baumann: A Century of Delight." *El Palacio* 87 (Spring 1981): 25–32.

Dargan, Marion. "New Mexico's Fight for Statehood, 1895–1912." Part 6. *New Mexico Historical Review* 18 (January 1943): 60–96.

Derleth, August. "Introduction." In Rudolph Dirks, *The Katzenjammer Kids: Early Strips in Full Color.* New York: Dover Publications, Inc., 1974.

Deutsch, Sarah. "Landscape of Enclaves: Race Relations in the West, 1865–1990." In *Under an Open Sky: Rethinking America's Western Past,* edited by William Cronon, George Miles, and Jay Gitlin, 110–31. New York: W. W. Norton and Company, 1992.

Deverell, William F. "To Loosen the Safety Valve: Eastern Workers and Western Lands." *Western Historical Quarterly* 19 (August 1988): 269–85.

Ehmann, F. A. "The Effect of the Railroad on New Mexico." *Password* 8 (Summer 1963): 56–69.

Eveleth, Robert W. "Gustav Billing, the Kelly Mine, and the Great Smelter at Park City, Socorro County, New Mexico." *New Mexico Geological Society Guidebook,* 89–95. Socorro, NM: n.p., 1983.

Faragher, John Mack. "Americans, Mexicans, Métis: A Community Approach to the Comparative Study of North American Frontiers." In *Under an Open Sky: Rethinking America's Western Past,* edited by William Cronon, George Miles, and Jay Gitlin, 90–109. New York: W. W. Norton and Company, 1992.

Fierman, Floyd S. "The Impact of the Frontier on a Jewish Family: The Bibos." *American Jewish Historical Quarterly* 59 (June 1970): 460–522.

———. "The Triangle and the Tetragrammaton: A Note on the Cathedral at Santa Fe." *New Mexico Historical Review* 37 (October 1962): 309–21.

Fontana, Bernhard L. "A Dedication to the Memory of Adolph Bandelier, 1840–1914." *Arizona and the West* 2 (Spring 1960): 1–5.

George, Sadie L. "Frontier Town." *New Mexico Magazine* 29 (December 1951): 18–19, 43–46.

Gerber, David A. "'You See i Speak Wery Well Englisch': Literacy and the Transformed Self as Reflected in Immigrant Correspondence." Review Essay. *Journal of American Ethnic History* 12 (Winter 1993): 56–62.

Gilman, Rhoda R. "Exploring Multicultural Perspectives in History." *Minnesota History* 53 (Summer 1993): 225–29.

Gordon, Milton M. "Assimilation in America: Theory and Reality." *Daedalus* 90 (Spring 1961):

Greer, Richard R. "Origins of the Foreign-Born Population of New Mexico during the Territorial Period." *New Mexico Historical Review* 17 (October 1942): 281–87.

Griswold, Robert L. "Anglo Women and Domestic Ideology in the American West in the Nineteenth and Early Twentieth Centuries." In *Western Women: Their Land, Their Lives*, edited by Lillian Schlissel, Vicki Ruiz, and Janice Monk, 15–33. Albuquerque: University of New Mexico Press, 1988.

Gutiérrez, Ramón A. "Charles Fletcher Lummis." In *Nuevomexicano-Cultural Legacy: Forms, Agencies, and Discourse*. Edited by Francisco A. Lomelí, Victor A. Sorell, and Genaro M. Padilla. Albuquerque: University of New Mexico Press, 2002, 11–27.

Habermas, Jürgen. "Heidegger—Werk und Weltanschauung." In *Heidegger und der Nationalsozialismus*, by Victor Faría, 11–37. Frankfurt a.M.: S. Fischer, 1989.

Handke, Peter. "Erste Lese-Erlebnisse." In *Karl May*, edited by Helmuth Schmiedt, 35. Frankfurt a.M.: Suhrkamp Verlag, 1983.

Hering, Christoph. "Otto Ruppius, der Amerikafahrer, Flüchtling, Exilschriftsteller, Rückwanderer." In *Amerika in der deutschen Literatur* (Stuttgart: Philipp Reclam Jun., 1975), edited by Sigrid Bauschinger, Horst Denkler, and Wilfried Malsch, 124–134.

Hilton, O. A. "Public Opinion and Civil Liberties in Wartime 1917–1919." *Southwestern Social Science Quarterly* 28 (December 1947): 201–24.

Hoerig, Karl A. "The Relationship between German Immigrants and the Native Peoples in Western Texas." *Southwestern Historical Quarterly* 47 (January 1994): 423–51.

Hollick, Julian Crandall. "The American West in the European Imagination." *Montana: The Magazine of Western History* 42 (Spring 1992): 17–21.

Hyde, Anne F. "Cultural Filters: The Significance of Perception in the History of the American West." *Western Historical Quarterly* 24 (August 1993): 351–74.

Jacobsen, Joel K. "An Excess of Law in Lincoln County: Thomas Catron, Samuel Axtell, and the Lincoln County War." *New Mexico Historical Review* 68 (April 1993): 133–51.

Jaehn, Thomas. "Charles Blumner: Pioneer, Civil Servant, and Merchant." *New Mexico Historical Review* 61 (October 1986): 319–27.

————. "The Priest Who Made Schools Bloom in the Desert: Peter Küppers, 1911–1957." In *Seeds of Struggle-Harvest of Faith: The Papers of the Archdiocese of Santa Fe Catholic Cuarto Centennial Conference on the History of the Catholic Church in New Mexico.* Edited by Thomas J. Steele, Paul Rhetts, and Barbe Awalt, 291–310. Albuquerque, NM: LPD Press, 1998.

Jaffee, David. "Peddlers of Progress and the Transformation of the Rural North, 1760–1860." *Journal of American History* 78 (September 1991): 511–35.

Jensen, Joan. "Butter Making and Economic Development in Mid-Atlantic America, 1750–1850." 1988. Reprint. In Jensen, *Promise to the Land: Essays on Rural Women*, 170–205. Albuquerque: University of New Mexico Press, 1991.

————. "New Mexico Farm Women, 1900–1940." In *Labor in New Mexico: Unions, Strikes and Social History since 1880*, edited by Robert Kern, 61–81. Albuquerque: University of New Mexico Press, 1983.

————, and Darlis A. Miller. "The Gentle Tamers Revisited: New Approaches to the History of Women in the American West." *Pacific Historical Review* 2 (May 1980): 173–213.

Johnson, Mark A. "Capital Accumulation and Wage Rates: The Development of the California Labor Market in the Nineteenth Century." *Review of Radical Political Economics* 21 (Fall 1989): 76–81.

Jones, Charles Irving. "William Kronig, New Mexico Pioneer." Parts 1, 2. *New Mexico Historical Review* 19 (July, October 1944): 185–224, 271–311.

"Karl der Deutsche." *Der Spiegel* (12 September 1962): 54–74.

Keith, Genry. "Crossroads." *New Mexico Magazine* 18 (February 1940): 21, 35–37.

Kessler-Harris, Alice, and Virginia Yans-McLaughlin. "European Immigrant Groups." In *Essays and Data on American Ethnic Groups*, edited by Thomas Sowell, 107–37. [Washington, D.C.: Urban Institute], 1978.

Kleppner, Paul. "Voters and Parties in the Western States, 1876–1900." *Western Historical Quarterly* 14 (January 1983): 49–68.

Kloberdanz, Timothy J. "Plainsmen of Three Continents: Volga German Adaptation to Steppe, Prairie and Pampa." In *Ethnicity on the*

Great Plains, edited by Frederick C. Luebke, 54–72. Lincoln: University of Nebraska Press, 1980.

Kuester, Martin. "American Indians and German Indians: Perspectives of Doom in Cooper and May." *Western American Literature* 23 (November 1988): 217–22.

Lamar, Howard R. "Political Patterns in New Mexico and Utah Territories 1850–1900." *Utah Historical Quarterly* 28 (October 1960): 363–87.

———. "The Santa Fe Ring." In *New Mexico, Past and Present: A Historical Reader*, edited by Richard N. Ellis, 148–62. Albuquerque: University of New Mexico Press, 1971.

Landale, Nancy S., and Avery M. Guest. "Generation, Ethnicity, and Occupational Opportunity in Late 19th Century America." *American Sociological Review* 55 (April 1990): 280–96.

Latimer, Roman L. "Bankers and Merchants to New Mexico Territory." *Numismatic Scrapbook Magazine* 38 (25 February 1972).

Lee, Hector. "Tales and Legends in Western American Literature." *Western American Literature* 9 (Winter 1975): 239–54.

Lummis, Charles F. "The White Indian." *The Land of Sunshine* 13 (June 1900).

Lutz, Hartmut. "German Indianthusiasm: A Socially Constructed German National(ist) Myth." In *Germans and Indians: Fantasies, Encounters, Projections*, edited by Colin G. Calloway, Gerd Gemünden, and Susanne Zantop, 167–184. Lincoln: University of Nebraska Press, 2002.

McWilliams, Carey. "Does Social Discrimination Really Matter?" In *Sociological Analysis*, edited by Logan Wilson and William L. Kolb, 500–509. New York: Harcourt, Brace and Co., 1949.

Melzer, Richard. "Stage Soldiers of the Southwest: New Mexico's Four Minute Men of World War I." *Military History of the Southwest* 20 (Spring 1990): 23–42.

Miller, Darlis A. "Cross-Cultural Marriages in the Southwest: The New Mexico Experience, 1846–1900." *New Mexico Historical Review* 57 (October 1982): 335–59.

———. "Foragers, Army Women, and Prostitutes." In *New Mexico Women: Intercultural Perspectives*, edited by Joan M. Jensen and Darlis A. Miller, 141–68. Albuquerque: University of New Mexico Press, 1986.

———. "The Perils of a Post Sutler: William H. Moore at Fort Union, New Mexico, 1859–1879." *Journal of the West* 32 (April 1993): 7–17.

———. "The Women of Lincoln County." In *New Mexico Women: Intercultural Perspectives*, edited by Joan M. Jensen and Darlis A. Miller, 169–200. Albuquerque: University of New Mexico Press, 1986.

Moltmann, Günter. "American-German Return Migration in the Nineteenth and Early Twentieth Centuries." *Central European History* 13 (December 1980): 378–92.

Montoya, Maria E. "The Dual World of Governor Miguel A. Otero: Myth and Reality in Turn-of-the-Century New Mexico." *New Mexico Historical Review* 67 (January 1992): 13–31.

Mosse, George L. "Jewish Emancipation: Between Bildung and Respectability." In *The Jewish Response to German Culture: From the Enlightenment to the Second World War*, edited by Jehuda Reinharz and Walter Schatzberg, 1–16. Hanover, NH: University Press of New England, 1985.

Nash, Gerald D. "European Images of America: The West in Historical Perspective." *Montana: The Magazine of Western History* 42 (Spring 1992): 2–16.

———. "New Mexico in the Otero Era: Some Historical Perspectives." *New Mexico Historical Review* 67 (January 1992): 1–12.

"New Mexico's Prospects: Past and Future of Her Sheep Industry." *Wool Record* (9 November 1897): 1, 27.

Noggle, Burl. "Anglo Observers of the Southwest Borderland, 1825–1890: The Rise of a Concept." *Arizona and the West* 1 (Summer 1959): 105–31.

Nugent, Walter. "The People of the West since 1890." In *The Twentieth-Century West: Historical Interpretations*, edited by Gerald D. Nash and Richard W. Etulain, 35–70. Albuquerque: University of New Mexico Press, 1989.

"Old Shatterhand am Elbestrand." *Zeitmagazin* (28 June 1991).

Parish, William J. "The German Jew and the Commercial Revolution in Territorial New Mexico, 1850–1900." Sixth Annual Research Lecture, University of New Mexico, 1 May 1959.

Peterson, Brent O. "How (and Why) to Read German-American Literature." In *The German American Encounter: Conflict and*

Cooperation between Two Cultures, 1800–2000, edited by Frank
Trommler and Elliott Shore, 88–102. New York: Berghahn
Books, 2001.

Pomeroy, Earl. "On Becoming a Westerner: Immigrants and Other
Migrants." In *Jews of the American West*, edited by Moses Rischin
and John Livingston, 190–212. Detroit: Wayne State University
Press, 1991.

Portes, Alejandro, and Min Zhou. "Should Immigrants Assimilate?" *The
Public Interest* 116 (Summer 1994): 18–33.

Quinn, D. Michael, "Religion in the American West." In *Under an Open
Sky: Rethinking America's Western Past*, edited by William Cronon,
George Miles, and Jay Gitlin, 145–66. New York: W. W. Norton
and Company, 1992.

Quintana, Frances Leon. "Land, Water, and Pueblo-Hispanic Relations
in Northern New Mexico." *Journal of the Southwest* 32 (Autumn
1990): 288–99.

Raphael, Marc Lee. "Beyond New York: The Challenge to Local
History." In *Jews of the American West*, edited by Moses Rischin
and John Livingston, 48–65. Detroit: Wayne State University
Press, 1991.

Ritter, Alexander. "German-American Literature: Critical Comments on
the Current State of Ethnic Writing in German and Its
Philological Description." In *America and the Germans: An
Assessment of a Three-Hundred-Year History*, edited by Frank
Trommler and Joseph McVeigh, 1:343–56. Philadelphia: University
of Pennsylvania Press, 1985.

Rodriguez, Arnold L. "New Mexico in Transition." *New Mexico
Historical Review* 24 (July 1949): 184–222.

Schwantes, Carlos A. "The Concept of the Wageworkers' Frontier: A
Framework for Future Research." *Western Historical Quarterly* 18
(January 1987): 39–55.

Schweikart, Larry. "Early Banking in New Mexico from the Civil War to
the Roaring Twenties." *New Mexico Historical Review* 63 (January
1988): 1–24.

Seligmann, Raphael. "Die Juden Leben." *Der Spiegel*, 16 November 1992.

Shore, Elliott. "A New Look at the Nineteenth Century." In *The German-
American Encounter: Conflict and Cooperation between Two*

Cultures, 1800–2000, edited by Frank Trommler and Elliott Shore, 3–5. New York: Berghahn Books, 2001.

Simmons, Marc. "Settlement Patterns and Village Plans." In *New Spain's Far Northern Frontier: Essays on Spain in the American West, 1540–1821*, edited by David J. Weber, 97–115. Albuquerque: University of New Mexico Press, 1979.

Somma, Mark. "Ecological Flight: Explaining the Move from Country to City in Developing Nations." *Environmental History Review* 15 (Fall 1991): 1–26.

Spence, Mary Lee. "They Also Serve Who Wait." *Western Historical Quarterly* 14 (January 1983): 5–28.

Stadler, Ernst. "Karl May: The Wild West under the German Umlaut." *Missouri Historical Society Bulletin* 21 (July 1965): 295–307.

Stern, Fritz. "The Political Consequences of the Unpolitical German." 1960. Reprint. In *The Failure of Illiberalism: Essays on the Political Culture of Modern Germany*, 1–25. New York: Alfred A. Knopf, 1972.

Sterns, Will-Amelia. "A Memoir of Walter Ufer, N.A." *Southwest Art* 5 (February 1976): 70–73.

Taft, Robert. "The Pictorial Record of the Old West: Heinrich Balduin Möllhausen." Part 6. *Kansas Historical Quarterly* 32 (October 1948): 225–45.

Theisen, Lee Scott, ed. "Frank Warner Angel's Notes on New Mexico Territory, 1878." *Arizona and the West* 18 (Winter 1976): 333–70.

Tobias, Haven. "New Mexico Labor Legislation, 1912–1949." In *Labor in New Mexico: Unions, Strikes, and Social History since 1881*, edited by Robert Kern, 277–312. Albuquerque: University of New Mexico Press, 1983.

Tobias, Henry, and Charles E. Woodhouse. "New York Investment Bankers and New Mexico Merchants: Group Formation and Elite Status among German Jewish Businessmen." *New Mexico Historical Review* 65 (January 1990): 21–47.

Torrez, Robert J. "The San Juan Gold Rush of 1860 and its Effect on the Development of Northern New Mexico." *New Mexico Historical Review* 63 (July 1988): 257–72.

"Trade between Missouri and Mexico: Answers of Augustus Storrs to Queries Addressed to Him by the Hon. Thomas H. Benton." *Niles Register* 27 (15 January 1825): 312–16.

Tuckel, Peter, and Richard Maisel. "Voter Turnout among European Immigrants to the United States." *Journal of Interdisciplinary History* 24 (Winter 1994): 407–30.

Walter, Paul A. F. "Necrology: Arthur Seligman." *New Mexico Historical Review* 8 (1933): 306–16.

———. "The Santa Fe–Taos Art Movement." *Art and Archaeology* 4 (December 1916): 330–38.

Weber, David J. "'Scarce more than apes': Historical Roots of Anglo American Stereotypes of Mexicans in the Border Region." In *New Spain's Far Northern Frontier: Essays on Spain in the American West, 1540–1821*, edited by David J. Weber, 295–307. Albuquerque: University of New Mexico Press, 1979.

Weigle, Marta. "Exposition and Mediation: Mary Colter, Erna Fergusson, and the Santa Fe/Harvey Popularization of the Native Southwest, 1902–1940." *Frontiers* 12 (Fall 1991): 117–50.

Wessel, Thomas R. "Agricultural Depression and the West, 1870–1900." In *The American West: As Seen by Europeans and Americans*, edited by Rob Kroes, 72–80. Amsterdam: Free University Press, 1989.

White, Richard. "Race Relations in the American West." *American Quarterly* 38 (Bibliography 1986): 396–416.

Whiteside, James. "Coal Mining, Safety, and Regulation in New Mexico, 1882–1933." *New Mexico Historical Review* 64 (April 1989): 159–84.

Wittke, Carl. "The American Theme in Continental European Literature." *Mississippi Valley Historical Review* 28 (June 1941): 3–26.

Wolfinbarger, Harold A. "Captain Richard Charles Deus, 1822–1904." Reprint, edited by Milton Callon. Denver: Westerners Brand Books, 1968.

Wolfinger, Raymond E. "The Development and Persistence of Ethnic Voting." *American Political Science Review* 59 (December 1965): 896–908.

Zantop, Susanne. "Close Encounters: Deutsche and Indianer." In *Germans and Indians: Fantasies, Encounters, Projections*, edited by Colin G. Calloway, Gerd Gemünden, and Susanne Zantop, 3–14. Lincoln: University of Nebraska Press, 2001.

Zimmerman, Jonathan. "Ethnics against Ethnicity: European Immigrants and Foreign-Language Instruction, 1890–1940." *The Journal of American History* 88 (March 2002): 1383–1404.

BOOKS AND PAMPHLETS

Abrams, Lynn. *Workers' Culture in Imperial Germany: Leisure and Recreation in the Rhineland and Westphalia*. New York: Routledge, 1992.

Albuquerque City Directory. [Publishers vary], 1896–1921.

Allgemeine Deutsche Biographie. Vol. 31. Leipzig: Dunker und Humblot, 1890.

Amerikanische Bürgertreue von Bürgern deutscher Abkunft. Washington, D.C.: Government Printing Office, 1917.

Anderson, Margo J. *The American Census: A Social History*. New Haven, CT: Yale University Press, 1988.

Armand [Friedrich Armand Strubberg]. *Amerikanische Jagd- und Reiseabenteur*. 1858. Reprint. München: Lothar Borowsky Verlag, n.d.

Bancroft, Hubert H. *History of Arizona and New Mexico*. 1889. Reprint. Albuquerque, NM: Horn and Wallace, 1962.

Barrera, Mario. *Race and Class in the Southwest: A Theory of Racial Inequality*. Notre Dame, IN: University of Notre Dame Press, 1979.

Bartolosch, Thomas A., ed. *"Wir hatten ein Schlechtes Schiff . . .": Briefe eines Westerwälder Amerika-Auswanderer*. Altenkirchen, Germany: Archiv Altenkirchen Veröffentlichung, 1984.

Baxter, John O. *Dividing New Mexico's Waters, 1700–1912*. Albuquerque: University of New Mexico Press, 1997.

Bickerstaff, Laura M. *Pioneer Artists of Taos*. Revised and enlarged edition. Denver: Old West Publishing Co., n.d.

Billington, Ray Allen. *Land of Savagery, Land of Promise: The European Image of the American Frontier*. New York: W. W. Norton and Company, 1981.

Bloom, Lansing B., ed. *New Mexico in the Great War*. Santa Fe, NM: El Palacio Press, 1927.

Bohme, Frederick G. *A History of the Italians in New Mexico*. New York: Arno Press, 1975.

Born, Karl Erich. *Von der Reichsgründung bis zum Ersten Weltkrieg*. Stuttgart: Klett Verlag, 1970.

Brandt, Peter. *Preussen: Zur Sozialgeschichte eines Staates*. 5 vols. Hamburg: Rowohlt Taschenbuch Verlag, 1981.

Broder, Patricia Janis. *Taos: A Painter's Dream*. Boston: New York Graphic Society, 1980.

Brown, Dee. *The Gentle Tamers: Women of the Old Wild West*. 1958. Reprint. Lincoln: University of Nebraska Press, 1981.

Bureau of Immigration [of the Territory of New Mexico]. *New Mexico. Winter Edition*. Las Vegas, NM: J. A. Carruth, Printer, 1889.

———. *Report as to Socorro County*. Socorro, NM: Socorro Daily News Office, 1881.

———. *Report of San Miguel County*. Santa Fe: New Mexican Print, 1882.

———. *Resources of New Mexico: Prepared under the Auspices of the Territorial Bureau of Immigration*. 1881. Reprint. Santa Fe, NM: William Gannon, 1973.

Cactus. *Roswell High School Yearbook*, Roswell, NM, 1914.

Calloway, Colin G., Gerd Gemünden, and Susanne Zantop, eds. *Germans and Indians: Fantasies, Encounters, Projections*. Lincoln: University of Nebraska Press, 2002.

Carlson, Alvar W. *The Spanish-American Homeland: Four Centuries in New Mexico's Rio Arriba*. Baltimore, MD: The Johns Hopkins University Press, 1990.

Chávez, Thomas E. *Manuel Alvarez 1794–1856: A Southwestern Biography*. Niwot: University Press of Colorado, 1990.

Cinel, Dino. *From Italy to San Francisco: The Immigrant Experience*. Stanford, CA: Stanford University Press, 1982.

Cleaveland, Agnes Morley. *No Life for a Lady*. Boston: Houghton Mifflin Company, 1941.

Clever, Charles P. *New Mexico: Her Resources, Her Necessities for Railroad Communication with the Atlantic and Pacific States, Her Great Future*. Washington, DC: McGill & Witherow, Printers, 1868.

Conzen, Kathleen. *Immigrant Milwaukee, 1836–1860: Accommodation and Community in a Frontier City*. Cambridge, MA: Harvard University Press, 1976.

———. *Making Their Own America: Assimilation theory and the German Peasant Pioneer*. New York: Berg Publishers, 1990.

Cooper, James Fenimore. *The Last of the Mohicans: A Narrative of 1757*. 1826. Reprint. New York: Signet Classic, 1962.

———. *The Pioneers or the Sources of the Susquehanna: A Descriptive Tale*. 1823. Reprint. New York: Signet Classic, 1964.

Cronon, William, George Miles, and Jay Gitlin, eds. *Under an Open Sky: Rethinking America's Western Past.* New York: W. W. Norton and Company, 1992.

Daniels, Roger. *Coming to America: A History of Immigration and Ethnicity in American Life.* New York: HarperCollins Publishers, 1990.

De Vos, George, and Lola Romanucci-Ross, eds. *Ethnic Identity: Cultural Continuities and Change.* Palo Alto, CA: Mayfield Publishing Company, 1975.

Deutsch, Sarah. *No Separate Refuge: Culture, Class, and Gender on an Anglo-Hispanic Frontier in the American Southwest, 1880–1940.* New York: Oxford University Press, 1987.

Dinkelacker, Horst. *Amerika zwischen Traum und Desillusionierung im Leben und Werk des Erfolgsschriftstellers Balduin Möllhausen, 1825–1905.* New York: Peter Lang, 1990.

Doerflinger, Thomas M. *A Vigorous Spirit of Enterprise: Merchants and Economic Development in Revolutionary Philadelphia.* Chapel Hill: University of North Carolina Press, 1986.

Doerries, Reinhard R. *Berlin-Washington, 1908/1917.* Düsseldorf: Athenaeum Verlag, 1975.

———. *Iren und Deutsche in der Neuen Welt: Akkulturations-prozesse in der Amerikanischen Gesellschaft im Späten Neunzehnten Jahrhundert.* Stuttgart: Rudolf Steiner Verlag, 1986.

Doti, Lynne Pierson, and Larry Schweikart. *Banking in the American West: From the Gold Rush to Deregulation.* Norman: University of Oklahoma Press, 1991.

DuBois, W. E. B. *The Philadelphia Negro: A Social Study.* 1899. Reprint. New York: Schocken Books, 1967.

Duden, Gottfried. *Bericht über eine Reise nach den westlichen Staaten Nordamerika's und einen mehrjährigen Aufenthalt am Missouri.* Elberfeld: S. Lucas, 1829.

Eldridge, Charles C., Julie Schimmel, and William H. Truettner. *Art in New Mexico, 1900–1945: Paths to Taos and Santa Fe.* New York: Abbeville Press, Publishers, 1986.

Emmons, David M. *The Butte Irish: Class and Ethnicity in an American Mining Town, 1875–1925.* Urbana: University of Illinois Press, 1989.

Erdoes, Richard. *Saloons of the Old West.* New York: Alfred A. Knopf, 1979.

Evans, Richard J. *The Feminist Movement in Germany, 1894–1933.* London: Sage Publications, 1976.

————, and W. R. Lee, eds. *The German Peasantry: Conflict and Community in Rural Society from the Eighteenth to the Twentieth Century.* New York: St. Martin's Press, 1986.

Fierman, Floyd S. *The Spiegelbergs: Pioneer Merchants and Bankers of the Southwest.* Waltham, MA: American Jewish Historical Society, 1967.

Finsch, Norbert. *Die Goldgräber Kaliforniens: Arbeitsbedingungen, Lebenstandard und politisches System um die Mitte des 19. Jahrhunderts.* Göttingen: Vandenhoeck & Ruprecht, 1982.

Francaviglia, Richard, and David Narrett, eds. *Essays on the Changing Images of the Southwest.* College Station: Texas A&M University Press, 1994.

Fröbel, Julius. *Aus Amerika: Erfahrungen, Reisen und Studien.* 2 vols. Leipzig: Verlagsbuchhandlung von J. J. Weber, 1857.

Garcia, F. Chris, and Paul L. Hain, eds. *New Mexico Government.* Albuquerque: University of New Mexico Press, 1976.

Gerstäcker, Friedrich. *Georg, der Kleine Goldgräber in Kalifornien.* Berlin: Verlag von Neufeld und Henius, n.d.

————. *Streif- und Jagdzüge durch die Vereinigten Staaten Nord-Amerikas.* Dresden: Arnold, 1844.

Gibson, Arrell Morgan. *The Santa Fe and Taos Colonies: Age of the Muses, 1900–1942.* Norman: University of Oklahoma Press, 1983.

Gjerde, Jon. *The Minds of the West: Ethnocultural Evolution in the Rural Middle West, 1830–1917.* Chapel Hill: University of North Carolina Press, 1997.

Goetzmann, William H., and William N. Goetzmann. *The West of the Imagination.* New York: W. W. Norton and Company, 1986.

Gregg, Josiah. *Commerce of the Prairies.* 2 vols. 1844. Reprint. Philadelphia, PA: J. B. Lippincott Company, 1962.

Gregg, Josiah. *Wanderungen durch die Prärien und das nördliche Mexiko.* Stuttgart: Verlag der Frankh'schen Buchhandlung, 1847.

Grimes, Ronald L. *Symbol and Conquest: Public Ritual and Drama in Santa Fe, New Mexico.* Ithaca, NY: Cornell University Press, 1976.

Grove, Pearce S., Becky J. Barnett, and Sandra J. Hansen. *New Mexico Newspapers: A Comprehensive Guide to Bibliographical Entries and Locations.* Albuquerque: University of New Mexico Press, 1975.

Hall, Thomas D. *Social Change in the Southwest, 1350–1880*. Lawrence: University Press of Kansas, 1989.

Higham, John. *Send These to Me: Jews and Other Immigrants in Urban America*. New York: Atheneum, 1975.

———. *Strangers in the Land: Patterns of American Nativism, 1860–1925*. New York: Atheneum, 1971.

Holmes, Jack E. *Politics in New Mexico*. Albuquerque: University of New Mexico Press, 1967.

Horn, Maurice, ed. *The World Encyclopedia of Comics*. New York: Chelsea House Publishers, 1976.

Huning, Franz. *Trader on the Santa Fe Trail: The Memoirs of Franz Huning*. Albuquerque, NM: University of Albuquerque, 1973.

Iverson, Peter. *The Navajo Nation*. 1981. Reprint. Albuquerque: University of New Mexico Press, 1984.

Jackson, W. Turrentine. *The Enterprising Scot: Investors in the American West after 1873*. Edinburgh: Edinburgh University Press, 1968.

Jeffrey, Julie Roy. *Frontier Women: The Trans-Mississippi West, 1840–1880*. New York: Hill and Wang, 1979.

Jordan, Terry G. *German Seed in Texas Soil: Immigrant Farmers in Nineteenth-Century Texas*. Austin: University of Texas Press, 1966.

Kamphoefner, Walter D. *The Westfalians: From Germany to Missouri*. Princeton, NJ: Princeton University Press, 1987.

Kazal, Russell A. *Becoming Old Stock: The Paradox of German-American Identity*. Princeton, NJ: Princeton University Press, 2004.

Keleher, Julia, and Elsie Ruth Chant. *The Padre of Isleta*. Santa Fe, NM: Rydal Press, 1940.

Keleher, William A. *Turmoil in New Mexico, 1846–1869*. 1952. Reprint. Albuquerque: University of New Mexico Press, 1982.

Kern, Robert, ed. *Building New Mexico: The Experience of a Carpenter Union in the Southwest*. Albuquerque: New Mexico Humanities Council and the District Council of the United Brotherhood of Carpenters, 1983.

———, ed. *Labor in New Mexico: Unions, Strikes, and Social History since 1881*. Albuquerque: University of New Mexico Press, 1983.

Kessner, Thomas. *The Golden Door: Italian and Jewish Immigrant Mobility in New York City, 1880–1915*. New York: Oxford University Press, 1977.

Klasner, Lily. *My Girlhood among Outlaws*, edited by Eve Ball. Tucson: University of Arizona Press, 1972.

Koch, Ekkehard. *Karl May's Väter: Die Deutschen Im Wilden Westen*. Husum: Hansa Verlag, 1982.

Kusmer, Kenneth L. *A Ghetto Takes Shape: Black Cleveland, 1870–1930*. Urbana: University of Illinois Press, 1970.

La Farge, Oiver. *Santa Fe: The Autobiography of a Southwestern Town*. Norman: University of Oklahoma Press, 1959.

Lamar, Howard R. *The Far Southwest, 1846–1912: A Territorial History*. New Haven, CT: Yale University Press, 1966.

Lange, Charles H., and Carroll L. Riley, eds. *The Southwestern Journals of Adolph F. Bandelier, 1883–1884*. Albuquerque: University of New Mexico Press, 1970.

———, and Elizabeth M. Lange, eds. *The Southwestern Journals of Adolph F. Bandelier, 1889–1892*. Albuquerque: University of New Mexico Press, 1984.

Langston, LaMoine "Red." *A History of Masonry in New Mexico*. Roswell, NM: Hall-Poorbaugh Press, [1977].

Larson, Robert W. *New Mexico Populism: A Study of Radical Protest in a Western Territory*. Boulder: Colorado Association University Press, 1974.

———. *New Mexico's Quest for Statehood, 1846–1912*. Albuquerque: University of New Mexico Press, 1968.

Leighly, John. *Land and Life: A Selection from the Writings of Carl Ortwin Sauer*. Berkeley: University of California Press, 1965.

Lesinsky, Henry. *Letters Written by Henry Lesinsky to His Son*. New York: n.p., 1924.

Levine, Bruce. *The Migration of Ideology*. Occasional Paper No. 7. Washington, DC: German Historical Institute, 1992.

Limerick, Patricia Nelson. *The Legacy of Conquest: The Unbroken Past of the American West*. New York: W. W. Norton and Company, 1987.

Long, Priscilla. *Where the Sun Never Shines: A History of America's Bloody Coal Industry*. New York: Paragon House, 1989.

Lorence, James J. *The Suppression of Salt of the Earth: How Hollywood, Big Labor, and Politicians Blacklisted a Movie in Cold War America*. Albuquerque: University of New Mexico Press, 1999.

Lowitt, Richard. *Bronson M. Cutting: Progressive Politician.* Albuquerque: University of New Mexico Press, 1992.

Luebke, Frederick C. *Bonds of Loyalty: German Americans and World War I.* DeKalb: Northern Illinois University Press, 1974.

———, ed. *Ethnic Voters and the Election of Lincoln.* Lincoln: University of Nebraska Press, 1971.

———. *Germans in the New World: Essays in the History of Immigration.* Urbana: University of Illinois Press, 1990.

———. *Immigrants and Politics: The Germans of Nebraska, 1880–1990.* Lincoln: University of Nebraska Press, 1969.

Malone, Michael P., and Richard W. Etulain. *The American West: A Twentieth-Century History.* Lincoln: University of Nebraska Press, 1989.

Mann, Thomas. *Betrachtungen eines Unpolitischen.* Berlin: S. Fischer Verlag, 1918.

Mauch, Christof, and Joseph Salmons, eds. *German-Jewish Identities in America.* Madison, WI: Max Kade Institute for German-American Studies, 2003.

May, Karl. *Karl May's Gesammelte Werke.* 74 vols. Bamberg: Karl-May Verlag, 1951.

McCaffery, Robert Paul. *Islands of Deutschtum: German-Americans in Manchester, New Hampshire and Lawrence, Massachusetts, 1870–1942.* New York: Peter Lang, 1996.

McWilliams, Carey. *North of Mexico: The Spanish-Speaking People of the United States.* 1948. Reprint, New York: Greenwood Press, 1968.

Meinig, D. W. *Southwest: Three Peoples in Geographical Change, 1600–1970.* New York: Oxford University Press, 1971.

Meketa, Jacqueline D. *Louis Felsenthal: Citizen-Soldier of Territorial New Mexico.* Albuquerque: University of New Mexico Press, 1982.

Meyer, Beatrice Ilfeld. *Don Luis Ilfeld.* Albuquerque, NM: Albuquerque Historical Society, 1973.

Meyer, Michael C. *Water in the Hispanic Southwest: A Social and Legal History, 1550–1850.* Tucson: University of Arizona Press, 1984.

Möllhausen, Balduin. *Reisen in die Felsengebirge Nordamerikas.* 2 vols. 1861. Reprint. München: Lothar Borowsky Verlag, n.d.

————. *Wanderungen durch die Prärien und Wüsten des westlichen Nordamerika vom Mississippi nach den Küsten der Südsee.* 1858. Reprint, München: Lothar Borowsky Verlag, n.d.

Moneta, Daniela, ed. *Chas. F. Lummis: The Centennial Exhibition,Commemorating His Tramp across the Continent.* Los Angeles: Southwest Museum, 1985.

Morrill, Claire. *A Taos Mosaic: Portrait of a New Mexico Village.* Albuquerque: University of New Mexico Press, 1973.

Myres, Sandra L. *Westering Women and the Frontier Experience 1800–1915.* Albuquerque: University of New Mexico Press, 1982.

Nadel, Stanley. *Little Germany: Ethnicity, Religion, and Class in New York City, 1845–1880.* Urbana: University of Illinois Press, 1990.

The New Mexico Blue Book or State Official Register, 1919. Santa Fe, NM: n.p., [1919].

Parish, William J. *The Charles Ilfeld Company: A Study of the Rise and Decline of Mercantile Capitalism in New Mexico.* Cambridge, MA: Harvard University Press, 1961.

Parsons, Stanley B. *The Populist Context: Rural Versus Urban Power on a Great Plains Frontier.* Westport, CT: Greenwood Press, 1973.

Paul, Rodman Wilson. *Mining Frontiers of the Far West, 1848–1880.* 1963. Reprint, Albuquerque: University of New Mexico Press, 1974.

Pearce, T. M., ed. *New Mexico Place Names.* Albuquerque: University of New Mexico Press, 1965.

Pisani, Donald. *From Family Farm to Agribusiness: The Irrigation Crusade in California and the West, 1850–1931.* Berkeley: University of California Press, 1984.

Plischke, Hans. *Von Cooper bis Karl May: Eine Geschichte des Völkerkundlichen Reise- und Abenteurromans.* Düsseldorf: Droste-Verlag, 1951.

Pollard, Sidney. *The Genesis of Modern Management.* Baltimore, MD: Penguin Books, 1968.

Pomeroy, Earl. *The Pacific Slope: A History of California, Oregon, Washington, Idaho, Utah, and Nevada.* New York: Alfred A. Knopf, 1965.

Proceedings of the Constitutional Convention of the Proposed State of New Mexico Held At Santa Fe, New Mexico. Albuquerque: Press of the *Morning Journal*, 1910.

Reeve, Agnesa Lufkin. *From Hacienda to Bungalow: Northern New Mexico Houses, 1850–1912.* Albuquerque: University of New Mexico Press, 1988.

Reeve, Frank D. *History of New Mexico.* 2 vols. New York: Lewis Historical Publishing Company, 1961.

Remley, David. *Bell Ranch: Cattle Ranching in the Southwest, 1824–1947.* Albuquerque: University of New Mexico Press, 1993.

Reports of Cases Argued and Determined in the Supreme Court of the Territory of New Mexico. Vols. 1–4, 19, 25. [Publishers and publication dates vary].

Report of the Secretary of the Territory, 1903–1904, and Legislative Manual, 1905. Santa Fe: The New Mexican Printing Company, 1905.

Rischin, Moses, and John Livingston, eds. *Jews of the American West.* Detroit, MI: Wayne State University Press, 1991.

Ritch, W. G., comp. *The Legislative Blue-Book of the Territory of New Mexico.* Santa Fe, NM: Charles W. Greene, Public Printers, 1882.

Rosenbaum, Robert J. *Mexicano Resistance in the Southwest: "The Sacred Right of Self-Preservation."* Austin: University of Texas Press, 1981

Rossbacher, Karlheinz. *Lederstrumpf in Deutschland.* München: Wilhelm Fink Verlag, 1972.

Rouck, Joseph S., and Bernhard Eisenberg, eds. *America's Ethnic Politics.* Westport, CT: Greenwood Press, 1982.

Scala, John. *The Lady of the Casa.* Santa Fe, NM: Rydal Press, 1959.

Schieder, Theodore. *Vom Deutschen Bund zum Deutschen Reich, 1815–1871.* Stuttgart: Klett Verlag, 1970.

Schlagintweit, Robert. *Die Santa Fe- und Südpacificbahn in Nordamerika.* Köln: Verlag von Eduard Heinrich Mayer, 1884.

Schlissel, Lillian, Vicki Ruiz, and Janice Monk, eds. *Western Women: Their Land, Their Lives.* Albuquerque: University of New Mexico Press, 1988.

Segale, Blandina. *At the End of the Santa Fe Trail.* Milwaukee, WI: Bruce Publishing Company, 1948.

Sheppard, Carl D. *Creator of the Santa Fe Style: Isaac Hamilton Rapp, Architect.* Albuquerque: University of New Mexico Press, 1988.

Sorin, Gerald. *Tradition Transformed: The Jewish Experience in America.* Baltimore: Johns Hopkins University Press, 1997.

Steffens, Lincoln. *The Shame of the Cities.* New York: Hill and Wang, 1957.

Szasz, Ferenc Morton. *The Protestant Clergy in the Great Plains and Mountain West, 1865–1915*. Albuquerque: University of New Mexico Press, 1988.

Thernstrom, Stephan. *The Other Bostonians: Poverty and Progress in the American Metropolis, 1880–1970*. Cambridge, MA: Harvard University Press, 1973.

———. *Poverty and Progress: Social Mobility in a Nineteenth Century City*. Cambridge, MA: Harvard University Press, 1964.

———, ed. *Harvard Encyclopedia of American Ethnic Groups*. Cambridge, MA: Harvard University Press, 1980.

Thompson, Richard H. *Theories of Ethnicity: A Critical Appraisal*. Westport, CT: Greenwood Press, 1989.

Tobias, Henry. *A History of the Jews in New Mexico*. Albuquerque: University of New Mexico Press, 1990.

———, and Charles E. Woodhouse. *Santa Fe: A Modern History, 1880–1990*. Albuquerque: University of New Mexico Press, 2001.

Trommler, Frank, and Elliott Shore, eds. *The German-American Encounter: Conflict and Cooperation between Two Cultures, 1800–2000*. New York: Berghahn Books, 2001.

Tuchman, Barbara W. *The Zimmermann Telegram*. New York: Ballantine Books, 1985.

Twitchell, Ralph E. *Leading Facts of New Mexico History*. 2 vols. Albuquerque, NM: Horn and Wallace, Publishers, 1963.

Utley, Robert M. *High Noon in Lincoln: Violence on the Western Frontier*. Albuquerque: University of New Mexico Press, 1987.

Weber, David J., ed. *New Spain's Far Northern Frontier: Essays on Spain in the American West, 1540–1821*. Albuquerque: University of New Mexico Press, 1979.

Weber, Max. *Economy and Society: An Outline of Interpretive Sociology*. 3 vols. Edited by Guenther Roth and Claus Wittich. New York: Bedmister Press, 1968.

———. *The Protestant Ethic and the Spirit of Capitalism*. Translated by Talcott Parsons. New York: Charles Scribner's Sons, 1958.

West, Elliott. *Growing Up with the Country: Childhood on the Far Western Frontier*. Albuquerque: University of New Mexico Press, 1989.

Westphall, Victor. *The Public Domain in New Mexico, 1845–1891*. Albuquerque: University of New Mexico Press, 1965.

Weyl, Nathaniel. *The Jew in American Politics*. New Rochelle, NY: Arlington, 1968.

White, Robert R., ed. *The Taos Society of Artists*. Albuquerque: University of New Mexico Press, 1983.

Wiebe, Robert H. *The Search for Order, 1877–1920*. New York: Hill and Wang, 1967.

Wied, Maximilian. *Reise in das Innere Nordamerika in den Jahren 1832 bis 1834*. Reprint. München: Lothar Borowsky Verlag, n.d.

Wilken, Robert L. *Anselm Weber, O.F.M.: Missionary to the Navaho, 1898–1921*. Milwaukee, MI: Bruce Publishing Company, 1955.

Wilson, Chris. *The Myth of Santa Fe: Creating a Modern Regional Tradition*. Albuquerque: University of New Mexico Press, 1997.

Wislizenus, Frederick A. *Ein Ausflug nach den Felsen-Gebirgen im Jahre 1839*. St. Louis, MO: Wilhelm Weber, 1840.

———. *Denkschrift über eine Reise nach Nord-Mexico, verbunden mit der Expedition des Oberst Doniphan, in den Jahren 1846 und 1847*. Braunschweig: F. Vieweg und Sohn Verlag, 1850.

———. *A Journey to the Rocky Mountains in the Year 1839*. 1912. Reprint, Glorietta, NM: Rio Grande Press, 1969.

———. *Memoir of a Tour to Northern Mexico: Connected with Col. Doniphan's Expedition in 1846 and 1847*. 1848. Reprint, Albuquerque, NM: Calvin Horn Publisher, Inc., 1969.

Worster, Donald. *Rivers of Empires: Water, Aridity, and the Growth of the American West*. New York: Pantheon Books, 1985.

Württemberg, Paul Wilhelm. *Reise nach dem nördlichen Amerika in den Jahren 1822 bis 1824*. 1835. Reprint, München: Lothar Borowsky Verlag, n.d.

Zeleny, Carolyn. *Relations between the Spanish-Americans and Anglo-Americans in New Mexico*. New York: Arno Press, 1974.

Zelinsky, Wilbur. *The Cultural Geography of the United States*. Englewood Cliffs, N.J.: Prentice-Hall, Inc., 1973.

THESES AND DISSERTATIONS

Atkins, Jane C. "Who Will Educate: The Schooling Question in Territorial New Mexico, 1846–1911." Ph.D. diss., University of New Mexico, 1982.

Balch, Royce Jane. "Jacob Korber, Early Businessman of Albuquerque, New Mexico 1881–1921." M.B.A. thesis, University of New Mexico, 1955.

Fincher, Ernest B. "Spanish-Americans as a Political Factor in New Mexico, 1912–1950." Ph.D. diss., New York University, 1950.

Lehmann, Terry J. "Santa Fe and Albuquerque 1870–1900: Contrast and Conflict in the Development of Two Southwestern Towns." Ph.D. diss., Indiana University, 1974.

McDowell, Archie M. "The Opposition to Statehood within the Territory of New Mexico." M.A. thesis, University of New Mexico, 1940.

Miller, David H. "Balduin Möllhausen: A Prussian's Image of the American West." Ph.D. diss., University of New Mexico, 1970.

Parker, Kate H. "'I Brought With Me Many Eastern Ways': Euro-American Income-Earning Women in New Mexico, 1850–1880." Ph.D. diss., University of New Mexico, 1984.

Rebord, Bernice Ann. "A Social History of Albuquerque, 1880–1885." M.A. thesis, University of New Mexico, 1947.

Saxton, Russell. "Ethnocentrism in the Historical Literature of Territorial New Mexico." Ph.D. diss., University of New Mexico, 1980.

Thomas, Dorothy E. "The Final Years of New Mexico's Struggle for Statehood, 1907–1912." M.A. thesis, University of New Mexico, 1939.

—⋙—

Index

—⊸⊷⊸—

References to tables or figures are indicated by an
italic *t* or *f* following the page number.

—∿—